Using Computers in the Translation of Literary Style

This volume argues for an innovative interdisciplinary approach to the analysis and translation of literary style, based on a mutually supportive combination of traditional close reading and 'distant' reading, involving corpus-linguistic analysis and text-visualisation. The book contextualises this approach within the broader story of the development of computer-assisted translation – including machine translation and the use of CAT tools – and elucidates the ways in which the approach can lead to better informed translations than those based on close reading alone. This study represents the first systematic attempt to use corpus linguistics and text-visualisation in the process of translating individual literary texts, as opposed to comparing and analysing already published originals and their translations. Using the case study of his translation into English of Uruguayan author Mario Benedetti's 1965 novel *Gracías por el Fuego*, Youdale showcases how a close and distant reading (CDR) approach enhances the translator's ability to detect and measure a variety of stylistic features, ranging from sentence length and structure to lexical richness and repetition, both in the source text and in their own draft translation, thus assisting them with the task of revision. The book reflects on the benefits and limitations of a CDR approach, its scalability and broader applicability in translation studies and related disciplines, making this key reading for translators, postgraduate students and scholars in the fields of literary translation, corpus linguistics, corpus stylistics and narratology.

Roy Youdale teaches undergraduate translation at Bristol University, UK, where he completed his PhD in 2017. He is researching the use of corpus linguistics and text-visualisation in literary translation and has presented his work at the universities of East Anglia and Swansea, and the Link Campus University in Rome.

Routledge Advances in Translation and Interpreting Studies

35 **Perspectives on Retranslation**
Ideology, Paratexts, Methods
Edited by Özlem Berk Albachten and Şehnaz Tahir Gürçağlar

36 **A (Bio)Semiotic Theory of Translation**
The Emergence of Social-Cultural Reality
Kobus Marais

37 **A Sociological Approach to Poetry Translation**
Modern European Poet-Translators
Jacob S. D. Blakesley

38 **Complexity Thinking in Translation Studies**
Methodological Considerations
Edited by Kobus Marais and Reine Meylaerts

39 **Translating and Interpreting in Korean Contexts**
Engaging with Asian and Western Others
Edited Ji-Hae Kang and Judy Wakabayashi

40 **Hybrid Englishes and the Challenges of/for Translation**
Identity, Mobility and Language Change
Edited by Karen Bennett and Rita Queiroz de Barros

41 **Translating the Visual**
A Multimodal Perspective
Rachel Weissbrod and Ayelet Kohn

42 **Using Computers in the Translation of Literary Style**
Challenges and Opportunities
Roy Youdale

For more information about this series, please visit https://www.routledge.com/Routledge-Advances-in-Translation-and-Interpreting-Studies/book-series/RTS

Using Computers in the Translation of Literary Style
Challenges and Opportunities

Roy Youdale

NEW YORK AND LONDON

First published 2020
by Routledge
605 Third Avenue, New York, NY 10017

and by Routledge
2 Park Square, Milton Park, Abingdon, Oxon, OX14 4RN

First issued in paperback 2020

Routledge is an imprint of the Taylor & Francis Group, an informa business

© 2020 Taylor & Francis

The right of Roy Youdale to be identified as author of this work has been asserted by him in accordance with sections 77 and 78 of the Copyright, Designs and Patents Act 1988.

All rights reserved. No part of this book may be reprinted or reproduced or utilised in any form or by any electronic, mechanical, or other means, now known or hereafter invented, including photocopying and recording, or in any information storage or retrieval system, without permission in writing from the publishers.

Trademark notice: Product or corporate names may be trademarks or registered trademarks, and are used only for identification and explanation without intent to infringe.

Library of Congress Cataloging-in-Publication Data
A catalog record for this title has been requested

ISBN 13: 978-0-367-72742-0 (pbk)
ISBN 13: 978-0-367-14123-3 (hbk)

Typeset in Sabon
by codeMantra

To my partner Graciela and my father Bill, for their
unstinting love and support throughout this project

Contents

List of Figures	ix
List of Tables	xi
Acknowledgements	xiii
List of Abbreviations	xv

Introduction   1
1.0 Style in Translation 2
2.0 Traditional Methodologies: Strengths and Limitations 5
3.0 What a New Approach Has to Offer 7
4.0 The Case Study: Gracias por el Fuego (1965)
by Mario Benedetti 9

1 Using Computers in Literary Translation   11
1.1 Computers and Translation: An Overview 12
1.2 CAT Tools, MT and Literary Translation 17
1.3 Computers and the CDR Approach to the
Translation of Style 23
1.4 The Relationship of the Methodology to
Other Disciplines 40

2 Analysing the Source Text: Structure and Style   46
2.1 The Author, the Novel and Its Reception 46
2.2 Using a Set of 'Standard' CDR Analyses 50
2.3 The Title 54
2.4 Characterisation 57

3 CDR, Translation Theory and the Attempt to Create an
'English Benedetti'   72
3.1 CDR and Translation Philosophy 74
3.2 Equivalence of Stylistic Effect and the Creation of
an 'English Benedetti' 81
3.3 Existing Benedetti Translations: Comparison
and Analysis 91

viii *Contents*

4   **Applying the Methodology (Part 1): The Translation of Culture**   98
    4.1 The Translation of CSIs: Flexible Foreignisation 99
    4.2 Multilingualism: Preservation, a Glossary
       and Typography 106
    4.3 Usted and the Translation of Tonal Register 114

5   **Applying the Methodology (Part 2): The Translation of**
    Punctuation   121
    5.1 Sentence Length in Gracias por el Fuego 124
    5.2 Short Sentences and the Creation of an
       English Benedetti 128
    5.3 Long Sentences: ST Style and TL Conventions 137

6   **Applying the Methodology (Part 3): Comparing Source**
    Text and Draft Translation   151
    6.1 Comparison Using Standard CDR Analyses 152
    6.2 Comparing Sentence Length 155
    6.3 Comparing Repetitions 162
    6.4 Comparing the Use of 'small' Words 166

7   **Applying the Methodology (Part 4): The Auto-analysis of**
    Translator Style   178
    7.1 Analysing One's Own Translation Style 179
    7.2 Assessing the Impact of Stylistic Auto-analysis on
       How One Translates 189

8   **Conclusions: Assessing the Potential of the Methodology**   199
    8.1 Assessing the Strengths and Limitations of the
       Methodology 200
    8.2 Relevance of the Methodology for
       Translation Scholars, Students and Professional
       Literary Translators 206

    Appendix A: Research Data   211
    Appendix B: Translations used for Chapter 7   217
    References   221
    Index   237

List of Figures

1.1	Word list and KWIC view in CATMA	27
1.2	Node word highlighted in the full text	28
1.3	English and Spanish parallel corpus in Sketch Engine	29
1.4	Example of a Word Sketch in Sketch Engine	30
1.5	(a) Raw word frequency view in Sketch Engine. (b) Word frequency distribution view in Sketch Engine	35
1.6	Corpus summary view in Voyant Tools	36
1.7	The Text Visualization Browser	38
2.1	Characters in Hamlet (Moretti 2011:12)	62
2.2	The networks of Ramón and Edmundo	64
2.3	Relationships between the five principal characters	65
2.4	Character relationships in Chapter 9	66
5.1	Proportions of sentences in *Gracias por el Fuego* by length	124
5.2	Average sentence length in *Gracias por el Fuego* by chapter	125
5.3	Distribution of the sentences of 101 words or more in *Gracias por el Fuego*	138
5.4	Graphic representation of the distribution of *y*, *et* and *and* in Microsoft Word 2010	148
5.5	Voyant Tools representation of the frequency and distribution of *y*, *et* and *and*	149
6.1	The LF Aligner 4.1 workspace	154
6.2	Parallel corpus search results in Sketch Engine	156
6.3	Visualisation of the average sentence length of two corpora of books written by Jack London and Mark Twain, using the LiteratureVis programme. (Keim and Oelke 2007:4)	158
6.4	The results of a CATMA search for ST sentences of six words or less in Chapter 14	160
6.5	CATMA search for instances of the lemma *estallar*	163
6.6	The 105 instances of *Y* and *y* in Chapter 14 of *Gracias por el Fuego*	171

List of Tables

1.1	Comparison chart of CL software for use in literary translation	32
1.2	A provisional model of CDR applied to the process of literary translation	41
2.1	Results of CATMA search for 'fuego'	55
2.2	Top seven keywords in Edmundo's discourse	60
3.1	Quantitative analysis of 'Familia Iriarte' and three English translations	93
3.2	Quantitative analysis of *La Tregua* and two English translations	94
4.1	Sources used for an analysis of the translation of *usted*	116
5.1	Average sentence length in four major Boom novels	126
5.2	Raw and normalised frequency analysis of occurrences of 'tan' + adjective in *Gracias por el Fuego* and four major Boom novels	127
5.3	Occurrences of the 30 sentences of 101 words or more in *Gracias por el Fuego* shown in narrative and chapter context	139
5.4	Summary of long sentences in Chapters 9, 10 and 13 of *Gracias por el Fuego*	140
5.5	Raw, normalised and average frequency analysis of commas in *Gracias por el Fuego* and four major Boom novels	142
6.1	Standard CDR statistical comparisons of ST and draft TT	152
6.2	Percentages of short and long sentences: ST and draft TT	159
6.3	Average sentence lengths: ST and draft TT	159
6.4	Word count: ST and draft TT	159
6.5	Short sentences which are longer in the TT than in the ST	161
6.6	Short sentences which are longer in the ST than in the TT	162
6.7	Occurrences of *estallar* and its draft translations	164
6.8	Raw and normalised frequency analyses of *Y/y* in *Gracias por el Fuego*, the *Corpus del Español*, the *Frequency Dictionary of Spanish* and four major Boom novels	169

xii *List of Tables*

6.9 Relative word frequency in *Gracias por el Fuego*, the *Frequency Dictionary of Spanish*, the *Corpus del Español* and four major Boom novels 169
6.10 The ten most frequently used words in *Gracias por el Fuego* and the draft translation 172
6.11 Comparison of occurrences of *Y/y* in the ST and *And/and* in the draft TT 173
7.1 Comparison of the two translations of the extract from *El Discurso Vacío* 185
7.2 Sentence length bands in my TT and C.C.'s TT 186
7.3 CQL queries used to identify possible specific translation habits 191
A1 Sentence length and word count in *Gracias por el Fuego* by chapter and overall 211
A2 Sentence length and word count in the 2014–15 draft translation of *Gracias por el Fuego* by chapter and overall 212
A3 Word frequency in *Gracias por el Fuego* by chapter and overall 213
A4 Word frequency in the draft translation by chapter and overall 214
B1 Extract from Chapter 13 of *Gracias por el Fuego* and my 2015 draft translation 217
B2 Extract from *El Discurso Vacío* and my translation, 2014 219

Acknowledgements

I would like to thank various copyright holders for their permission to include different kinds of material in this book: Guillermo Schavelzon and the Schavelzon Graham Agencia Literaria, S.L., for extracts from *Gracias por el Fuego* by Mario Benedetti; Professor Jan Christoph Meister and his team at the University of Hamburg for screenshots of the CATMA website; Michal Cukr and the Sketch Engine team for screenshots of the Sketch Engine website; Kostiantyn Kucher and Andreas Kerren at Linnaeus University in Sweden for screenshots of the TextVis Browser website; and Professor Stéfan Sinclair and Dr. Geoffrey Rockwell at the University of Alberta for screenshots of the Voyant Tools website.

A number of senior academics have gone out of their way to help and support me in the process of proposing and then writing this book, and I want them to know how grateful I am. Dr. Carol O'Sullivan, Director of Translation at the University of Bristol, first suggested the idea for the book after steering me patiently through my PhD. Jean Boase-Beier, Professor Emerita of Translation at the University of East Anglia, guided me through the proposal process and read parts of the draft, providing helpful comments. Andrew Rothwell, Professor of French and Translation at Swansea University, and Tom Cheesman, Professor of German – also at Swansea University – have been more than generous with their time in reading and commenting on parts of the draft manuscript, and also in inviting me to participate in workshops and an international summer school on the theme of the use of computers in literary translation, which have allowed me to present this research to a wider audience.

I would also like to thank staff at Routledge – Elysse Preposi, Editor in Linguistics, and Alexandra Simmons, Editorial Assistant – for their help and patience in answering all my questions and guiding me through the process of publishing an academic monograph. The author, however, retains full responsibility for all errors and omissions.

List of Abbreviations

BNC	British National Corpus
CALT	computer-assisted literary translation
CAT	computer-aided translation
CATMA	Computer-Aided Textual Markup and Analysis
CDR	close and distant reading
CL	corpus linguistics
CQL	corpus query language
CTS	corpus-based translation studies
DTS	Descriptive Translation Studies
ETN	Emerging Translators Network
MT	machine translation
NMT	neural machine translation
POS	part of speech
SL	source language
SMT	statistical machine translation
ST	source text
TAUS	Translation Automation Users Society
TL	target language
TMX	Translation Memory eXchange
TS	Translation Studies
TT	target text
TTR	type-token ratio

Introduction

Why do literary translators, and their trainers, often give the impression that they are at best ambivalent about the use of technology in literary translation, and at worst simply antagonistic? While explaining some of the reasons for this view, this book argues the case for a new approach to the translation of literary style which combines traditional close reading with computer-aided literary analysis, or 'distant reading', to use a term coined by Franco Moretti in his studies of nineteenth-century English literature (Moretti 2013a), in other words a 'close and distant reading' (CDR) approach. The approach does not employ machine translation (MT) or computer-aided translation (CAT) tools. It does, however, locate itself within the framework of an open invitation to the scholarly translation community and the practitioners of literary translation to engage in a wider debate about how technology might productively be integrated into the practice of literary translation, a debate which would also include uses of MT and CAT tools in this context. Chapter 1 sets out an overview of the use of computers in literary translation. It covers translator attitudes to the use of MT and CAT tools, some examples of the use of these in a literary translation context and a summary of the translation-relevant functionalities of leading text analysis software. A possible model of the various stages of the literary translation process is also put forward, with suggestions as to which software tools and techniques might profitably be used at each stage.

The focus in this book is on the use of corpus-linguistic tools and techniques, and visualisations linked to them, in the process of translating literary style. It represents a way in which translators can interact with technology as part of the translation process – a way which neither dilutes nor deskills the art of translation, but actually enhances it by revealing information about a text which even close reading is unlikely either to measure accurately or to detect at all. The methodology is applied to the complete translation into English by the author (for the first time) of *Gracias por el Fuego*, a novel by the Uruguayan author Mario Benedetti, published in 1965. The case study is used to support the argument that this approach can result in a stylistically better informed translation than one which relies on close reading alone. Chapters 2–6 focus

2 Introduction

on applying the CDR approach to the case study translation, illustrating through the use of a number of detailed examples how the information it revealed resulted in a deeper understanding of the text, which then led to significant revisions of the initial translation. Chapter 7 illustrates another possible use of the CDR approach, the auto-analysis of translator style, enabling translators to detect and analyse hitherto unconscious elements of their *own* translatorial style.

1.0 Style in Translation

Style is important to literature because it focuses not just on *what* is said, but on *how* it is said, and why a text may be shaped in a particular way. As Terry Eagleton remarks, literary writing 'is the kind of writing in which content is inseparable from the language in which it is represented. Language is constitutive of the reality or experience, rather than simply a vehicle for it' (2014:3). If style is important to literature, and is 'what is unique to a text' (Boase-Beier 2011:2), the style of a source text (ST) will have an important bearing on the shape of the target text (TT). Jean Boase-Beier argues that

> a "stylistically-aware"... reading of the source text can lead to a better translation. While the trend in translation studies... has since the 1980s been towards examining how translation has been done rather than evaluating it, many scholars would consider that stylistics also has an important role to play *as a tool to aid translation*.
>
> (2014b:401, emphasis added)

If stylistic awareness is something which can, in principle at least, lead to better informed translation, then the ability to detect and analyse the greatest possible range of stylistic features of a text is clearly desirable. In order to be able to do this, the use of a combination of close reading and quantitative (computer-aided and predominantly corpus-linguistic) analysis is beneficial, and is likely to be more effective than a reliance on close reading alone. This approach relates theory directly to practice by arguing that its methodology is relevant to, and usable by, three groups: translation scholars, MA students of translation and practising literary translators. It is also scalable: translation scholars may have the time to use a variety of analytical techniques and to explore specific stylistic features in depth, while students and practising literary translators may want to limit themselves, at least initially, to a smaller number of quick and easy-to-use analyses such as word and phrase frequencies, collocations and sentence length.

In order to discuss the translation of literary style we need a working definition of 'style'. In *Style in Fiction* Geoffrey Leech and Mick Short suggest that 'in its most general interpretation, the word "STYLE" has

Introduction 3

a fairly uncontroversial meaning: it refers to the way in which language is used in a given context, by a given person, for a given purpose, and so on' (2007:9, emphasis in original). In *A Dictionary of Stylistics*, Katie Wales opts for a basic definition of style as 'the perceived distinctive manner of expression' (2001:371).

Literary style has persuasively been shown to consist of both conscious and unconscious elements. The long-established applied linguistics sub-discipline of stylometry, which has mainly focused on authorship attribution, has demonstrated through various studies that an author's stylistic 'fingerprint' can often be reliably detected by the corpus-linguistic analysis of their use of small, high-frequency function words such as 'and' and 'the' (Mosteller and Wallace 1964; Burrows 1997; Holmes 1998; Stamatatos 2009; Jockers 2013). The use of such words is argued to be largely outside the realm of conscious control and to form part of an author's writing habits. This broadens the notion of literary style to include not only features which are prominent due to their salience, but also features which are not prominent to the reader at all, but are nevertheless detectable and significant. This is explored in more detail in Chapter 7. I therefore propose to define textual literary style as 'the distinctive linguistic characteristics of a particular text, which comprise both conscious and unconscious elements of language use' (Youdale 2017:9). I also propose to adopt Wales' summary formulation of the discipline of stylistics:

> The goal of most stylistics is not simply to describe the formal features of texts for their own sake, but in order to show their functional significance for the interpretation of the text, or in order to relate literary effects to linguistic 'causes' where these are felt to be relevant.
>
> (Wales 2001:453)

There is still no agreed definition of what translation is, but as with literary style, we need a working definition if we are to discuss it, and I find the suggestion put forward by Boase-Beier very serviceable:

> In its simplest, most intuitive sense, translation can be said to involve the translator conveying across a language (or genre) boundary whatever she or he understands to be essential to the meaning of the text, its function, and the way it achieves its effects.
>
> (2011:1)

Within translation studies there are a range of approaches to the issue of style. Gabriela Saldanha argues that 'traditionally, in discussions of literary translation, the stylistic domain has been restricted to the source text' (2014:96), but suggests that the approaches of leading theorists

4 Introduction

in the field can be located on a continuum between ST-orientation and TT-orientation. At the ST end she locates Tim Parks (2014) because he examines translations with the aim of arriving at 'a better appreciation of the original's qualities' (Parks 2014:14). She places Boase-Beier and Kirsten Malmkjaer in between the two ends on the basis that they are both 'concerned with style as reflection of a subjective interpretation of the world that explains the choices made by the writer and translator' (Saldanha 2014:99).

Boase-Beier champions a cognitive approach, seeing style as 'a set of textual elements which represent the attitude or state of mind of the reconstructed figure of the author, narrator or character' (2014b:402). Malmkjaer coined the term *translational stylistics* to describe the search for 'recurrent patterns in the relationships between the source text and the translation' (2004:22). Saldanha places herself and Mona Baker at the TT-oriented end of the continuum:

> rather than seeing style as a way of responding to the source text [we] propose to find stylistic idiosyncrasies that remain consistent across several translations by one translator *despite* differences among their source texts. In other words, we could say that Malmkjaer and Boase-Beier are concerned with the style of the *text* (translation style), and Baker and I with the style of the *translator*.
>
> (2014:100, emphasis in original)

Jeremy Munday's work is also concerned with the possible homogeneity of translator style across different authors, but specifically focuses on the translator's ideology and how this may be detected in their translations. This relates to the work of Giuliana Schiavi (1996), Theo Hermans (1996, 2014) and Cecilia Alvstad (2014) on the detection of the translator's attitude towards what they translate. It is against the background of this brief survey of current approaches to style in translation that I outline my own stylistic approach, in the context not of an analysis of existing translations as products, but of the process of translating the style of a mid-twentieth-century Latin American novel for an early twenty-first-century British readership.

So far, I have looked at the notion of style from four perspectives:

(a) its communicative importance because it focuses on how and why things are said, not just on what is said
(b) a provisional definition of style as 'the distinctive linguistic characteristics of a particular text, which comprise both conscious and unconscious elements of language use'
(c) its role as a bridge between the formal linguistic features of a text and possible interpretations of how those features create effects on the reader

Introduction 5

(d) its relatively underdeveloped place in translation theory, where the focus – particularly in corpus-based translation studies (CTS) – has moved away from the style of the text to the style of the translator.

What underlie all these ways of looking at style are the twin ideas of choices and their effects: why did the author or translator make such-and-such a set of linguistic choices, and how do those choices relate to the effects on the reader of the ST or TT? Ernst-August Gutt suggests that 'the point of preserving stylistic properties in translation lies not in their intrinsic value, but rather in the fact that they provide *clues* that guide the audience to the interpretation intended by the communicator' (1991:127, emphasis in the original). Starting from a similar premise, Boase-Beier argues that it is possible to consider style in translation from at least four potential viewpoints:

i) the style of the source text as an expression of its author's choices
ii) the style of the source text in its effects on the reader (and on the translator as reader)
iii) the style of the target text as an expression of choices made by its author (who is the translator)
iv) the style of the target text in its effects on the reader (2010a:5).

My overall approach to the translation of literary style is based closely on this idea of style as choices and effects, using the concept of 'creative reverse engineering'. I start by noting the effects which a text has on me as a reader; try to work out how the author created those effects, consciously and/or unconsciously; and then attempt to recreate those effects as far as possible in my translation. This leads to the idea of equivalence of stylistic effect as a primary translation goal, and this is the translation framework for the case study which is discussed in depth in Chapter 3.

2.0 Traditional Methodologies: Strengths and Limitations

Both stylistics and literary translation have traditionally relied on close reading as the foundation of their analysis of texts. Although now used to refer generally to the very careful reading of a text, the term 'close reading', as Mario Klarer notes, was

> often used synonymously with new criticism[1][...] It denotes the meticulous analysis of these elementary features [such as 'multiple meaning, paradox, irony, word-play, puns, or rhetorical figures'], which mirror larger structures in the text.
>
> (2004:86)

6 *Introduction*

In the context of the process of literary translation Boase-Beier argues that there is a special kind of reading, '"reading for translation" [...] a reading that not only takes the style into account, as any close critical reading will do, but that also hears in the text echoes of the translation it is about to become' (2010b:32).

This idea is supported by Gregory Rabassa, the well-known translator of Latin American fiction, who argues that 'translation is essentially the closest reading one can possibly give a text. The translator cannot ignore "lesser" words, but must consider every jot and tittle' (1989:6). Close reading forms the basis for an appreciation of style, an interpretation of communicative intention and the relationship between the two. The application of close reading to the process of translation also brings the translator's experience and accumulated linguistic and cultural knowledge into play, and it informs the deployment of what Michael Holman and Jean Boase-Beier call 'the translator's greatest skill, mastery of their own tongue' (2014:8). It is therefore clearly a *sine qua non* of literary translation.

When we read a lengthy text such as a novel we can register a wide range of linguistic and stylistic features such as register and word-play. But there are also a number of linguistic features, relevant to an understanding and appreciation of literary style, which we are simply incapable of either registering at all – like the patterns of use of high-frequency function words such as 'and' and 'that' – or registering with any degree of accuracy – such as sentence length or the occurrence of word clusters (repeatedly occurring sequences of words) and collocations. Roberto Busa, the acknowledged founder of humanities computing (Hockey 2004), argues in his Foreword to *A Companion to Digital Humanities* that modern computer-assisted textual analysis is valuable because 'one is afforded opportunities for perceiving and analysing patterns, conjunctions, connections, and absences that a human being, unaided by the computer, would not be likely to find' (Busa 2004:xxvi). Michaela Mahlberg makes a very similar observation:

> ...quantitative data can highlight linguistic phenomena that readers may not be aware of. Patterns may be present in a text and affect the readers' overall reaction to the text, but it might be difficult for readers to pinpoint what features contribute to which effect.
>
> (2014:389)

While it is true that the ordinary reader will often be less able to detect linguistic and stylistic patterns in a text than a trained stylistician or literary translator, the basic principle holds true. Without the introduction of some form of counting (computer-aided or manual) of features which can provide statistical support for a literary interpretation or judgement, traditional stylistic analysis is open, as Ronald Carter argues, to a major

Introduction 7

criticism, 'namely, that stylisticians select their examples and textual extracts to fit their interpretations, while paying little attention to the bulk of the works they purportedly analyse' (2012:5). And, crucially, their statements are less likely to be falsifiable. If a literary translator wishes to try to recreate the stylistic features of the ST in the TT as far as possible, and I think that many (probably most) do, then their interpretations of the ST and consequent choices for the TT are likely to be better informed if they have such data at their disposal.

Franco Moretti coined the term 'distant reading' to refer to the computer-aided analysis of large numbers of texts, arguing that 'distance [from a text or texts]... *is a condition of knowledge*: it allows you to focus on units that are much smaller or much larger than the text' (2013:48–49, emphasis in original). The methodology adopted in this book uses a distant reading approach as a tool for translating a *single* text, linking it closely and recursively with close reading. It is for this reason that I use the phrase 'close and distant reading' as a convenient way of referring to the methodological approach to the translation of literary style put forward in this book. To be quite clear, I am not arguing that literary translators cannot translate well unless they use quantitative methods. The work of translators like Gregory Rabassa, Edith Grossman, Suzanne Jill Levine and many others is testimony to the fact that they can and do. But the logic of my argument strongly suggests that literary translations of prose texts could benefit from the additional information which only distant reading can provide. A better informed translation will not automatically be a better translation, but it has the potential to be so.

3.0 What a New Approach Has to Offer

As I see it, there are several benefits of the approach. It can help translators with lexical choices. Anthony Kenny suggests that concordances – a 'display format that shows a "node" word in the centre with a specified amount of context on either side' (Mahlberg 2014:380) – 'are often more helpful than dictionaries for determining the precise sense of a word in an author's vocabulary, and they enable favourite phrases and tricks of style to be identified and catalogued' (1992:4). It can test stylistic hypotheses and 'hunches' about the importance, salience and frequency of occurrence of ST stylistic features initially identified through close reading. An example of this is the numerical confirmation of the suspected stylistic importance and prevalence of short sentences in *Gracias por el Fuego*, which is covered in depth in Chapter 5.

It can reveal the existence of potentially stylistically relevant linguistic patterns which close reading is either unlikely to reveal or is incapable of detecting, such as lexical variety and the use of words and phrases which are repeated, but are spread over a number of chapters. An example

8 Introduction

of this is given in Chapter 3. These patterns can then be subjected to qualitative investigation, which itself may give rise to further stylistic hypotheses that can in turn be investigated quantitatively. This is an example of what Leech calls 'the heuristic explanatory cycle of induction and deduction', whose goal is 'to arrive at... an evidentially warranted interpretation and appreciation of the text' (2008:195). The approach can also be used to make stylistic comparisons between the ST and the draft TT. This can help to evaluate, within clearly defined limits and against clearly established criteria, whether the draft TT has achieved certain translation goals set by the translator, and also whether unconscious shifts have taken place as a result of translation. In Chapter 5, I undertake such a comparison in relation to sentence length, and where a greater observed-than-expected variation between ST and TT is revealed, I investigate the draft TT qualitatively and suggest a possible explanation.

Finally, the approach dovetails with the current interest in translational style in CTS in that it can allow a translator to investigate and identify aspects of their *own* style. I undertook limited analyses of my own translatorial style, whose purpose was to start to answer two simple questions: What are my unconscious linguistic habits? Do they affect the way I translate, and if so, how? The methodology used and the results obtained are discussed in Chapter 7. It is worth noting here that the idea of computer technology, particularly in the form of artificial intelligence, tracking wider trends than can be achieved with close analysis alone, is often considered one of the major ways in which technology will change our lives over the next few years, in everything from medicine to traffic management, as Jim Al-Khalili's book *What's Next?* (2017) documents.

Limitations and Risks of the Methodology

An uncritical approach to a new methodology is dangerous and may undermine claims made for its proposed benefits, so listed below are what I see as the limitations and potential risks involved in its use. No stylistic analysis is ever complete, so it is necessary to choose particular features to investigate. In doing so it is important not to choose features just because they can be counted or processed computationally. This is because not every feature or pattern that can be counted is necessarily of stylistic or translational importance, and also because, as Anthony Kenny argues, 'it is important for humanists to adapt the software to the scholarship, not the scholarship to the software' (1992:9). Furthermore, as Jeremy Munday notes, 'word frequency lists and raw, even statistically-adjusted, figures inevitably decontextualize language. Any analysis must take into consideration the original context of those items' (1997:135–136). Linked to this point is the fact that, for the time being at least, there are many stylistically important linguistic phenomena that a computer

Introduction 9

cannot reliably detect, or detect at all. These include humour, irony, metaphors, similes and wordplay, to name but a few. However, it is important to note that these features can be counted manually by an analyst, which in some instances is perfectly feasible. It is the principle of providing evidence for stylistic judgements and statements by means of *counting* phenomena that is important, rather than the precise method by which this is done.

It is possible that the approach has more to offer the analysis and translation of prose than of poetry, since the longer the text, the harder it is for the human analyst or translator to notice and retain information about stylistically relevant linguistic patterns. However, even in the field of poetry the statistical analysis of certain features can be valuable, as Leech's analysis of tense usage in Dylan Thomas' poem *This bread I break* shows (2008:28–29). There is also a danger, when comparing a draft TT with its ST, that stylistic translational 'success' comes to be measured by the translator in terms of statistical closeness. In this context I cannot better Leech and Short's summary assessment of the balance needed between the digital and the humanities, the system and the human:

> ...the study of the relation between linguistic form and literary function, cannot be reduced to mechanical objectivity. In both the literary and the linguistic spheres much rests on the intuition and personal judgment of the reader, for which a system, however good, is an aid rather than a substitute. There will always remain, as Dylan Thomas says, 'the mystery of having been moved by words'.
>
> (2007:3)

4.0 The Case Study: *Gracias por el Fuego* (1965) by Mario Benedetti

I based my choice of ST on four main criteria. As a Spanish speaker and someone who has been involved with Latin America in a variety of ways for over 30 years, I was looking for a Latin American novel by a well-known writer which had not been translated into English, and which interested me. *Gracias por el Fuego*, in addition to being a gripping narrative, fulfilled all four criteria, interesting me for several reasons. Mario Benedetti was very well-known in Uruguay and was a prize-winning author in both Latin America and Spain, yet less than 10% of his considerable multi-genre body of work, including this novel, has been translated into English. Benedetti's work has been translated into 26 languages, and this novel itself has been translated into 10 European languages, but not English. So, given the dominant position of English as a world language into which many authors strive to be translated, there was on the face of it a literary conundrum.

10 *Introduction*

The novel is also an example of what Benedetti called *literatura com-prometida*, or politically committed literature. Written contemporaneously with the Latin American 'Boom' in the 1960s, it shares the left-wing perspective of renowned writers such as Gabriel García Márquez and Julio Cortázar, but is distinctive in that it primarily addresses its social and political message to a highly specific and localised audience, namely the Montevidean middle class to which Benedetti belonged. In relation to Benedetti's earlier novels, *Gracias por el Fuego* is more experimental and demonstrates how the dominant use of the interior monologue as a narrative style provided an effective vehicle for the transmission of that political message.

A complete translation of the novel was undertaken as part of the study, both because I felt it necessary to do this from a research point of view, and also because I wanted to see it published as a contribution to raising Benedetti's profile in the Anglophone canon of twentieth-century Latin American literature. In Chapters 3–6, I compare extracts of the ST with my draft translation, and it is important to clarify when this translation was done. The first draft of the translation was completed between August 2014 and May 2015, before I had begun to use computer-assisted methods as a translation tool. This first draft therefore constitutes a 'before' in relation to the 'after' which involved applying both close and distant reading to the translation. Unless otherwise indicated, all TT extracts come from this first draft, and these are frequently compared to drafts revised in the light of the application of the methodology. When I originally applied the methodology I only used the CATMA programme[2] (Youdale 2017), while subsequent research and analysis has also involved the use of Sketch Engine and Voyant Tools.

Notes

1 A mid-twentieth-century school of literary criticism which included figures such as I. A. Richards, and Wimsatt and Beardsley.
2 Please see Meister et al. (2018) in References.

1 Using Computers in Literary Translation

The focus of this book is on combining close reading with corpus linguistics (CL) and text-visualisation tools and techniques in the process of literary translation. The role of this chapter is to actively encourage the opening up of a wider debate about the various ways in which computer technology could be productively incorporated into this process, without involving either deterioration in quality of translation or translator deskilling. The close and distant reading (CDR) approach is contextualised by looking at the development and current usage of the two most widely adopted translation technologies: computer-aided translation (CAT) tools and machine translation (MT). The impact of these technologies on translators is summarised, and evidence is provided of varying attitudes towards their use on the part of both commercial and literary translators.[1] Some examples of the employment of both MT and CAT tools in literary translation are then given to show that these technologies need to be considered as part of the wider debate referred to above, particularly in the light of some current developments.

The third section of the chapter sets out the practical detail of the CDR approach as it relates to computer-aided literary analysis and literary translation. The functionalities of a number of software programmes which can be used in literary translation – CATMA (Computer-Aided Textual Markup and Analysis),[2] Sketch Engine[3] and Voyant Tools[4] – are listed and illustrated by examples of possible uses. These functionalities are then brought together, listed in a software comparison chart and linked to a provisional four-stage model of the process of literary translation. This shows how the software tools and approaches can expand the range and type of stylistic and narratological information available to the translator by interrogating both the source text (ST) and the draft target text (TT), in addition to their uses in the search for immediate translation solutions for given words and phrases. The chapter concludes by making the case for the relevance of the CDR approach to a range of neighbouring disciplines, and it is suggested that both they and Translation Studies (TS) would benefit from closer dialogue.

12 Using Computers in Literary Translation

1.1 Computers and Translation: An Overview

The Development of Translation Technologies

In a chapter from the *Routledge Encyclopedia of Translation Technology* (2015) the editor, Sin-Wai Chan, makes the blunt observation that 'In terms of the means of production, all translation nowadays is computer-aided as virtually no one could translate without a computer' (2015b:44). He also notes that 'It is estimated that with the use of translation technology, the work that was originally borne by six translators can be taken up by just one' (2015b:45). How we have arrived at this situation and an overview of what the impact of technology on translators has been, form the focus of this section and provide a context within which to examine the actual and potential uses of computers in literary translation.

Warren Weaver of the Rockefeller Foundation and Andrew Booth of London University are held to have been the first two scholars to suggest using the newly invented computer to automate translation between natural languages, in 1947 (Chan 2015a:3). Over the next 20 years substantial resources were devoted to developing this idea, but with disappointing results. It was believed by the research funders that the achievement of the stated goal of MT – the ability to produce fully automated, high-quality translation – was unattainable. In 1966 the Automatic Language Processing Advisory Committee (ALPAC) report of the US National Academy of Sciences concluded that there was 'no immediate or predictable prospect of useful machine translation'.[5] Although this delayed the progress of MT, it is held to have led directly to the development of CAT for the human translator in the form of the translation memory (TM) (Chan 2015a:5).

MT research was given a boost in the 1970s by the needs of the Canadian and European Community governments to find a way of producing a large volume of acceptable multilingual translations of administrative documents (Qun and Xiaojun 2015:107). In the 1980s the original MT systems based on linguistic rules were supplemented by the use of example-based MT, which took advantage of enlarged databases to allow better automated string-matching searches. This was followed by the development of statistical machine translation (SMT), sometimes called data-driven MT, which is 'a machine translation system that uses algorithms to establish probabilities between segments in a source and target language document to propose translation candidates'.[6] Before they can be used SMT systems, like all MT systems, need to be 'trained': they are 'fed' bilingual parallel corpora of texts related to the field and text-type being translated to analyse. They then search for probable matches amongst these corpora for ST segments (usually sentences), and

Using Computers in Literary Translation   13

these searches can be word-based, phrase-based or syntax-based (Qun and Xiaojun 2015:113). Despite this apparent technical sophistication, most MT still requires human intervention in the form of post-editing of translations, which is fast becoming a standard part of commercial translation. Two of the most recent developments in the field of MT are neural machine translation (NMT) – so-called due to an analogy with the human brain's neural network – which performs analysis and output based on weights and biases; and a growing convergence between MT and CAT's main tool, the TM (Choudhury and McConnell 2013:53).[7]

Born in a sense from the apparent failure of MT in the 1960s, the development of TMs and other CAT tools was boosted in the 1990s by the desire of corporations and institutions to widen their markets in goods and services (Garcia 2015:68). Whilst varying in the range of tools they offer and how they interact with other systems,

> every CAT system divides a text into "segments" (normally sentences, as defined by punctuation marks) and searches a bilingual memory for identical (exact match) or similar (fuzzy match) source and translation segments. Search and recognition of terminology in analogous bilingual glossaries are also standard. The corresponding search results are then offered to the human translator as prompts for adaptation and reuse.
>
> (Ibidem)

While the fundamental principles of TMs have remained the same, there have been significant changes in the context within which they are used and the features they can now offer. These include the following:

- a predominantly web-based rather than hard drive-based working environment, involving translation teams rather than lone translators
- large online databases can now be accessed, such as TDA (TAUS Data Association)[8] and the Google Translate Toolkit[9]
- term extraction tools can now bring language-specific knowledge to a CAT environment, which was previously like an empty shell waiting to be filled by TMs
- speech recognition text input is now being integrated into some CAT tools
- some sub-segmental matching from internal databases is now possible, as well as the use of predictive typing
- the convergence of MT with TM is growing, with advantages accruing from using a suggested MT version of a segment where there is 'no match' in the CAT tool or a fuzzy match below 70% similarity.[10]

(Garcia 2015:82–85)

14   *Using Computers in Literary Translation*

The Impact of Translation Technologies on Translators: Some Key Issues

The discussion so far has dealt with the development of translation technologies in purely technical terms, without regard to the effects these technologies have had on human translators, but a consideration of this is vital in any discussion of technology and translation. Even a brief review of the development of translation technologies will have made it clear that they have transformed the working lives of translators, particularly since the widespread introduction of CAT tools from the 1990s onwards. There now exists a body of studies on the impact of these technologies which reveals a mixed picture (Olohan 2011; Pym 2011; Screen 2016; Kenny 2017; LeBlanc 2017; Vieira and Alonso 2018). In broad terms, as Anthony Pym notes, the impact of translation technology on commercial translation is plain to see:

> whereas much of the translator's skillset and effort was previously invested in *identifying* possible solutions to translation problems (i.e., the *generative* side of the cognitive process), the vast majority of these skills and efforts are now invested in *selecting* between available solutions (i.e., the *selective* side of the cognitive processes).
> (Pym 2013:493, emphasis in the original)

While TMs have undoubtedly increased productivity, improved consistency and eliminated some boring and repetitive tasks (LeBlanc 2017:48), they have also led to some adverse consequences: 'TMs render the translator's work more mechanical and, when misused, may lead to deskilling and may have an effect on the translator's professional satisfaction' (Ibidem) as well as lowering rates of pay.

According to the UK Translators Survey 2017, involving 588 respondents, 65% of translators used TMs and 22% used MT (2017:26). In relation to TMs, while two thirds rated them as important to their work, there were mixed views on their impact:

> I use translation memories when required to do so by clients, but find them of little benefit.
> (2017:28)

> Many of my (agency) clients would not work with me if I did not use a CAT tool, it is therefore an essential skill to learn.
> (2017:41)

With MT, there was more overt hostility: 'Post-editing, which some agencies use a lot, is not improving quality, just reducing what the translator is paid' (2017:32). There were also examples of suggested strategies

Using Computers in Literary Translation 15

for ameliorating the impact of MT: 'Machine translation will be the natural evolution of the translation industry, to a certain extent. By fearing MT, we can make it worse. It should be embraced, but sold to clients as a different service to human translators' (Ibidem). Given the rapid development of both the translation technologies themselves and changes in the contexts in which they are being used and integrated, perhaps the survey's most surprising finding is that only a fifth of 585 respondents felt that technology would reduce the importance of human translators (2017:39). What is clear is that the future of translation technology is not entirely straightforward to predict, and that it is probably unwise to adopt either what Dorothy Kenny terms 'cyber-utopian visions of a world without language barriers' (2016:online) or the sweeping assumption that most translators will soon become just post-editors of MT (Pym 2013:488).

So far we have only looked at translation technology in the context of commercial translation, which is estimated to account for 90% of all translation worldwide (Chan 2015b:44). The focus of this book, however, is on computers and literary translation, and before turning to literary translators' attitudes to technology it is necessary to clarify some differences – and similarities – between the kinds of texts belonging to each type of translation. It is widely held that commercial and technical texts are 'simpler' and more repetitive than literary texts and are therefore more suited to MT and CAT applications. This is something of an oversimplification. The language of many literary texts in terms of lexical variety is often relatively simple and straightforward, as in the case of *Gracias por el Fuego*, and it is in the unconventional ways that language is used that literary complexity and originality are to be found. Conversely, medical and legal texts, for example, often contain much greater lexical variety and even complex conceptual structures, but are much more rule-bound in terms of modes of expression. It is this latter factor which makes such texts more amenable to the use of CAT tools in particular rather than any inherent simplicity. It is the relative lack in literary texts of consistent terminology and standardised phraseology, rather than inherent 'complexity' that makes the use of these tools less obviously attractive.

This helps to explain why there appears to be an almost wholesale rejection by literary translators of the use of CAT tools and MT in their craft. The following comments taken from the 2017 survey referred to above are representative:

> In my main field of literary translation, fortunately neither CAT tools nor MT are of any use as MT can translate words, but not meaning.
>
> (2017:32)

16   *Using Computers in Literary Translation*

> I find CAT tools useful for general commercial translation, but for creative work and literature they are irrelevant.
>
> (Ibidem)

Such sentiments were also strongly echoed in a 2017 thread on the use of CAT tools on the Emerging Translators Network (ETN), an online forum for literary translators.

There are, however, some dissenting voices which argue that CAT tools at least can be useful in a literary context:

> CATs can also be useful for glossary management [...] Maybe a character uses certain lingo and you want to be true to that by using the same equivalents and register in the translation, so it's important to stay consistent with the vocabulary.
>
> (Lombardino 2014:online)

Another literary translation blogger, Riccardo Schiaffino, has changed the segmentation rules in his CAT tool to segment at paragraph rather than sentence level, and he then exports the output to a word-processor for revision (Schiaffino 2016), thus allowing him to translate within a wider context. In Section 1.2 some specific examples are given of the use of both CAT tools and MT in literary translation.

The Use of Computers in TS

No overview of computers and translation would be complete without a consideration of the field of corpus-based translation studies (CTS). This area of study began in the 1990s as a result of the convergence in the 1980s and 1990s of two developments. The first was the increased feasibility of compiling corpora of texts, a corpus being defined as 'a large collection of machine-readable texts compiled with a specific purpose that can be retrieved with particular computer software for linguistic research' (Lan 2015:465). The second was the ability to analyse such texts with the use of CL, 'a research approach that facilitates empirical descriptions of language use' (Biber 2011:15). Originally developed for monolingual text analysis, scholars such as Mona Baker (1993, 1995) and Jan-Mirko Maczewski (1996) showed how corpus-linguistic literary analysis could be successfully applied to translation.

Early CTS research saw the linking of Descriptive Translation Studies (DTS) to CL with a view to deepening our understanding of what happens in the translation process (Laviosa 2004:8). Shoshana Blum-Kulka's (1986) explicitation hypothesis and Gideon Toury's suggestion that there might be 'universal' laws of translation (2012) are perhaps two of the best-known examples. In the second half of the 1990s Mona Baker focused on the investigation of whether there were identifiable

Using Computers in Literary Translation 17

features that could distinguish translated from non-translated language, and set up the Translational English Corpus at Manchester University.

Since 2000 one of the main areas of investigation, following Mona Baker's seminal article 'Towards a methodology for investigating the style of a literary translator' (2000), has been that of translator style, as opposed to the style of a translated text (Saldanha 2014:100). This has provided evidence (Malmkjaer 2004; Winters 2009; Saldanha 2011) that it is possible to identify features of an individual translator's style which recur across different translations and can distinguish her/him from other translators (see Chapter 7 for a fuller treatment of this topic). A defining feature of CTS, however, is the fact that it has only analysed already completed and published translations. What makes the CDR approach new is that it uses many of the tools and techniques developed in CL and CTS as part of the *process* of translation, and a detailed summary of the approach is provided in Section 1.3.

1.2 CAT Tools, MT and Literary Translation

The conventional wisdom strongly suggests that CAT tools and MT are simply not appropriate for literary translation. The need for creativity in translation solutions and the inability of computers to deal with polysemy, idioms and various forms of linguistic complexity common in literary language are all cited in support of this view. There is also the simple fact, noted by Carl et al., that 'understanding human language relies on information which is not present in the words which make up the message' (Carl, Bangalore and Schaeffer 2016:226). Yet despite this dismissive assessment there have in recent years been a few interesting experiments designed to see whether these technologies might in fact have a role to play in literary translation, and a range of these are reviewed in this section.

These experimental studies are divided into those related to CAT tools and those concerned with various applications of MT, of which there appear to be a greater number. Rather than viewing the use of MT as 'all or nothing' – if it cannot fully automate literary translation it is useless – researchers have taken a variety of approaches. At one end of the spectrum Antonio Toral and Andy Way (2015) pursue the holy grail of fully automated high-quality translation of a novel between two closely related languages, Spanish to Catalan, with cautiously optimistic results. Laurent Besacier and Lane Schwartz (2015) explore the time-saving potential of post-edited MT as an alternative to full human translation. Ruth Jones and Ann Irvine (2013) use a comparison of human and machine translation of the same text to help identify points of difficulty in translation; and in similar vein Andrew Rothwell (2009) shows how MT, when applied to Dadaist texts, can reveal key aspects of the contrastive linguistics of French and English, throwing light on common translation challenges.

18 *Using Computers in Literary Translation*

CAT Tools and Literary Translation

A TM, the quintessential CAT tool, has been shown to work best on texts which are repetitive, linguistically regular and contain fairly short sentences. The system draws on a parallel bilingual database of translated texts and automatically suggests a possible translation for each new segment of text, usually a sentence. As indicated above, literary works generally do not fit the profile of TM-friendly texts and are therefore widely considered not to be able to benefit from TM translation systems. Andrew Rothwell questions this sweeping assumption and shows how TM can be useful in the retranslation of a classic literary text, Émile Zola's 1884 novel *La Joie de vivre*, which he argues represented 'an urgent and, at the time, radical manifesto for the rational, scientific education of girls, and the open acknowledgement of female sexuality' (Rothwell 2018:2).

The original translation into English, *The Joy of Life* (1901) is by Ernest Vizetelly and was published at a time when much of the ST content was considered criminally pornographic in England, resulting in heavy self-censorship in the translation. In preparation for the recent retranslation both ST and TT were digitised, divided into chapter files and aligned at segment level using the free LF Aligner 4.1.[11] Each aligned chapter was then exported in Translation Memory eXchange (TMX) format and imported into the memoQ CAT tool. Rothwell argues that the use of a TM in the context of the retranslation of a classic text can benefit the translator 'by making instantly and consistently available for scrutiny the solutions chosen by an earlier translator' (2018:1), rather than having to search the ST and original TT manually.

Reflecting on his experience of translating this way, Rothwell observes that

> Correcting the initial automatic alignments, then working with the resultant TMs, became a fascinating process of dual reading, matching up segments of ST and TT and interpreting them in the light of one another. This served both to confirm and occasionally correct my own understanding, but also to create a more three-dimensional vision of the ST and near-contemporary TT in their shared historical era, as twin texts handling the same narrative and psychological material from different but convergent angles, and only accidentally, as it were, deployed in different languages and voices.
>
> (2018:5)

He concludes by hoping that 'the present case-study will encourage further experiments, eventually allowing translation memory to find its legitimate place in the toolkit of the literary translator' (2018:6).

MT and Literary Translation

Toral and Way (2015) challenge the view that MT is of no use in literary translation, using the fully automated translation of a novel from Spanish to Catalan as a case study, aimed at measuring 'the translatability of literary text' (2015:123). Their methodology is based on the view that

> the applicability of MT to a given type of text can be assessed by analysing parallel corpora of that particular type and measuring (i) the degree of freedom of the translations (how literal the translations are), and (ii) the narrowness of the domain (how specific or general that text is).
>
> (Ibidem)

The researchers built an MT system, possibly the first specifically designed to translate a novel, to translate *The Prisoner of Heaven* (2011) by Carlos Ruiz Zafón, from Spanish into Catalan. They trained the system on Spanish and Catalan translations of two other novels by the same author and Spanish to English translations of novels by the author and by Gabriel García Márquez. The evaluation of the output involved the use of automated metrics[12] and two bilingual speakers in Spanish and Catalan, who were asked to judge the quality of two sets of 101 translation segments which they thought were both produced by MT, when in fact one set had been produced by a professional translator.

Their results provide evidence that

> MT can be useful to assist with the translation of novels between closely-related languages, namely (i) the translations produced by our best system are equal to the ones produced by a professional human translator in almost 20% of cases with an additional 10% requiring at most 5 character edits, and (ii) a complementary human evaluation shows that over 60% of the translations are perceived to be of the same (or even higher) quality by native speakers.
>
> (2015:123)

They concluded that MT translated short sentences relatively well, but that human translation produced higher quality translations of longer sentences, and that 'Regarding translation freedom, the main variable is not related to the type of data but to the level of relatedness of the pair of languages involved' (2015:130). In subsequent studies they experimented with translations from two less closely related languages (English to Catalan) and produced two interesting findings. In terms of post-editing a literary text which had been translated using two MT variants – phrase-based SMT and NMT – there were productivity gains (higher for NMT in both cases) in time taken and number of keystrokes used, as compared to

20 Using Computers in Literary Translation

post-editing a professional human translation undertaken from scratch (Toral, Wieling and Way 2018). In a separate experiment with the same language pair, involving the translation of randomly selected passages from 12 well-known English novels spanning a period from the 1920s to today, they found that 'between 17% and 34% of the translations, depending on the book, produced by NMT [...] are perceived by native speakers of the target language to be of equivalent quality to translations produced by a professional human translator' (Toral and Way 2018:1).

In their study Besacier and Schwartz (2015) set out to discover whether post-edited SMT would be feasible for the translation of a literary work. Specifically, they ask if this approach would be quicker than full human translation, and whether the results would be acceptable to readers (2015:114). They selected an essay by the author Richard Powers, *The Book of Me*, originally published in GQ magazine in 2008, and used SMT to translate this into French. The methodology involved recursive MT and post-editing in a three-stage process:

- The first third of the document was translated from English to French using Moses [...], a state-of-the-art phrase-based machine translation system. This machine translation output was then post-edited.
- The post-edited data from the third of the document was used to train an updated domain-adapted English-French MT system.
- Then, the second third of the text was translated with the adapted MT system, then the results were post-edited and a second adapted MT system was obtained starting from the new data. This second system was used to translate the third and last part of the text.

(2015:115)

The post-editing was done by a postgraduate student of translation, and the result was revised by a native French speaker who had good English (2015:116). Nine French readers read the final version and answered a questionnaire. The key finding was that eight of the nine considered the text to be 'overall readable (5 Very Good and 3 Good), comprehensible (8 yes, 1 not) and containing few errors (8 seldom, 1 often)' (2015:119). Richard Powers' official French translator was also asked to evaluate the final text. He considered it unacceptable due to errors arising from syntactic calque, unidiomatic phrasing and an inability to take account of cultural references (2015:120). However, the researchers found that while the post-edited MT version took 25 human hours to complete (total post-editing and revising time), the professional translator estimated that he would need approximately 48 hours to do a full translation of the 10,731 words (Ibidem). They concluded that post-edited MT was capable in principle of increasing productivity in literary translation. All the data featured in their article is available in French at https://github.com/powersmachinetranslation/DATA.

Using Computers in Literary Translation 21

In another study of the MT post-editing of a literary text from English to Catalan by six experienced literary translators, Joss Moorkens et al. (2018) looked at translator attitudes to MT post-editing as compared to translating from scratch. They concluded that 'While all participants prefer to translate from scratch, mostly due to the freedom to be creative without the constraints of segment-level segmentation, those with less experience find the MT suggestions useful' (240). Interestingly, the translators still preferred to translate from scratch even where using NMT measurably saved them time and cognitive effort.

The last two studies compare the ways in which human translation and MT produce a text, and suggest that the value of MT is not its capacity to produce a high-quality literary translation, but in the way its *in*capacity to do so highlights linguistic differences between languages which are often a challenge for translators. Jones and Irvine (2013) link the issue of MT in literary translation to translation theory – specifically the domestication vs. foreignisation debate – and take as their starting point the idea that 'one objective in literary translation is to preserve the *experience* of reading a text when moving to the target language' (2013:96, emphasis in the original). In this process a range of factors external to the text come into play, including translators' attitudes to their role as cultural mediators, something for which it would be extremely difficult to programme an MT engine.

The researchers analyse translations from two samples of French literature, one of which is an extract from Albert Camus' 1955 novel *L'étranger*, with its 1989 English translation *The Stranger* by Camus and Ward. The human translation is compared to two SMT versions, one trained on the Canadian Hansard data[13] and the other produced by Google Translate. An example shows how and where human and machine translators diverge:

ST	Hansard MT	Google SMT	Ward translation
je crois que j'ai dormi parce que je me suis réveillé avec des étoiles sur le visage.	i think i slept because i woke up with stars on your face.	i think i slept because i woke up with stars on her face.	i must have fallen asleep, because i woke up with the stars in my face.

The SMT translations 'drop the indefinite article and assume a second person in the scene' (2013:99). On the basis of this and two other similar examples, the authors argue that 'The discrepancies between the human and MT versions of Camus' text suggest that the MT systems might, at the least, be able to identify the difficulties of translating certain stylistic elements of the French' (Ibidem).

22 *Using Computers in Literary Translation*

They also draw a number of broader conclusions about the inherent limitations of MT as a method of literary translation. They point out that linguistic features such as tense usage are subtly different in English and French; that the human translator has to decide 'when to make exceptions to convention for the sake of the reader's experience of the translated text, and the question of the exception is difficult for the machine to account for' (2013:100); and that decisions about explicitation, for example, are defined by the translator rather than the text. It would be very hard to design a reliable computational model which could take factors like these into account. In short, they argue, 'There is a constant trade-off between fluency and faithfulness. Although SMT can deal with fluency it cannot handle ideas of domestic and foreign' (Ibidem).

The final example is, paradoxically, of an unusual form of literary translation for which MT would actually seem to be *more* appropriate than human translation. Rothwell (2009) poses the question of how Dadaist works from the early twentieth century, deliberately intended by their authors to produce texts that 'challenge and frustrate the reader's desire to find coherence in them' (2009:260) can be translated. Arguing that a human translator would instinctively try to remove ambiguity and create coherence not present in the original, he suggests that an unthinking (and therefore unbiased) machine would actually be more likely to produce a 'faithful' translation, and puts this to the test. He uses Systran 4 Premium to automatically translate the Préface to Francis Picabia's *Pensées sans langage* (1919) and compares translation and original. An example is given below:

ST: Les pierres précieuses ont la même dimension accidentellement et en dessous.
TT: The invaluable stones have same dimension accidentally and below (2009:262 and 265, emphasis in the original).

Rothwell makes the observation that 'Systran's "failure" to translate *pierres précieuses* by the expected collocation '*precious* stones' (as in Lowenthal's translation) draws attention to the ossified nature of such collocations in both languages, and therefore in the thought patterns of their users' (2009:266, emphasis in the original). Furthermore, he notes, in this and other instances 'the software has again drawn attention to a translation decision [...] which might otherwise have passed unnoticed' (2009:268).

The picture that emerges from this brief review of research on CAT tools, MT and literary translation is more nuanced than the translator survey responses might suggest. A strong case has been made for the usefulness of a TM in the retranslation of a classic text (Rothwell 2018), and it is possible to summarise both the clear limitations and some of the potential benefits of using MT in different ways.

Using Computers in Literary Translation   23

Limitations	Potential Benefits
• to date, MT has only been shown to have potential benefits where it is used with linguistically simple texts, is trained on highly specific translations which stick closely to the ST language and style and is used with fairly closely related languages • powers of syntactic analysis and reproduction are still relatively crude • typical features of literary language such as polysemy, ambiguity, humour, metaphor, idioms and long sentences are still poorly handled • MT systems are not currently programmed to take account of metatextual factors such as translator approach, author/publisher briefs and cultural references, all of which would represent significant challenges for system designers	• when trained on highly genre- and domain-specific translation databases, and applied to related language pairs, MT may be capable of producing near-human quality translation in certain circumstances • if the initial MT error rate can be reduced to a minimal level, it would appear that there could be potential time-saving gains to be made by post-editing MT as opposed to using full human translation from scratch, also in certain circumstances • comparisons of human translation and MT of the same text have the potential to highlight aspects of translator decision-making and the contrastive linguistics of language pairs • the idea of using MT interactively, whereby 'the translator is provided with MT suggestions as he/she types the translation' (Toral and Way 2015:264) may solve some of the problems associated with fully automated MT

It will have been noted that this chapter has excluded any consideration of the use of translation technology to translate poetry. This is partly because research in this area is even scarcer than for prose,[14] and partly because the limitations listed above relating to prose apply with even greater force to poetry, which by its nature is often semantically and syntactically complex and unusual, as well as highly ambiguous.

1.3 Computers and the CDR Approach to the Translation of Style

The Philosophy of CDR

In the Introduction I outlined my approach to the translation of literary style as being based on the choices made by the ST and TT authors, and the effects those choices may have on the ST and TT readers, respectively. Specifically, I aim to creatively 'reverse engineer' the effects I experience as a reader of the ST by trying to work out how those effects were

24 *Using Computers in Literary Translation*

achieved and then attempting to recreate them in my translation. That is easier said than done. It is one thing to register the effects a literary work has on you as a reader, but often quite another to understand how those effects were created by the text.

Literary style is fundamentally based on patterns of language use, and a pattern 'is essentially repetition' (Hunston 2010:152), though not necessarily frequent repetition. While certain stylistic features will be foregrounded and noticed by the reader, such as frequently repeated phrases used by a particular character, many will not. There are several reasons why some stylistic patterns are unlikely to be noticed by even the closest reader. Attempting to retain an accurate count of sentence length while reading a novel, for example, would only be possible at the expense of destroying any kind of normal reading experience. When we read, we simply do not register or retain this kind of information. Susan Hunston also suggests that as language users we 'have relatively untuned intuitions about frequency, about frequency of co-occurrence in particular' (2010:154), and that

> repetition in naturally occurring conversations is transient, fleeting; it may have no perceptible effect, or its effects may not be ascribed to the repetition itself. In other words, it is not noticed.
>
> (Ibidem)

Computers, however, are very good at detecting linguistic patterns and presenting them to an analyst (or translator-as-analyst) for qualitative investigation and assessment. And it is their ability to reveal these 'hidden' layers of information about a text that makes them valuable tools for translators. The more stylistic information a translator has at their disposal, the greater the likelihood that they will be able to understand how the text has created its effects and how to attempt to recreate them. The field of CTS has used the tools provided by CL to analyse some of these hidden aspects of author and translator style in already completed and published translations. The CDR approach uses these and other computer-aided methods in the translation process itself, and this is what makes it new.

The approach concentrates on the use of CL and text-visualisation tools, which in some cases are beginning to converge, rather than MT and CAT tools. While the latter may have a role to play, as evidenced by some of the studies discussed in the previous section, they have been developed in the context of a commercial translation industry driven by pressures to increase productivity and reduce both translation costs and the role of the human translator in the translation process. By contrast the use of CL and text-visualisation in CDR is consciously designed to support and enhance the literary translator's creativity by maximising the amount of stylistic (and frequently narratological) information

Using Computers in Literary Translation 25

they have at their disposal. Translation options are increased rather than decreased.

In practical terms the CDR approach can be used in three specific ways as part of the literary translation process, and one more general way:

1 In analysing the ST after (and possibly even during) initial reading, and in helping the translator to formulate specific translation goals.
2 In undertaking the first draft of the translation.
3 In comparing the ST and draft translation, with a view to seeing if certain translation goals have been achieved, and what has actually happened in the translation process.
4 In the auto-analysis of translator style. This can be done at any time, but is more likely to yield meaningful results after a translator has completed several translations.

In the remainder of this section I will show how CL and text-visualisation can be used in different ways as aids in literary translation. The use of specific software programmes will be explained and illustrated, and their functionalities linked to a provisional four-stage model of the translation process.

Using CL and Corpus Stylistics to Translate Literary Style

The term 'corpus' has been defined in various ways (Saldanha 2009) but essentially refers to a body of text (often in the form of multiple texts) selected for the purposes of linguistic analysis and stored in searchable electronic form. According to Douglas Biber, 'corpus linguistics is a research approach that [...] has the goal of describing the patterns of language use in the target textual domain' (2011:15). The use of this approach to study aspects of literary style has become known as corpus stylistics, where

> The computer does not provide a single method of text analysis, but offers a range of exploratory techniques for investigating features of texts and corpora. The findings of corpus stylistics (comparative frequencies, distributions and the like) sometimes document more systematically what literary critics already know (and therefore add to methods of close reading), but they can also reveal otherwise invisible features of long texts.
>
> (Stubbs 2005:22, emphasis added)

CL and corpus stylistics are both concerned with finding linguistic patterns, which involve repetition, and repetition is measured in frequency terms: 'in corpus linguistics it is frequency of occurrence that takes pride

26 *Using Computers in Literary Translation*

of place' (Tognini Bonelli 2010:19). This applies to individual words and groups of words, and explains why the first steps in analysing a corpus 'generally involve two related processes: the production of frequency lists (either in rank order, or sorted alphabetically) and the generation of concordances' (Evison 2010:122). Concordances are the results of searches for specific words or phrases, which are displayed with the target term(s) – or 'node(s)' – vertically centred, and a pre-set (but usually alterable) number of words on either side. These vertically displayed concordance lines are also known as key-word-in-context (KWIC) views. The words either side of the node can be sorted alphabetically, and this often helps to reveal further patterns. An example of a word frequency list and its related KWIC view are shown in Figure 1.1.

It is worth noting that the results of CL analysis are normally presented in a way which decontextualises them, as lists of words or very short text extracts. This is a form of 'distant reading'. However, programmes such as CATMA allow alternation between distant and close reading at the click of a button. In Figure 1.1 a word is first shown in a simple word list, then in its immediate context as part of a KWIC list. If the user double-clicks on the highlighted node word in KWIC view, the word is then shown underlined in the context of the full document, as shown in Figure 1.2, allowing for close reading in the light of anything suggested by the distant reading results.

It should now be easier to see how this kind of frequency search functionality for words and phrases could be useful to the translator. Finding out how often and in what contexts a word or phrase occurs can help, for example, with individual translation decisions (see the discussion of how to translate the word 'fuego' in the case study novel's title, in Chapter 2). Another useful tool involves the analysis of collocation: 'the way in which particular words are associated with each other, as shown empirically by their tendency to co-occur more frequently than would be expected by chance' (Biber 2011:18). This type of analysis may help a translator assess, for instance, whether a word is being used in an unusual way by an author, or whether it tends to demonstrate a particular semantic prosody, 'an underlying evaluative meaning' (Ibidem), often categorised as simply positive or negative. As Jane Evison notes, 'it is useful both for hypothesis testing and hypothesis generation' (2010:129).

The last standard analytical tool offered by most CL software programmes is *keyword* analysis (not to be confused with 'key word in context', where 'key' simply refers to the word highlighted as the node of a concordance line). Keywords are words which occur more often ('positive' keywords) or less often ('negative' keywords) in the corpus being analysed than in a comparable reference corpus containing texts of a similar type and genre. Positive keywords can give valuable clues about themes in a text and help to reveal linguistic devices used to achieve particular effects (Biber 2011:17), thus assisting the translator with the stylistic reverse engineering process referred to earlier.

Result by Phrase	Result by Tag		

Phrase	Frequency		Visible in Kwic
▸ era	128	▾	☐
▸ ya	128		☐
▸ Ramón	127		☑
▸ tiene	127		☐
▸ hay	126		☐
▸ A	126		☐
▸ Viejo	125		☐
▸ dos	119		☐
▸ algo	119		☐
▸ sé	118		☐
▸ puede	117		☐
▸ este	117		☐
▸ ojos	115		☐
▸ todos	113		☐
Total count: 11,992	Total frequency: 92,936		

D	Left Context	Keyword	Right Context	Start Point	End Point
G	. Yo lo quería a	Ramón	. ¿Acaso no sabés	448,178	448,183
G	vacías. Acaso el pobre	Ramón	, piensa Gloria, se	446,396	446,401
G	verdaderamente, el suicidio de	Ramón	lo había golpeado fuerte.	444,379	444,384
G	—La muerte de	Ramón	me ha golpeado fuerte.	444,069	444,074
G	a raíz del suicidio de	Ramón	. Simplemente, ha envejecido	442,357	442,362
G	. Un día, cuando	Ramón	era un muchacho, me	437,730	437,735
G	que matarse. —Para	Ramón	, sí. Era bueno	433,972	433,977
G	no podrá ser aquel que	Ramón	me fue quitando, y	429,759	429,764
G	tenga mi piel acariciada por	Ramón	. Pero tampoco. Nunca	429,391	429,396
G	memoria, que no tenga	Ramón	, que no tenga mi	429,348	429,353
G	fue la desgracia mayor.	Ramón	tonto, tontísimo, claro	428,066	428,071
G	. Ramón, Ramón,	Ramón	. ¿Y ahora?	427,218	427,223
G	, seguir. Ramón,	Ramón	. Ramón. ¿Y	427,211	427,216
G	. Oh, seguir.	Ramón	. Ramón, Ramón.	427,204	427,209
G	que empezaste a convencerme.	Ramón	tonto. Viejito. Seguramente	422,320	422,325

Figure 1.1 Word list and KWIC view in CATMA.

28 Using Computers in Literary Translation

Lindos. Ya no lo son. Ahora la piel tiene más de cuarenta. Ahora los hombros tienen pecas. Y están caídos. Y ella está cansada. Y tiene urgencia. Y aunque los hombros tengan pecas y su piel tenga más de cuarenta años, ella necesita que un hombre, no un viejo, use esos hombros, no para apoyar las manos cuando esté cansado, no para hacer frases famosas, sino para atraerla, para usarla a ella toda, no sólo sus hombros, para usarla a ella en alma y cuerpo, no como instrumento, no como un mueble; un hombre, no un viejo que dice aspirar a que lo maten y sin embargo está loco de miedo; no un viejo sino un hombre verdadero y común, un hombre que no se crea infalible, poderoso; un hombre y no un viejo relleno de plata y de rencores.

—No valía la pena. Yo lo quería a Ramón. ¿Acaso no sabés que lo quería? Tenía miedo a la oscuridad y me miraba con una carita agradecida cuando yo venía a auxiliarlo, a confortarlo. Y una vez le compré diez cajas de soldados de plomo. Y tenía una expresión de asombro. No, si yo no me olvido. ¿Sabés por qué no me mató, a pesar de que puso el revólver sobre la mesa? No me mató, porque en el fondo me seguía queriendo, me seguía necesitando. Era mi hijo, era mi hijo. Y yo lo vi allá abajo, con la cabeza en un charco de sangre.

Figure 1.2 Node word highlighted in the full text.

So far we have looked at standard CL analysis of lexical frequency from a purely semantic point of view. However, programmes such as CATMA and Sketch Engine also allow users to conduct grammatical analyses using corpus query language (CQL). This involves setting criteria for complex searches which cannot be carried out using the standard user interface controls, employing a series of standard codes. If, for example, the ST or draft TT being analysed has been 'tagged' for parts of speech (POS) – a process whereby each word in a text is assigned a POS by a computer programme – then it is possible to search for particular grammatical categories. A search for all the proper nouns in a text, for instance, would extract all the names of people and places mentioned, thus yielding a list of characters. Average and banded sentence length can also be easily extracted using CQL, and this is analysed in relation to the case study translation in Chapter 5 in some detail. The use of CL tools within a corpus stylistic framework thus offers a literary translator ways of detecting and analysing 'the functional and aesthetic associations of linguistic patterns' (Biber 2011:21).

The contribution of CL to the process of literary translation is not confined to the identification and assessment of linguistic patterns and stylistic features. It also encompasses powerful aids to solving specific translation challenges. This is important given that there is evidence that translators can spend 'over half their time looking for information of various kinds' (Kübler and Aston 2010:501). At the same time there is strong evidence that very few professional translators actually use corpora at all in their work (Scott 2010; Gallego-Hernández 2015; Frérot

Using Computers in Literary Translation   29

2016). There are three main kinds of corpora that a translator could use to look up problematic words and phrases:

- monolingual SL corpora such as the *Corpus del Español*[15]
- comparable bilingual corpora: 'corpora compiled using similar design criteria but which are not translations' (Zanettin 2002:10), such as the TenTen Corpus Family[16]
- parallel bilingual corpora: 'texts in one language aligned with their translation in another' (Ibidem) as illustrated in Figure 1.3.

As Federico Zanettin points out, it is important to understand that corpora cannot be seen simply as large dictionaries: 'While dictionaries favour a synthetic approach to lexical meaning (via a definition), corpora offer an analytic approach (via multiple contexts)' (Zanettin 2002:11). Parallel corpora in particular differ from bilingual dictionaries since the latter are 'repertoires of lexical equivalents', whereas parallel corpora are '<u>repertoires of strategies deployed by past translators, as well as repertoires of translation equivalents</u>' (Ibidem, emphasis added).

The other kind of corpus a literary translator could profitably use is one they create themselves. When preparing to translate a text, the translator could assemble a corpus of other texts by the same author (copyright permitting) or a corpus of secondary sources about her/him. Sketch Engine allows users to upload their own documents and then automatically 'compiles' them into a fully searchable corpus. The programme will even automatically conduct a web search and then create a searchable corpus for the user, based on a recommended range of 3–20 'seed' words or

2. La Unión ofrecerá a sus ciudadanos un espacio de libertad, seguridad y justicia sin **fronteras** interiores, en el que esté garantizada la libre circulación de personas conjuntamente con medidas adecuadas en materia de control de las fronteras exteriores, asilo, inmigración y de prevención y lucha contra la delincuencia.	2. The Union shall offer its citizens an area of freedom, security and justice without internal frontiers, in which the free movement of persons is ensured in conjunction with appropriate measures with respect to external border controls, asylum, immigration and the prevention and combating of crime.
2. La Unión ofrecerá a sus ciudadanos un espacio de libertad, seguridad y justicia sin fronteras interiores, en el que esté garantizada la libre circulación de personas conjuntamente con medidas adecuadas en materia de control de las **fronteras** exteriores, asilo, inmigración y de prevención y lucha contra la delincuencia.	2. The Union shall offer its citizens an area of freedom, security and justice without internal frontiers, in which the free movement of persons is ensured in conjunction with appropriate measures with respect to external border controls, asylum, immigration and the prevention and combating of crime.
c) mantener la paz, prevenir los conflictos y fortalecer la seguridad internacional, conforme a los propósitos y principios de la Carta de las Naciones Unidas, así como a los principios del Acta Final de Helsinki y a los objetivos de la Carta de París, incluidos los relacionados con las **fronteras** exteriores;	(c) preserve peace, prevent conflicts and strengthen international security, in accordance with the purposes and principles of the United Nations Charter, with the principles of the Helsinki Final Act and with the aims of the Charter of Paris, including those relating to external borders;

Figure 1.3 English and Spanish parallel corpus in Sketch Engine.

30 *Using Computers in Literary Translation*

terms which the user inputs. A particularly good use of Sketch Engine's corpus creation functionality from a CDR point of view is the conversion of an ST and draft TT into a parallel corpus. Once aligned and converted into TMX format (not a difficult process: see Section 1.2 for details of the free LF Aligner 4.1 software), the ST and draft TT can quickly be converted into a searchable parallel corpus, allowing the translator to search, review and analyse their translation with ease and in detail.

There is a very useful, and possibly unique, feature of Sketch Engine called *Word Sketch*, which displays an at-a-glance overview of a word's 'behaviour', as illustrated in Figure 1.4.

In the course of preparing to undertake another translation I came across the Spanish phrase *soga y cabrito* [rope and little goat] with which I was not familiar and which made no semantic sense in context. I thought that it must be an idiomatic expression. Print and online dictionaries threw no light on the phrase, nor did internet searches. Searching a ten-billion word monolingual Spanish corpus provided by Sketch Engine yielded only three hits for the phrase. The results suggested a possible meaning and also suggested that the phrase was probably fairly uncommon. A further search using Sketch Engine's Word Sketch feature to find collocates for *soga* threw up the closely related phrase *soga y cabra* [rope and nanny goat]. A subsequent search in the same monolingual Spanish corpus for this phrase yielded 71 results, strongly suggesting a translation of the phrase as *everything*, which made good sense in the context of the translation. However, it seemed to me that if the SL expression was probably uncommon, it made stylistic sense to translate it using a correspondingly uncommon TL expression, and after reviewing various

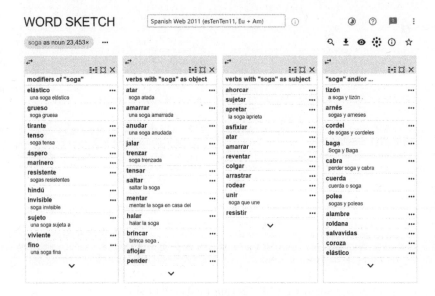

Figure 1.4 Example of a Word Sketch in Sketch Engine.

Using Computers in Literary Translation 31

possibilities I settled on 'the whole shebang'. This example supports the argument put forward by Frankenberg-Garcia that corpora can 'help both translation trainees and professionals cope better with unfamiliar terminology and phraseology, and with the styles and idiolects they may need to reproduce in a translation' (Frankenberg-Garcia 2015:352).

It is also important to note that the CDR approach can be applied to a wide variety of other language pairs. In recent years the range of languages which can be processed in corpus linguistic software has grown significantly. ParaConc, specifically designed for translation,[17] can handle Arabic, Farsi, Chinese, Russian, Czech and nearly all the Nordic languages, in addition to other European languages. CATMA[18] can also process Korean, Greek, Irish, Hebrew, Albanian, Hindi, Japanese and Vietnamese. Sketch Engine[19] boasts a capacity to handle over 90 languages.

To conclude this overview of the uses of CL and corpus stylistics in literary translation I would like to make two observations. First, it is clear that the use of corpora and CL analysis offers the translator a range of powerful tools and methods which can be applied at all three key stages of the translation process:

- during and/or after initial reading of the ST to undertake ST analysis
- during initial translation
- during translation revision, by facilitating direct and searchable comparison of the ST and TT and the opportunity to assess whether certain translation goals have been achieved.

Second, there is ample evidence of calls for, and studies of, the use of corpora in commercial translator training, which still seems patchy at best (Zanettin 2002; Hyde-Parker 2008; Gallego-Hernández 2015; Frérot 2016). I believe that the use of corpora should also form part of the training of literary translators.

CL Software for Use in Literary Translation: A Comparison

The software programmes listed in the comparison chart in Table 1.1 all offer the following basic CL analytical functionalities:

- word frequency lists
- KWIC view concordance displays
- collocation analysis
- keyword lists.

In addition, they offer a range of other tools, some of which are unique to a particular programme. These include various forms of text-visualisation, which will be discussed separately in the following subsection. The chart does not pretend to be exhaustive, but I believe that

Table 1.1 Comparison chart of CL software for use in literary translation

Tool	Functionality	AntConc	CATMA	ParaConc	Sketch Engine	WordSmith Tools	Voyant Tools
Word list	Lists all words in a corpus by frequency or alphabetically	•	•	•	•	•	•
Word/phrase search	Allows the user to search for any word or phrase in the corpus	•	•	•	•	•	•
KWIC concordance	Lists occurrences of a search word/phrase with a small amount of text either side	•	•	•	•	•	•
Collocation	Allows the user to investigate words co-occurring with a search term in the corpus	•	•	•	•	•	•
Keyword list	Displays the words which occur more or less frequently than in a comparable reference corpus	•	•	•	•	•	•
N-grams	Allows the user to search for sequences of words of a set length or range (e.g. 2–5 words) without using a search term	•	X	X	•	•	•
Word clusters	Allows the user to search for a word or pattern, and group (cluster) the results together with the words immediately to the left or right of the search term	•	•	X	•	•	•
Multilingual use	Allows the user to analyse corpora in different languages	•	•	•	•	•	•
Monolingual corpora	Allows the user to consult built-in reference corpora	Allows the user to import a reference corpus	X	X	•	Allows the user to import a reference corpus	X
Comparable corpora	Allows the user to search for translations of a search term in corpora of a similar text type in another language	X	X	X	•	X	X
Parallel corpora	Allows the user to search segment-aligned ST and TT	X	X	•	•	X	X

Word Sketch	Provides a one-page, automatic, corpus-derived summary of a word's grammatical and collocational behaviour	X	X	X	•	X	X
Word Sketch difference	Allows the user to compare and contrast two words by analysing their collocations and by displaying the collocates divided into categories based on grammatical relations	X	X	X	•	X	X
Thesaurus	Allows the user to generate a list of related words from a lemma, [20] from a user-created or reference corpus	X	X	X	•	X	X
Custom dictionaries	Allows the user to generate a headword list, providing POS labels, usage labels, generating candidates for sentences, collocations, synonyms and thesaurus entries, definitions and/or translations	X	X	X	•	X	X
Corpus tagging	Allows the user to search a corpus in a variety of specialised and non-semantic ways	Allows the user to import lemma lists to produce lemmatised word counts	Offers manual tagging and user-defined annotation	X	Offers automated POS-tagging and lemmatisation	Allows the user to import tag files	X
Corpus summary	A 'one-stop' overview containing basic corpus statistics such as word count and average sentence length, plus some text visualisations	X	X	X	Offers word, sentence, lemma, word type and document count	Allows the user to generate summary statistics for specific analyses	•

• = the functionality is offered by the programme.
X= the functionality is not offered by the programme.

34   *Using Computers in Literary Translation*

it represents a useful starting point from which a literary translator, student or translation scholar can explore the field of corpus-assisted translation. In Chapter 8, I deal with the objection sometimes raised that the use of these and other computer-aided approaches is impractical for literary translators on the grounds of cost, complexity and the time and effort required to learn and use them.

Website, Cost and Mode of Use

AntConc: http://www.laurenceanthony.net/software/antconc/ (free, downloadable)
CATMA: https://portal.catma.de/catma/ (free, online)
ParaConc: http://paraconc.com/ ($49, downloadable)
Sketch Engine: https://www.sketchengine.eu/ (free via a European higher education institution;[21] from 4.83 euros/month for non-commercial use; from 8.33 euros/month for commercial activity; online)
Voyant Tools: https://voyant-tools.org/docs/#!/guide (free, online and downloadable)
WordSmith Tools: http://www.lexically.net/wordsmith/ (£50, downloadable)

The CDR Approach and Text-Visualisation

The CDR approach involves the use of two distinct but complementary methods in a partnership of equals, operating in a recursive way to both test and generate stylistic hypotheses, which themselves can be tested and so on. To use the approach successfully it is important to take account of Stefan Jänicke et al.'s observation that

> While close reading retains the ability to read the source text without dissolving its structure, distant reading does the exact opposite. It aims to generate an abstract view by shifting from observing textual content to visualizing global features of a single or of multiple text(s).
> (Jänicke et al. 2015:online)

It has become clear that Digital Humanities scholars value the ability to switch between close and distant reading views of texts within the same software programme (Ibidem), and in particular to move from a global, abstract view to a close-up of specific portions of a text or texts. This was summarised by Ben Schneiderman as the Information Seeking Mantra: 'Overview first, zoom and filter, details-on demand' (1996:337).

The results of analyses conducted with CL tools are very valuable, but because they are decontextualised and in many cases impossible to display on a single screen, it can be difficult to get an overview of them. For example, knowing that a particular word appears x number of times

Using Computers in Literary Translation

in a text can be useful, but it would often be even more useful to be able to visualise how those occurrences are distributed across the text. The contrast between the two forms of display is shown in Figures 1.5a and b.

The same frequency information about the word 'años' [years] is presented from different perspectives, yielding different but complementary insights. The word is one of the highest frequency 'content' words in the text (words which have lexical meaning, as opposed to 'function' words which explain or create grammatical relationships between content words), which suggests that time may be an important theme in this text, a collection of short stories by the same author.[22] The distribution display shows where in the text the word appears, indicating that it is commonly used across the text, and by using the coarse-grained/fine-grained slider it would be possible to identify in which stories it appears most prominently. Amongst the programmes listed in Table 1.1 Voyant Tools is unique in providing a combination of visualisations, traditional tabular results and a scrolling view of the full text on a single screen, as shown in Figure 1.6.

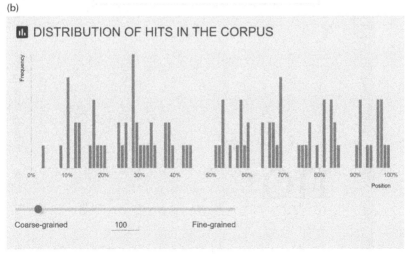

Figure 1.5 (a) Raw word frequency view in Sketch Engine. (b) Word frequency distribution view in Sketch Engine.

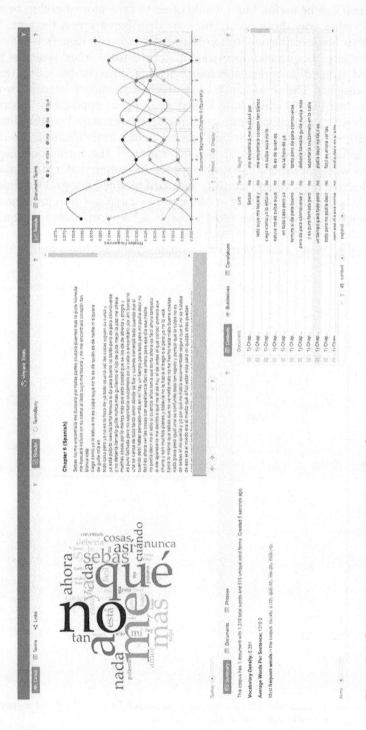

Figure 1.6 Corpus summary view in Voyant Tools.

Using Computers in Literary Translation 37

In their review of ten years of research on visualisations that support the close and distant reading of textual data in the Digital Humanities Jänicke et al. provide a useful summary of some of the key forms that these visualisations have taken:

- 'Structure overviews illustrate the hierarchy of an individual text or an entire corpus'.
- 'Heat maps or block matrices are often used to highlight textual patterns'.
- 'Tag clouds are intuitive visualizations to encode the number of occurrences of words within a selected section, a whole document or an entire text corpus by using variable font size'.
- 'Maps are widely used to display the geospatial information contained in a text'.
- 'Timelines are appropriate techniques to visualize historical text corpora carrying various types of temporal information'.
- 'Graphs are the most often applied method to visualize certain structural features of a text corpus' (2015:online).

While text-visualisation techniques have been developed since the 1990s (Nan and Cui 2016:11), their growth has been much more rapid since around 2007 (Kucher and Kerren 2015:120). The range of software is now so great that Kostiantyn Kucher and Andreas Kerren have developed the Text Visualization Browser[23] interactive visual tool for viewing 400 different programmes, as shown in Figure 1.7.

Researchers can use the interactive panel on the left to filter entries according to four different kinds of categories (Kucher and Kerren 2014:online): 'by task [...], by data to be visualized, by application domain, and by style of visualization design' (Nan and Cui 2016:12).

In contrast to CL programmes, a number of which actively cater for different languages and also specifically for translation, text-visualisation software appears to be overwhelmingly monolingual and Anglocentric. Furthermore, much of it is not available for general use, having been developed by research teams for highly specific projects but never released (see Keim and Oelke 2007 as an example). Practitioners wishing to adopt a CDR approach can use the limited and fairly traditional visualisations offered by programmes such as CATMA and Sketch Engine, or the wider variety of possibilities included in programmes such as Voyant Tools which offers 15 different visualisation tools.

In conclusion, it is worth noting that there have been some groundbreaking text-visualisation studies in the field of literary translation, which may well help to inspire designers and result in the development of tools that can be used by translators in the future. An example of this is the ShakerVis tool that was developed by a team of translation scholars and computer scientists at Swansea University to study multiple German

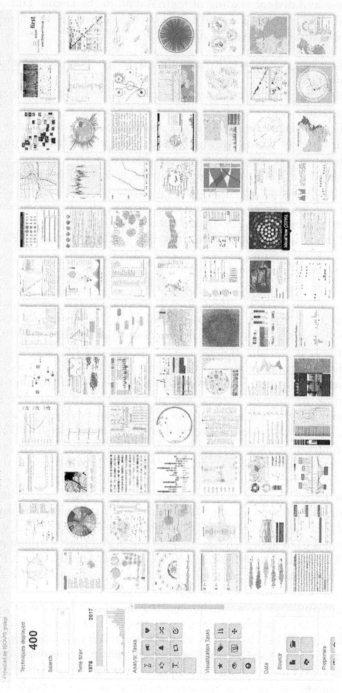

Figure 1.7 The Text Visualization Browser.

Using Computers in Literary Translation 39

translations of Shakespeare's play, *Othello*. Zhao Geng et al. digitised 32 translations, prepared them as a parallel corpus and developed 'an interactive visualization system to present and explore the parallel segment variations between multiple translations' (Geng et al. 2015:275). These retranslations 'all embody variant interpretations of their source texts' and 'document cross-cultural relations between source and target cultures' (2015:282). But in addition, 'the patterns of variation among translations can also shed new light on translated texts themselves' (Ibidem).

A Provisional Four-Stage Model of the Application of CDR to Literary Translation

The aim of the final part of this section is to flesh out the three-stage translation process outlined at the beginning, linked to CDR. This involves adding a fourth stage and making suggestions about which CL and text-visualisation tools might be productively used in the analysis of literary style at each stage. The result is a provisional four-stage model of how the CDR approach could be used in practice.

To carry out practical stylistic analysis, which I would argue all literary translators need to be able to do to some degree, we need to have a reasonably detailed idea of which lexical, grammatical and text-structural features of a prose work might potentially be relevant. While no exhaustive list of these exists, the checklist produced by Geoffrey Leech and Mick Short in Chapter 3 of their highly regarded book *Style in Fiction* (1981 and 2007) can be seen as a very good place from which to start. Although produced in the context of monolingual English stylistic analysis, this is very useful for translators wanting to analyse both an ST and their own TT. In their preface to the checklist the authors note that

> There is no infallible technique for selecting what is [stylistically] significant. We have to make ourselves newly aware, for each text, of the artistic effect of the whole, and the way linguistic details fit into this whole. Nevertheless, it is useful to have a checklist of features which may or may not be significant in a given text [...] It is not exhaustive, of course, but is rather a list of 'good bets': categories which, in our experience, are likely to yield stylistically relevant information.
> (2007:60–61)

They divide the list into four main categories, each with a series of subcategories, which I have summarised below (2007:60–66).

A: <u>Lexical categories</u>: general, nouns, adjectives, verbs, adverbs
B: <u>Grammatical categories</u>: sentence types, sentence complexity, clause types, clause structure, noun phrases, verb phrases, other phrase types, word classes, general

40 *Using Computers in Literary Translation*

C: <u>Figures of speech</u>: grammatical and lexical, phonological, tropes
D: <u>Context and cohesion</u>: cohesion, context

They go on to apply the checklist to worked examples of the stylistic analysis of three short stories by Joseph Conrad, D.H. Lawrence and Henry James (2007:66–88).[24]

In Table 1.2 I have borrowed from the checklist and adapted it to produce a model, which is provisional for at least two reasons. Literary translators work in different ways and so this can only be a prototypical representation of their working practice. Well-respected translators from Spanish and Portuguese to English such as Gregory Rabassa and Daniel Hahn, for example, have written about their preference for not reading a ST before starting to translate. Second, I have only given examples at each stage of the model and make no claim for it being in any way an exhaustive account of the possibilities.

I am not suggesting that all the above features should be investigated, merely that they are all *potentially* stylistically relevant. Having an overview of the possibilities and the 'good bets' provides a starting point and increases the chances of arriving at a better informed translation. I see the model as a tentative first step in operationalising the approach, in the hope that literary translators, students and scholars will find it sufficiently interesting to try out, modify and improve.

1.4 The Relationship of the Methodology to Other Disciplines

Viewed from a wider perspective the CDR approach is essentially a 'mixed methods' approach, combining qualitative (close reading) and quantitative (distant reading) methodologies. It can be seen as forming part of the Digital Humanities and in particular the field of digital literary studies. Originally concerned with the need to provide quantifiable evidence for literary judgements and interpretations (Hoover 2004; Rommel 2004; Leech and Short 2007), this field has broadened and I would argue that it now encompasses both corpus stylistics and computational narratology, each of which can be shown to be relevant to the computer-aided translation of literary style.

Style is about the 'how' of a literary work, the way linguistic choices are employed and the effects they can create. But that 'how' needs to be understood in relation to the 'what' it is used to present, in other words the story and the plot, traditionally the province of narratology. The 'what' and the 'how' are both relevant to translation because both have to be reproduced in the TT. While there seems to be increasing interest in the relationship between style and translation, relatively little work has been published on what stylistics and narratology may have to offer each other. The separation between the two is based, as Monika

Table 1.2 A provisional model of CDR applied to the process of literary translation

Translation process stage	Potential stylistically relevant features			
	Narratological[a]	Lexical	Grammatical	Context and cohesion
1. ST analysis (part 1): making notes during and after initial reading	• Plot structure • Character names, attributes, dialogue registers, etc. • Narration type (interior monologue, third person, etc.) • Treatment of time and space	• Use of particular parts of speech • Unusual words or collocations • Idiomatic expressions • Culture-specific references and terms	• Sentence length and type • Sentence complexity • Clause type and structure • Phrase type • Use of punctuation	• Paragraph length • Repetition of words and phrases • Semantic prosody • Use of co-ordinating conjunctions etc. • Use of typographical features
2. ST analysis (part 2): preparing to translate	**Following up Stage 1** • Analysing any of the features noted in Stage 1 • Preparing one or more custom corpora • Running CQL complex queries where relevant • Using visualisations	**Doing 'standard' analyses[b]** • Corpus summary • Word list/word cloud • Keyword list • Average sentence length • Lexical richness • N-grams and word clusters	**Setting translation goals** It is part of the CDR philosophy that pre-translation ST analysis can help to suggest and feed into the formulation of specific translation goals, against at least some of which the draft TT can be assessed, e.g. the degree of foreignisation/domestication	
3. Initial translation	**Looking up words and phrases** • Monolingual corpora • Comparable corpora • Parallel corpora • Word Sketch/Word Sketch Difference • Thesaurus		**Investigating patterns** • Following up any of the analyses from Stages 1 and 2 • Collocations • Further n-grams and word clusters • Running CQL queries on specific features • Using visualisations to make ST-TT comparisons clearer	
4. Comparing ST and draft TT with a view to translation revision	• Assessing the extent to which measurable translation goals may have been achieved, e.g. by running duplicate analyses on both texts separately to see if, for example, the TT has preserved comparable lexical richness and sentence length parameters[c] • Creating a segment-aligned parallel corpus of both texts and uploading it to Sketch Engine, allowing for a range of searches and analyses to be undertaken			

a Although not included by Leech and Short in their checklist as such, narratological features of a literary text are mentioned in their analyses and are in practice inextricably linked to style, providing the framework within which this is expressed (see Chapter 5 for an analysis of how sentence length and a predominantly interior monologue narrative format interact stylistically in the case study translation).

b One of the aspects of the CDR approach which I would like to see tested is whether it is appropriate to suggest a standard set of initial analyses to conduct for works of literary prose prior to translation, or whether each text should always be treated on its merits.

c I am aware that the whole question of evaluating translations is subject to considerable debate, and discuss some of the limitations involved in attempting this, in Chapter 5.

42 *Using Computers in Literary Translation*

Fludernik notes, on the premise that 'in principle, points of style are language specific, whereas phenomena like flashback or focalization are not restricted to any one language but... may occur in a variety of languages and cultures' (2009:69). However, there are areas where style and narrative overlap, and also have clear implications for translation. For example, while in English maintaining gender ambiguity in first-person narration is linguistically relatively straightforward, it is much more difficult in languages like French and Spanish where adjectives are gender-marked. Studies that have linked stylistics and narratology, although they mainly relate to what narratology can offer stylistics, include Short (1999), Herman (2002), Simpson (2004), Shen (2005a, 2005b, 2014), Leech and Short (2007) and Fludernik (2009). Dan Shen represents the broad consensus of these studies when he argues that 'in order to interpret and appreciate more comprehensively the techniques of narrative fiction, we need to take advantage of the findings of both stylistics and narratology' (2014:203).

In their introduction to a 2014 special issue of *Language and Literature* on 'Narration and Translation', Lars Bernaerts, Liesbeth De Bleeker and July De Wilde suggest that 'research into narratological issues has been relatively rare in translation studies' (2014:204). Studies that have looked at the relationship between narratology and translation have come from both disciplines and include Hermans (1996), O'Sullivan (2003), Alvstad (2014), Boase-Beier (2014a) and Prince (2014). They have provided evidence, particularly Prince (2014), that translation can lead to narrative shifts, and that, as Boase-Beier says, 'prose translators... even when they are highly sensitive to style, often seem relatively unaware of narrative structures in texts' (2014a:214). This point is also made by Susan Bassnett in *Translation Studies* (1994:109–120). I would argue that it would benefit all three disciplines to engage in greater dialogue and to be more open to each other's insights.

In my case this dialogue turned out to be game-changing. While attending a doctoral seminar on computational narratology in 2015 I realised that the CATMA software, specifically developed for collaborative narratological analysis, could also be used in the translation of a literary text. This was a use which the software's designers had not thought about, but could see the value of. As a result of the dialogue which ensued after the seminar between myself and the CATMA team I was given valuable help with a complex CL query to extract banded sentence length frequencies, and the team decided to incorporate a facility for sentence length analysis into the programme as they could see that it would be useful for narratology, too.

In the case study translation, my overall translation goal was to attempt to achieve equivalence of stylistic effect: in other words, to recreate in the TT the effects I had experienced as a reader of the ST, an approach which I believe is shared by many, possibly most, literary translators. It

Using Computers in Literary Translation   43

must be acknowledged from the start that this can only ever be a hopeful attempt, and that it is not possible to say that reproducing a given stylistic feature from one language in another will create the same effects in the reader of the translation as it did in the readers of the original. At present 'the reader' is a hypothetical construct, and it is both difficult and, for a translator, dangerous to make too many assumptions about how a given stylistic feature will affect her/him. Christiane Nord underlines this point when she argues that even 'one and the same person at different times in his or her life may "read" the same text in different ways' (1991:18).

Much of the research on reader response has relied on impressionistic self-reporting by readers. However, some recent research in the overlapping fields of cognitive stylistics (Stockwell 2002; da Costa 2007; Zunshine 2011; Sanford and Emmott 2012) and cognitive narratology (Bortolussi and Dixon 2003; Emmott, Sanford and Dawydiak 2007; Herman 2013) suggests that before too long it may be possible to predict aspects of reader response to certain textual features such as page layout and the use of linguistic devices such as cleft sentences, with increased confidence. This is due to developments in empirical experimental procedures which are falsifiable and repeatable, and which crucially do not rely on subjective self-reporting by readers. In *Mind, Brain and Narrative* (2012) Sanford and Emmott set out 'to show, by reference to relevant empirical work, how various stylistic devices employed by writers for rhetorical purposes serve to influence [reader] processing in ways that correspond to certain of the intuitions of analysts in the humanities' (2012:5). In earlier empirical work on reader reaction in text-change experiments,[25] for example, they conclude that

> The stylistic features which we felt intuitively to be attention-capturing were confirmed to be so, in terms of increasing the amount that the readers noticed... Also the fact that attention increased when information was split off into short sentences or sentence fragments makes sense in the context of the anomaly researchers' finding that information embedded in more complex structures is less detectable.
> (Emmott, Sanford and Dawydiak 2007:7)

Although the context of their research is monolingual, and there is no suggestion that what they have found in relation to English would automatically be transferable to other languages, their findings are of direct relevance to translation since, as Reuven Tsur argues, 'Cognitive poetics... offers cognitive theories that systematically account for the relationship between the structure of literary texts and their perceived effects' (2002:279). If, and it is an important 'if', this research proves to be robust, it has significant implications for translation, since it potentially offers translators, publishers and book designers the possibility of

44 *Using Computers in Literary Translation*

foregrounding certain parts or aspects of a text in such a way that they can have a degree of confidence in the effect this is likely to have on readers, for example, in relation to attention capture.

So, starting from the broad umbrella of literary and linguistic computing/digital literary studies, there is evidence that the CDR approach to literary translation draws upon, and can offer insights to, several neighbouring disciplines: corpus stylistics, cognitive stylistics, computational narratology and cognitive or psycho-narratology. The entire field of comparative literature – both in translation and in original languages – could also in principle be linked to the CDR approach, since the latter is a methodology and not confined to a specific language pair.

Notes

1 Many literary translators also do commercial translation, but there is evidence that their attitudes to the use of MT and CAT tools differ according to the type of translation involved (see section 1.1).
2 CATMA is available at: https://portal.catma.de/catma/
3 Sketch Engine can be accessed at: https://auth.sketchengine.eu/
4 Voyant Tools is available at: http://voyeurtools.org/category/voyant-tools/documentation/
5 ALPAC. 1966. Language and machines: computers in translation and linguistics. A report by the Automatic Language Processing Advisory Committee. Washington, DC: National Academy of Sciences. (cited in Hutchins, J., 2010. Machine translation: a concise history. *Journal of Translation Studies*, 13(1 & 2), pp.29–70. Available at: www.hutchinsweb.me.uk/CUHK-2006.pdf)
6 Translation Automation Users Society (TAUS) knowledge base: www.taus.net/knowledgebase/index.php/Statistical_machine_translation
7 For free, detailed information on developments in commercial translation technology, see Jost Zetzsche's 'The Tool Box Journal' at: www.internationalwriters.com/toolkit/; and John Hutchins' website containing lists of publications on machine translation, computer-based translation technologies, linguistics and other topics: www.hutchinsweb.me.uk/
8 www.tausdata.org/
9 https://translate.google.com/toolkit/list?hl=en#translations/active
10 This is the commonly used threshold below which suggested matches are felt to be unhelpful.
11 https://sourceforge.net/projects/aligner/
12 BLEU, TER and METEOR. For details see Agarwal and Lavie (2008).
13 A database of eight million parallel lines of text, freely available at: www.parl.gc.ca
14 Although see Greene et al. (2010) for a study of MT use in the translation of Dante's Divine Comedy into English.
15 Available at: www.corpusdelespanol.org/
16 Details available at: www.sketchengine.eu/documentation/tenten-corpora/
17 www.paraconc.com/
18 http://portal.catma.de/catma/
19 www.sketchengine.co.uk/
20 The lemma of a word is its base root, and a lemmatised list of word types would count the inflections of that lemma as a single type: for example, the

lemma *say* would represent instances of *say*, *says*, *saying* and *said*. The purpose of lemmatization is to help provide a more accurate representation of lexical variety. In Spanish, for instance, inflections are far more numerous than in English, but this does not mean that its higher raw type count indicates greater lexical variety.

21 At the time of writing this will last at least until the end of 2019.
22 Paz Soldán, E. 2018. *Desencuentros*, Madrid: Páginas de Espuma.
23 http://textvis.lnu.se/
24 Joseph Conrad, 'The Secret Sharer' (1910); D.H. Lawrence, 'Odour of Chrysanthemums' (1911); and Henry James, 'The Pupil' (1891).
25 The text change experiment 'uses pairs of textual materials which are either identical or identical apart from a change of one word. The reader is asked whether or not a change has taken place. The detection or lack of detection of any changed word provides a task to check how attentive the reader is being to the text at that point. Each experiment generally tests one or two stylistic/narratological features that are thought to be "attention-controlling"' (Emmott, Sanford and Dawydiak 2007:210–211).

2 Analysing the Source Text
Structure and Style

In the context of translation, a source text analysis aims, as Leech says of the analysis of literary texts in general, 'to arrive at (a) an evidentially warranted interpretation and appreciation of the text, and (b) an understanding of how that interpretation/appreciation is supported by the way the text works as a linguistic and communicative phenomenon' (2008:195). This involves a consideration of both stylistics and narratology, and their relationship to translation, and illustrates the first use of the close and distant reading (CDR) approach in the translation process: source text analysis.

Section 1 of this chapter provides summary background information about Mario Benedetti, the novel *Gracias por el Fuego* and its reception. Section 2 shows how a potentially standard set of quick and straightforward computer-aided analyses of the source text (ST) – such as a word frequency list, a keyword list and average sentence length – can be undertaken, and how the results can be used to inform translation decisions. Sections 3 and 4 demonstrate the application of the CDR approach in more nuanced ways to two specific features of the text: the title and characterisation. These include the extraction of proper nouns in order to produce a list of characters, network visualisations of their relationships and discourse analysis of one character's direct speech. The decision to analyse the title and characterisation was based on selecting features which fulfilled four conditions: they can be expected to affect the reader, they relate to the presentation of the novel's subtext within the framework of a literary text, they have implications for translation and they illustrate the applicability of the CDR approach.

2.1 The Author, the Novel and Its Reception

The translation of a novel involves more than just dealing with the words on the page. Understanding something of the author's life and character, and the context of the production and reception of the text, will help to inform an appreciation of that text and an interpretation of the author's communicative intention. Mario Orlando Hamlet Hardy Brenno Benedetti Farrugia was born in Paso de los Toros in northern Uruguay on 14 September 1920 and died on 17 May 2009 in Montevideo at the age of

88. He published over 100 books including poetry, short stories, novels, essays, literary criticism, journalism, plays, screenplays and songs. He was also a translator. He received 13 literary prizes in seven countries – Uruguay, Mexico, Cuba, Chile, Spain, Bulgaria and Denmark – and was awarded four honorary doctorates by universities in Uruguay, Spain and Cuba. His work has been translated into 26 languages,[1] including braille. His work shares a number of characteristic features of the Latin American Boom,[2] such as 'the fact that human love never offers a means of escape from a spiritual malaise which at times borders on existential despair' (Shaw 2008:iv), and a desire to highlight social injustice. However, what distinguishes him is his focus on what he saw as the immorality and injustice plaguing his immediate community – that of the Montevidean middle class – in contrast to the flamboyant literary experimentalism of Cortázar's *Hopscotch*, for example, or the continental perspective of García Márquez' *One Hundred Years of Solitude*.

Gracias por el Fuego is Benedetti's third novel and was written between 1962 and 1963, at a time when he had already established his reputation as a writer, and had been deeply influenced by the Cuban Revolution of 1959, and the left in Uruguay had signally failed to make electoral headway in the November 1962 elections. In the face of a deepening political and economic crisis, he was grappling, both publicly and privately, with two issues: no longer believing that peaceful change through parliamentary democracy was possible, and yet understanding that the country was not ready for revolution, what was he and those on the left to do? And in particular, what was the role and responsibility of the writer and intellectual in promoting revolutionary change? In this chapter I argue that the novel was written as an appeal to the Montevidean middle class to re-examine both the political system under which they lived, and their own lives, in terms of the need for both moral and political change. It also represented Benedetti's own uncertainty about how to answer the two questions raised above.

Gracias por el Fuego: *Plot, Presentation and Interpretation*

In his entry on Benedetti in the *Encyclopedia of Latin American Literature*, the Uruguayan literary critic Jorge Ruffinelli summarises what he sees as a key aspect of the author's work, represented by *Gracias por el Fuego*:

> The author passes judgement on his country in all his texts; here, though, this becomes a theme. Through three generations of a family (grandson, son, father), he tells the story of an old newspaper boss, corrupt and venal, his cowardly sons and a cautiously rebellious grandson. The most dramatic aspects concern the old man's son, Ramón Budiño, who has a lovehate relationship with his father, and decides to kill him as a way of saving the country, or the multiple victims of this "terrible father".

(1997:211)

48   *Analysing the Source Text*

The main character in the novel is Ramón Budiño, 44, married with a 17-year-old son, a middle-class Montevidean undergoing an existential crisis. He is overshadowed, like the whole family, by his dominant and domineering father Edmundo, a powerful and unscrupulous newspaper and factory owner and prominent political figure. At the beginning of Chapter 2, Ramón summarises this:

> En la familia no hubo, ni hay, ni habrá sitio para otra persona importante que no sea el Viejo. Desplantes principistas, encendida oratoria, figura prócer. Nos ha absorbido a todos. Yo nunca fui Ramón Budiño sino el hijo de Edmundo Budiño. Mi hijo nunca será Gustavo Budiño sino el nieto de Edmundo Budiño.
>
> (Benedetti 2014:46)[3]

> [In this family, there wasn't, there isn't, there won't be room for anyone of importance except The Old Man. Pompous pronouncements, fiery speeches, heroic figure. He has subsumed us, all of us. I was never Ramón Budiño, just the son of Edmundo Budiño. My son will never be Gustavo Budiño, just the grandson of Edmundo Budiño.]

Ramón's relationships with women are either transient, as in his casual sexual encounters; or loveless, as in his marriage to Susana; or frustrated, as in his love for his sister-in-law Dolly. He has difficulty communicating with his son, Gustavo. The money to set up his travel agency came from a loan from his corrupt father, and during an altercation with Edmundo Ramón is made to see this as tainted money, whose stain will remain even after the debt is paid off. Unable to confront his father, and with a growing sense of desperation to resolve the pressures and contradictions in his life, Ramón realises that the only way to free himself is to kill his father, which he also sees as being a service to society. When the planned moment arrives, he cannot go through with it, and realising suddenly that there is another, equally final solution, he instead commits suicide by jumping from Edmundo's ninth floor office in central Montevideo.

The novel consists of 15 chapters, ranging in length from 5 to 44 pages, the majority being in the range of 10–20 pages. The total length is 298 paperback pages (2014 edition): 76,442 words. As Joan Rea Boorman observes, the narrative structure is circular (1976:82–83). Chapter 1 is effectively an extended prologue. Chapters 2–13 form the novel proper, beginning and ending in the ninth-floor office of Edmundo Budiño. Chapters 14 and 15 form an epilogue, each chapter being devoted to one of the two main female characters, Dolly and Gloria, Edmundo's secret, long-term mistress.

A number of writers and scholars, including both of Benedetti's biographers (Paoletti 1995; Campanella 2009), concur in viewing the political subtext of the novel as an appeal by the author to the Montevidean middle class to stop acquiescing in the perpetuation of a corrupt political system,

Analysing the Source Text 49

with its insidious effects on their own morality and relationships (Fornet 1975; Céspedes 1976; Fernández Retamar 1976; Lewis 1982; Soubeyroux 1986; Paoletti 1995; Campanella 2009; Lagos 2013). A link is also made between Ramón's political views, as expressed particularly in Chapter 8 in his dialogue with Gustavo, and Benedetti's own views as set out in his collection of essays *El País de la cola de paja* (Benedetti 1970). Bart Lewis suggests that '"El Viejo" [Edmundo] plainly represents Uruguay's morally bankrupt Establishment; Ramón, Benedetti's own frustrated but power-less generation; and Gustavo, radicalized, doctrinaire youth' (1982:7).

Commercial and Critical Reception

Gracias por el Fuego was published in 1965 in Montevideo and quickly became a best seller by the standards of the day. The first edition of 5,000 copies sold out within days, and the second edition print run was 10,000 copies (Rodríguez Monegal 1965:52). According to Benedetti himself the novel sold over 50,000 copies in Uruguay alone (Ruffinelli 2008:241). Twenty-one editions had been published by 1980: seven in Uruguay, eight in Mexico, four in Argentina, one in Cuba and one in Spain (Beberfall 1981:363–364). According to a 2015 literary blog[4] there have been 69 editions in all, and the novel is still in print. Between 1969 and 2006 it was translated into Russian (1969), Italian (1972), Hungarian (1973), Polish (1974), Czech (1976), Bulgarian (1978), French (1983), German (1987), Greek (1996) and Portuguese (2006) (Paoletti 1995 and updated list provided by Harry Morales, Benedetti's US translator).

When asked why *Gracias por el Fuego* had sold so well, one of the edi-tors from the novel's Montevideo publisher Alfa replied by saying 'Porque pinta la realidad de lo que es Uruguay hoy... Nosotros compramos este libro porque somos masoquistas: nos gusta vernos retratados y no poder hacer nada. Sólo decir: ché ¡qué bien pinta la situación Benedetti, qué mal que estamos!' (Mathieu 1983:13).[5] [Because he paints a truthful pic-ture of Uruguay today... We buy this book because we're masochists: we like to see ourselves portrayed and not be able to do anything. Just to say: ché, how well Benedetti describes the situation, how screwed up we are!]

The novel's treatment by critics was much more mixed. As well as the favourable reception (Dorfman 1966/1976; Promis 1966; Fernández Retamar 1969/1976; Carillo 1971/1976; Guyot 1972/1976; Spital-eri 1972), there were brickbats. In an article on 'The 1965 Literary Scene in Argentina and Uruguay' the US critic Ernest Lewald commented dis-paragingly that 'it is largely a pastiche composed of stock characters and contrived situations' (1966:148). Much closer to home was the harsh re-sponse to the novel's manuscript by Emir Rodríguez Monegal, a respected Montevideo literary critic and fellow member of the Benedetti's literary generation, whose opinion of the novel Benedetti was keen to have. According to Paoletti, Monegal's response was blunt: ' – ¿Querés una

50 *Analysing the Source Text*

opinión sincera? Quemala. Se llama *Gracias por el Fuego* ¿no? Bueno, quemala' (1995:110) [Do you want an honest opinion? Burn it. It's called *Thanks for the Light*, isn't it? So, burn it]. One of the reasons he gave was that no one in Montevideo commits suicide by jumping from a tall building. A story is told that on the day the novel was published a man did indeed commit suicide by jumping from a ninth-floor window, and Benedetti is said to have quipped that he 'hadn't hired him' (Butazzoni 2009).

Another criticism levelled at the novel, and one with which I agree, relates to Edmundo's apparent expressed desire in chapter 15 to provoke his own assassination, thereby purifying the country: 'Este país es una porquería. La prueba la tenés en que nadie haya tenido suficientes cojones como para matarme. Anotá esto. Si algún día alguien me mata, entonces puede ser que este país tenga salida, tenga salvación' (p. 307) [This country is rubbish. The proof is that no one's had the balls to kill me. Remember this. If one day someone kills me, then maybe this country's got hopes, got a future]. Paoletti suggests that the critics of the day considered this idea highly unlikely on the basis that 'los Edmundo Budiño de este mundo suelen tener una opinión estupenda de sí mismos y no creen, para nada, que su asesinato pueda marcar el comienzo de una era luminosa sino todo lo contrario' (Ibidem). [The Edmundo Budiños of this world usually have a very high opinion of themselves, and don't believe for a second that their assassination could mark the beginning of a new dawn, quite the opposite].

2.2 Using a Set of 'Standard' CDR Analyses

The aim of this section is to apply part of the four-stage model outlined in Table 1.2 to *Gracias por el Fuego* by performing a 'standard' set of analyses of the ST which would have been appropriate prior to translation.[6] Three criteria informed the selection of these analyses. They needed to be quick and easy to perform, to produce results which were likely to be able to inform translation decisions and goal-setting, and to be able to provide potential benchmarks against which to compare the draft translation. Collectively the results of these analyses should be able to help build a computer-aided stylistic profile of key structural and linguistic aspects of the text. To that end I want to suggest that there are five specific types of analysis which are likely to be particularly useful: corpus summaries, word lists, keyword lists, n-grams and simple measures of lexical richness. For each type of analysis there will be an explanation of the kind of data it can provide, the potential relevance of that data to translation and an example of information extracted that could not have been obtained by close reading alone.

1 **Corpus summaries**
    Both Sketch Engine and Voyant Tools offer one-click corpus summary screens, and both display total word and total token counts,[7]

Analysing the Source Text 51

word type count and average sentence length (Sketch Engine obliges you to do a very simple calculation to obtain this). In addition to these Voyant Tools displays a word cloud, a distribution visualisation of the five most frequently occurring words ('Trends'), a concordance of the most frequently occurring word and a vocabulary density measure (see 5. Lexical richness).

Translation relevance: The summaries provide two key measures which relate to the underlying structure of the text: average sentence length and the ratio of word types to total words, often referred to as the type-token ratio (TTR). Average sentence length gives a clue to grammatical complexity, as the longer sentences are the more likely they are to contain complex structures and numerous clauses and subclauses. It also gives a clue as to stylistic significance, since an average of 12 might well be significantly short, while an average of 25 might be significantly long (see Chapter 5). In the case of *Gracias por el Fuego* initial reading suggested that at least in certain chapters and sections there were a 'lot' of 'short' sentences. This prompted a desire to quantify sentence length and see if it was significantly shorter than that of Latin American fiction of the period. I also wanted to see to what extent sentence length contributed to the immersive effect of the dominant interior monologue narrative format, and therefore how important it might be to try to preserve this in the translation (see Chapter 5 for a fuller discussion of sentence length).

2   **Word lists**

Simple word lists are helpful in highlighting repetitions and allowing frequency searches for specific words. However, they can be considered misleading in two ways. By not differentiating between different forms of the same word, such as 'come' and 'comes', they can give an inaccurate picture of both frequency and lexical variety. It can be argued that for translation purposes a lemmatised word list offers a more accurate lexical profile of a text. The lemma of the verb 'to say', for example, consists of 'say', 'says', 'saying' and 'said', and all occurrences of these in a text will be counted as occurrences of one lemma. For inflected languages such as Spanish and French the variety of word forms is far greater than in English, and so the potential for distorted frequency and variety statistics if lemmas are not used is correspondingly higher. Sketch Engine automatically lemmatises a text as part of the 'compilation' process, while Computer-Aided Textual Markup and Analysis (CATMA) allows for searches for individual lemmas. The popular free corpus linguistics (CL) programme AntConc allows for the importing of freely available language-specific lemma lists (downloadable from the internet) which can then be used to produce a lemmatised word list of a text.

Translation relevance: The frequency and distribution of individual words can give thematic clues and either confirm or contradict subjective impressions arising from initial reading. In particular they

52 *Analysing the Source Text*

can help a translator to decide whether the same word needs to be translated consistently across a text or not. In *Gracias por el Fuego* Ramón's father Edmundo is referred to as *el Viejo* [the Old Man] 129 times. Concordances of the term confirmed my impression that far from corresponding to the affectionate way of referring to a father usually indicated by 'the old man', the semantic prosody of the description was entirely negative and often hate-filled. In the light of this I felt that consistency of translation was crucial, and chose to capitalise the article as well as the adjective and noun – giving The Old Man – as a way of distancing the description from any suggestion of affection.

3 Keyword lists

Keywords are those which occur more, or less, frequently in the text being analysed than in a comparable reference corpus. They are particularly useful for identifying key themes in a text. In her study of an Australian short story[8] Lourdes Gonçalves found that an unusually high proportion of the types of keywords were *hapax legomena*, or words which only occur once in a text, which are 'extremely difficult, if not impossible, to detect without computational methods' (Gonçalves 2016:42). By analysing the 558 hapax legomena in the text, she discovered that 'about one-fifth [sic] of these words were related to emotions, which, in turn, pointed to an undercurrent of emotion in the text, showing that the hapax may be used by an author to include a subliminal effect in the text' (2016:48).

Translation relevance: In addition to highlighting themes, keywords can point to features of a text which close reading alone may well not identify. Of the top 20 keywords in *Gracias por el Fuego*, 15 are character names. This is a high proportion and suggests two possibilities: that there are a lot of different characters in the novel (an aspect which is developed in Section 2.4), and/or that many of the names are unusual and may merit further investigation.

4 N-grams

N-grams are repeated sequences of words, searches for which specify the number of words or the ranges of words (2–4, 3–5, etc.). They reveal patterns which close reading alone may not detect and will certainly be incapable of quantifying. In CATMA and Sketch Engine it is also possible to search for n-grams containing a specified word or words. The distribution of particular n-grams across a text can also be visualised in Sketch Engine, and both the frequency result and the visualisation are linked to concordance displays, as with word and keyword lists.

Translation relevance: N-grams provide another way of revealing linguistic patterning and also help the translator to consider the question of whether it is stylistically important to translate a given phrase consistently across a section, chapter or an entire text. In *Gracias por el Fuego* the phrase *después de todo* [after all] emerged as the second highest three-word n-gram with 23 hits, occurring

Analysing the Source Text 53

right across the novel. Concordance investigation revealed that the phrase was used 19 times to emphasise the fact that Ramón was Edmundo's son, which in the context of the plot suggested the need for consistency of translation (see Chapter 6, Section 6.1).

5   **Lexical richness**

A number of different measures are used to give an indication of the degree of linguistic variety in a text, or lexical richness. One of the commonest is *lexical diversity*, or 'the ratio of different words (types) to the total number of words (tokens), the so-called type-token ratio, or TTR' (Johansson 2008:62). The higher the percentage figure, the greater the range of language used. The measure can be used to compare texts of a similar length, but one major weakness is that the longer the text, the greater the likelihood of words being repeated and therefore the lower the TTR, so comparison of texts of varying lengths is very likely to be misleading (Mitchell 2015:2). When applied to two languages this measure can also be misleading due to inflections, as mentioned earlier.

Another measure of vocabulary range and complexity involves dividing the number of hapax legomena by the total number of words. The higher the percentage, the greater the lexical variety. According to András Kornai 40%–60% of words in large corpora are hapax (Kornai 2008:72). There is also the measure of *lexical density*: 'the percentage of lexical as opposed to grammatical items in a given text or corpus of texts' (Baker 1995:237). 'Lexical' (or content) words are those which have a meaning that can be understood from the word alone, such as 'tree' or 'red'.[9] Grammatical (or function) words can only be fully understood in relation to other words in a sentence (Murray 1995), such as 'of' and 'by'. It is argued that 'lexical density is simply a way to measure how informative a text is' (Sari 2016:31) and that 'the greater the lexical density of a text, the more content heavy it is and more 'unpacking' it takes to understand' (Ibidem).

Translation relevance: In relation to *Gracias por el Fuego* the *lexical diversity* measure is 14.7%, suggesting that on the whole the vocabulary used in the novel is fairly common. This is consistent with Benedetti's well-known desire to be able to communicate easily with his readers (Bermejo 1973:40–41). This is further supported by the measure of hapax lemmas divided by the total number of lemmas in the novel, which at 48% falls in the middle of the 40%–60% range mentioned by Kornai. While lexical and grammatical differences between languages such as inflection must be taken into account, having an idea of the degree of lexical richness of a source text provides a possible benchmark against which to compare the draft translation. If there is a significant discrepancy between the same measures in ST and TT (target text) there is a possibility that key features of style – in this case possibly register and overall readability – may not have been successfully preserved.

54   *Analysing the Source Text*

Summary

The five different kinds of distant reading analyses described above are all quick to perform and draw on automated features of the software which are easy to use. Evaluating the results and assessing their stylistic importance then become tasks for close reading. Set out below is a summary of the potential benefits to a literary translator of using this set of computer-aided analytical tools, which can identify

- the frequency, distribution and context of occurrence of words and phrases, including words which only occur once (word lists and n-grams)
- themes and potentially hidden aspects of authorial style (word lists, keyword lists and n-grams)
- structural features of style such as sentence length and the range and register of vocabulary used (corpus summaries, lexical richness measures).

Taken as a whole, the use of these analyses can furnish the translator with information which close reading alone is either unlikely or unable to provide. This information has the potential to assist with the assessment of the stylistic relevance and importance of lexical, grammatical and structural features of a text. It can also inform the setting of translation goals by the translator and the establishment of ST benchmarks against which to compare the draft translation. In the case of *Gracias por el Fuego* this involved attempting to preserve sentence length and boundaries in the translation, and assessing the need for consistency of translation in relation to selected frequently and infrequently occurring words and phrases (see Chapters 5 and 6).

2.3 The Title

Titles are important because they provide a way for authors, translators and publishers to manage, and sometimes confound, reader expectations. Translators have commented on the difficulties and pitfalls presented by titles, particularly short ones (Rabassa 1989, 2005; Levine 2009). Rabassa cites the Spanish translation of William Faulkner's novel *Light in August* (1932), rendered as 'Luz en Agosto', commenting that it is 'perfect in a direct matching of words. What Mr. Will had in mind, however, was the country expression used for a cow who is "comin' in", expectant, "heavy in June, light in August"' (1989:11). In my case the problem was the word *fuego* which normally means *fire*, but here could also be translated as *light*, and my translation solution is the result of combining close reading and quantitative analysis, and both narratological and stylistic considerations.

Initial close reading of the novel revealed two instances of the title phrase, both spoken by Gloria to Ramón (see *Table 2.1* for details). The first, in

Analysing the Source Text 55

Chapter 7, very clearly relates to the lighting of a cigarette, 'Thanks for the light'. According to my interpretation the second, in Chapter 15, is an expression of gratitude to the dead Ramón for the fact that his suicide and Edmundo's reaction to it have finally given her the strength to leave him. At this stage, two meanings of *fuego* were satisfied by the word *light*: the light given by a cigarette lighter and the light of hope and inspiration provided by Ramón's suicide. This prompted a desire to see how many instances there were in the novel of the word *fuego* and what other associations it might have, and I ran a search query to this effect in CATMA. Double-clicking on the keyword in each instance allowed me to see the wider context, and I reproduce the results, with my draft translations, in *Table 2.1*, indicating that there were only four occurrences (underlined).

Table 2.1 Results of CATMA search for 'fuego'

Chapter/page	ST	TT
7/126	Ella tomó un cigarrillo y él le acercó el encendedor. «Gracias por el <u>fuego</u>», había dicho ella. Y nada más.	She took out a cigarette and he proffered her his lighter. "Thanks for the <u>light</u>", she had said. And nothing more.
8/144–145	Si estallamos, no por propia convicción, sino pura y exclusivamente porque estallan nuestros vecinos y el <u>fuego</u> se propaga, lo más probable es que las llamas recibidas no nos sirvan de nada, como no sea para destruirnos... mientras no adquiramos una conciencia visceral de la necesidad de nuestra propia explosión, de nuestro propio <u>fuego</u>, nada será hondo, verdadero, legítimo, todo será una simple cáscara, como ahora es cascarita, sólo cascarita, nuestra tan voceada democracia.	If we explode, not as a result of our own convictions, but purely and simply because our neighbours explode and the <u>fire</u> has spread, the most likely outcome is that the flames that reach us will only serve to destroy us... as long as we don't develop a visceral awareness of the need to have our own explosion, our own <u>blaze</u>, nothing will be deep, genuine, legitimate, it will all be just a shell, like a scab, only a scab, that is our much vaunted democracy now.
15/307–308	Acaso el pobre Ramón, piensa Gloria, se mató por cobardía... pero de todos modos consumó su venganza. Porque esa muerte ha vuelto vulnerable a Edmundo Budiño. Esa amenaza que no se cumplió ha colocado muchas amenazas en el aire. Gracias por el <u>fuego</u>.	Maybe poor Ramón killed himself out of cowardice, thinks Gloria... but all the same he got his revenge. Because that death has made Edmundo Budiño vulnerable. That threat he didn't carry out has left many threats hanging in the air. Thanks for the <u>light</u>.

56   *Analysing the Source Text*

The first and fourth instances repeat the title, and both are addressed to Ramón by Gloria, suggesting the translation of *fuego* as *light*. The second and third instances occur in successive sentences in Chapter 8, in the context of a discussion between Ramón and Gustavo about politics. They are significant because they are spoken by Ramón in a context where, as I argued in Section 2.1, they represent Benedetti's own views as expressed in his essay *El País de la cola de paja*. Here *fuego* is clearly a metaphor for a popular uprising. As María Jesús Antón argues:

> el fuego es un símbolo de la acción que supone la toma de conciencia del pueblo uruguayo ante la Revolución cubana, porque Ramón, metáfora política del pueblo, se purifica con su suicidio y se libera de un mundo inauténtico, ya que su muerte convierte a su padre en un ser débil y deja ver la verdadera cara de Edmundo Budiño' (1992:128). [fire is a symbol of the action which is implied by the political awakening on the part of the Uruguayan people in the light of the Cuban revolution, because Ramón, a political metaphor for the people, is purified through his suicide and liberated from an insincere world, since his death turns his father into a weak being and reveals the true face of Edmundo Budiño]

Joëlle Guyot also supports this analysis as it relates to the novel's title: 'Ese tema de la sublevación y de la violencia ligado al tema del fuego, lo encontramos en el título de la obra' (1976:143) [That theme of uprising and violence linked to the idea of fire is found in the title of the novel].

As a result of looking at these occurrences in a quantitative context, I changed my initial translation of the third instance of *fuego* from *blaze* – which in isolation seemed more expressive – to *fire*, on the basis that in this case consistency of translation was more important if the ST pattern of repetition was to be preserved. This is one of a number of instances where macro-level narrative considerations can conflict with micro-level stylistic preferences considered in isolation. It is interesting to note that the French translators of the novel, Claude Riva and Tomas Namer, chose to translate the two occurrences of the title phrase in different ways. The first is translated as 'Merci pour le feu' [Thanks for the light, in relation to a cigarette], while the second becomes 'Merci pour cette étincelle' [Thanks for that spark], which highlights the idea of Ramón's death as an inspiration. Indeed, the French title is simply *L'Étincelle* [The Spark] (Benedetti 1983), and this prompted me to consider the titles of the other translations as a further source of reference. Set out below are the titles of six of the ten translations by way of comparison.[10]

Language	Translation	Back translation
Czech (1976)[11]	Díhy Za Oheň	Thanks for the fire/light in relation to a cigarette
French (1983)	L'Étincelle	The Spark
German (1987)	Danke für das Feuer	Thanks for the light/fire
Greek (1996)	Ευχαριστώ για τη φωτιά (Efcharistó ya tee fotiá)	Thanks for the light (cigarette)/fire/anger
Italian (1972)	Grazie per il fuoco	Thanks for the fire (not used for a cigarette)
Russian (1969)	Spasibo Za Oghonyek (transliteration)	Thanks for the 'fire' (a diminutive derived from the word for 'fire', but colloquially a light for a cigarette)

While there are slight variations, four of the six translations clearly retain at least two meanings of 'fire', the general meaning and the lighting of a cigarette. It is also worth noting that the first edition of the novel in 1965[12] has as its cover illustration a smoking ashtray full of cigarette ends, and that the covers of 10 of the 25 editions published between 1965 and 2015 still available on the internet contain a representation of cigarette lighting or fire (Youdale 2017:65). The methodology has helped to confirm the validity of the translation of *fuego* as *light* in the novel's title, which allows for the full range of connotations suggested in the original. Lighting a cigarette, lighting the fire of rebellion, offering the light of hope and providing the light of an inspirational example are all contained in its ambit.

2.4 Characterisation

Characterisation is an important focus for study in both narratology and translation, and the use of both perspectives is likely to produce a more comprehensive picture of the nature of characterisation in a fictional text, and therefore in principle a better informed translation. I take as my starting point the view that 'since characters are shaped by their authors to attain certain ends and effects, it makes perfect sense to inquire why and to what end they endowed their characters with this particular selection of features' (Margolin 2007:68). In this section I apply the CDR approach to characterisation in *Gracias por el Fuego* in four different ways. The frequency and distribution of named character references to Ramón and Edmundo are analysed, and then two different ways of analysing an individual character are explored: a concordance list and discourse analysis of the character's direct speech. The final part of the section then examines the use of network analysis and visualisation to

58   *Analysing the Source Text*

plot a map of all the interacting characters in the novel and illustrates different ways of viewing their interactions and relationships.

Ramón and Edmundo

In Section 2.1, I argued that Edmundo represented the country's corrupt and hypocritical governing class, while Ramón stood for the alienated and morally contaminated Montevidean middle class, aware of the rottenness of the political system but unwilling or unable to take steps to change it. Quantitative analysis provides textual evidence for the centrality of these two characters. Ramón appears as an actor in 12 chapters (1–6 and 8–13), is referred to in Chapter 7 and forms the focus of attention in Chapters 14 and 15. He is also the actor-narrator in nine chapters. Edmundo appears as an actor in five chapters (2, 6, 7, 9 and 15) where he is primarily represented through dialogue, but also much talked about by seven other characters. In another four chapters (10–13), as Jacques Soubeyroux notes, 'il reste constamment au centre de l'histoire, et le prénom personnel <<lo>> suffit à le designer... sans qu'il y ait besoin d'autre précision' (1986:91) [he is always at the centre of the story, and the personal pronoun "him" is sufficient to refer to him... without need of further clarification]. In addition to their presence in terms of page and chapter count, these two characters can be considered central by virtue of their relationship, an irreconcilable conflict which forms the axis around which the entire narrative revolves.

A CDR analysis of named references to Edmundo and a sub-corpus of his direct speech will show how information can be gleaned from a text through distant reading that is relevant to the translation of character and voice, and to the choice of translation for individual words and phrases. Investigation of the contexts of occurrence and collocations of the 38 named references to 'Edmundo', using Sketch Engine's word list, concordance and collocations tools, reveals several facts. First, 30 of the 38 references are to his full name, Edmundo Budiño, and occur in the context of descriptions of his public and private personae and the strong contrast between the two. Over half the references (20) are made by Gloria, his secret, long-term mistress, in two chapters: Chapter 7 (14) and Chapter 15 (6). This identifies these two chapters as particularly fruitful sources of the portrayal of Edmundo's character as seen by a person who knows him very well indeed. In other words, the CDR approach elicited information about the location and nature of named references to Edmundo which could help with the translation of descriptions of him and his dialogue. It also acts as cross-referencing for the use of the term 'el Viejo' [The Old Man] already referred to.

The creation of a sub-corpus of Edmundo's direct speech in the novel – the only direct source of information about what and how he thinks,

Analysing the Source Text   59

since he has no interior monologues – allows for further character investigation through discourse analysis. Using the set of analytical tools discussed in Section 2.2, I was able to arrive at a deeper understanding of his character and both the themes of his discourse and the manner in which they are expressed. This informed specific translation decisions. There are two indications that the kind of language used by Edmundo is relatively straightforward. The average sentence length, calculated from Sketch Engine's corpus summary, is 11.4 words (for a text of 5,350 words), which is very close to that for the novel as a whole, and short sentences are generally less complex than long ones. Second, a review of the 200 most frequently occurring words in the word list showed them all to be very common. However, a more balanced picture of language variety also needs to take account of the least frequently used words – the hapax legomena – and computer-aided analysis is particularly helpful in this respect.

Close reading is, as has been said, effectively incapable of identifying words which are only used once in a text, unless they are particularly abstruse or outlandish, but CL software can quickly produce an alphabetical list of them which can be referred to during both initial translation and revision. Knowing which these words are can be of great assistance to the translator. First, with the exception of variants within a lemma, the translator does not need to be concerned with the issue of consistency of translation which arises with many repeated words. S/he does, however, need to decide whether a hapax in the ST needs to be translated as a hapax in the TT, and if the SL word is unusually rare or simply uncommon in relation to the general vocabulary used in the text.

The verb *arrebolarse* stood out for me in the list of hapax as being an uncommon word. It appears in Chapter 9 and is used by Edmundo to embarrass and humiliate Ramón in the course of a pompous and sarcastic homily about the fact that his (Edmundo's) shady dealings will not be allowed to drag the Budiño name through the mud. The context is:

> Y vos y Hugo [Ramón's brother] y Gustavo podrán seguir entregando su tarjetita de visita con el nombre de Budiño sin que las mejillas hipersensibles <u>se les arrebolen.</u>
>
> (p. 166, emphasis added)

> [And you and Hugo and Gustavo will be able to continue offering your precious Budiño visiting card without your hypersensitive cheeks <u>reddening</u>]

The essential meaning of the verb is *to redden* with shame or embarrassment, and this would be an obvious translation. However, the question arises as to why Benedetti chose to use *arrebolarse*, when there are at

60   *Analysing the Source Text*

least four other more common verbs which in this context would have almost exactly the same meaning. In the Spanish Web 2011, a ten-billion word general reference corpus of European and American Spanish built into Sketch Engine, these synonymous verbs have the following frequencies: *sonrojarse* (1,938); *ruborizarse* (1,165); *enrojecerse* (195); *abochornarse* (50); *arrebolarse* (2). This supports the idea that *arrebolarse* is a fairly uncommon verb.

Two possibilities occurred to me: either this is a verb more commonly used in the River Plate area than in other parts of the Spanish-speaking world, or, given Edmundo's pompous and scathing tone in this exchange with Ramón, it is possible that he wanted to use a rarefied word to show off his own erudition and emphasise his superiority. Either way, it seemed reasonable to look for an unusual rendering in English to mirror the ST. A search for synonyms of *to redden* in print and online dictionaries[13] yielded the following: *to go/turn red, to blush, to flush, to colour, to colour up, to burn* (with shame), *to bloom, to glow, to suffuse* (with colour) and *to rubify*, which is very uncommon. For the reasons given above I decided to use *rubify* and to translate the final part of the extract as '...without your hypersensitive cheeks rubifying'.

In terms of an overview of key themes and patterns in Edmundo's discourse, a lemmatised word frequency list suggests that he has a fairly black and white view of the world, and a preoccupation with money. The top three lexical words are 'todo' (30) [all], 'nada' (18) [nothing] and 'plata' (15) [money]; and there are 151 instances of 'no'. A keyword list also suggests that he focuses on the themes of morality, immorality and violence. The top seven keywords and their meaning or reference are shown in *Table 2.2*:

Close reading can confirm or contradict suggestions thrown up by distant reading, but the latter can give the translator a steer as to things to look for and help provide a wider context for the translation of individual words and phrases.

Table 2.2 Top seven keywords in Edmundo's discourse

Keyword frequency	Keyword	Raw frequency	Meaning or reference
1	Larralde	11	A journalist who attempts to expose Edmundo's corruption
2	Budiño	7	The well-known and respected family name
3	Labrocca	3	A strike organiser at Edmundo's factory
4	suciamente	3	'dirtily'
5	Friedmann	3	A journalist suspected of wanting to expose Edmundo's corruption
6	matarme	4	'to kill me'
7	detestaba	3	'he hated me', with reference to Ramón

Analysing the Source Text 61

Character Analysis, Network Theory and Visualisation

The analysis of literary texts, whether narratological, stylistic or a combination of both, has traditionally been conducted verbally rather than visually. However, in 2011 Franco Moretti and his colleagues at the Stanford Literary Lab began exploring ways of representing the plots and characters in plays and novels through visualisation. In this subsection I draw on his work to conduct a CDR analysis of the character set in *Gracias por el Fuego*, with the aim of answering two further questions about characterisation. Having established that Ramón and Edmundo are the two central characters, what does their centrality consist of? And what is the relationship between these two and the other characters?

In 'Network Theory and Plot Analysis' Moretti displays the characters in Hamlet in the form of a network diagram (2011:12), as shown in Figure 2.1, and explains that 'two characters are linked if some words have passed between them' (2011:3).

He goes on to say: 'Four hours of action [the play], that become this. Time turned into space' (Ibidem) and asks 'What do we gain, by turning time into space? First of all, this: when we watch a play, we are always in the present: what is on stage, is; and then it disappears. Here, nothing ever disappears... the past becomes the past, yes, but it never disappears from our perception of the plot' (2011:3–4). The same principle applies to the reading of a novel: as we turn the page one character's words are replaced by another's and slip into the past. It is true that in contrast to watching a play we can always turn back a page to reread a passage, but I would argue that the idea Moretti is advancing still holds true: the full network of characters in a novel and the relationships between them are almost never available to us as a single visual snapshot, and certainly not in *Gracias por el Fuego*.

The first benefit of such visualisation is 'making the past just as visible as the present' (Moretti 2011:4), in other words all the characters can be viewed simultaneously, irrespective of when they actually appear. The second benefit is that a network map is, as Moretti argues, 'a model that allows you to see the underlying structures of a complex object. It's like an X-ray' (2011:4). In other words, it visibly brings to the surface information which is often only partially seen and understood when we read a novel, even when that reading is the close reading of a translator and allows us to examine areas of the network in new ways. But in order to analyse the results which are displayed visually and to explore possible questions raised, we need to go back to focused close reading.

Figures 2.2–2.4 display the results of a quantitative visual analysis of the characters in the novel, which show different aspects of their relationships. My methodology involved a sequence of four steps. First, I extracted an alphabetical list of all the proper nouns in the novel using a corpus query language (CQL) search in Sketch Engine, downloaded the results in Excel format and removed all the entries which were not character names.[14] There have been several experiments with non-CL

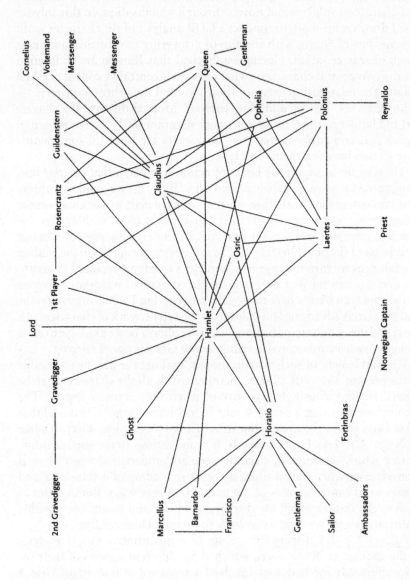

Figure 2.1 Characters in Hamlet (Moretti 2011:12).

software designed to extract character names from a literary text automatically (Elson, Dames and McKeown 2010; Lee and Yeung 2012; van Dalen-Oskam 2013; Sparavigna and Marazzato 2015) but to my knowledge there is still no publicly available software which will do this without the need for specialist computing knowledge.[15]

The results required manual 'cleaning' in various ways. Some characters are referred to in different ways, such as Edmundo who is variously called *Edmundo, Doctor, Papá* and *el Viejo*, and these all need to be aggregated to arrive at a figure for total named references. A few other characters are not given names at all, but only descriptions, such as *la húngara* [the Hungarian woman] and *la mujer de Sánchez* [Sánchez' wife]. I then ran a frequency query for each character and produced a table of results. It is important to acknowledge the limitations of this method of measuring the frequency of occurrence of character references, the most serious being its inability to register references contained in pronouns and inflected verbs. I am not aware of any software which can identify and extract such references at present.

The third step involved producing a foundation network map of the 87 plot-internal fictional characters who have at least one direct interaction (spoken, written or physical) with another character. This map excluded eight fictional and over ten non-fictional characters. It displays all the character names or descriptions with their frequency of named occurrence in brackets, and lines linking them to characters with whom they interact. The final stage involved adapting the foundation map to display three different subsets of relationships. Figure 2.2 shows the relationship networks of Ramón and Edmundo. Figure 2.3 shows the relationships between the five principal characters, as measured by a combination of named references, quantity of dialogue spoken and plot significance. Figure 2.4 shows the characters involved in each of eight 'scenes' in Chapter 9, defined as the narrative delimited by changes of place or character and where there is direct interaction between the characters, and linked to a specific page range.

Results of the Analysis

Figure 2.2 The networks of Ramón and Edmundo: The network visualisation produced two interesting results. The first was the sheer number of characters. Despite having read the novel at least three times and translated it, before counting I would have estimated the number of characters to be around 30 rather than 87. This supports the idea that as readers – even close readers – we either do not register or do not retain certain kinds of textual information, some of which can have a bearing on translation. The second was the nature of the inter-character relationships. Ramón links to 66 characters (76%) and Edmundo to 18 (20%). As Bal argues, one criterion for identifying the 'hero' character

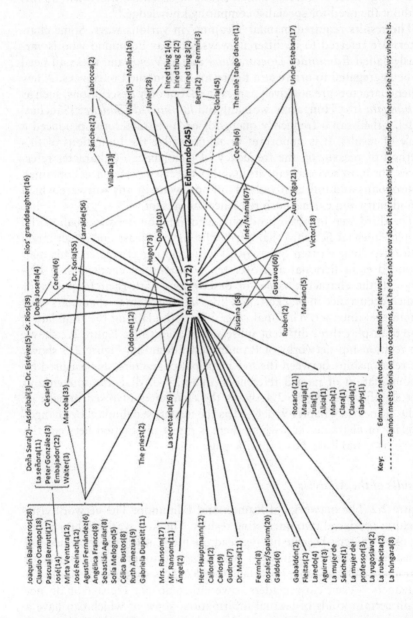

Figure 2.2 The networks of Ramón and Edmundo.

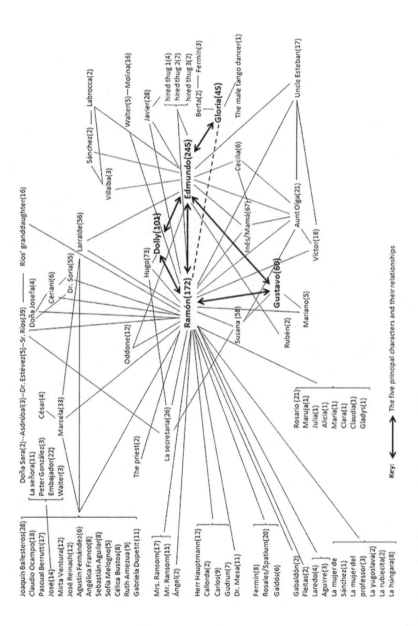

Figure 2.3 Relationships between the five principal characters.

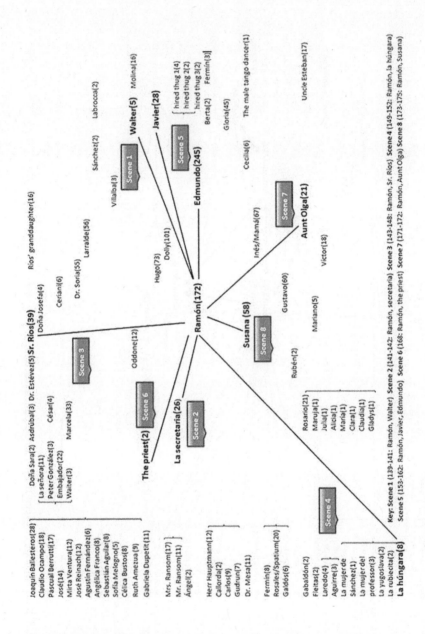

Figure 2.4 Character relationships in Chapter 9.

Analysing the Source Text 67

is that 's/he maintains relations with the largest number of characters' (1997:132). Their centrality is defined by an overwhelming centre-periphery relationship to the other characters. There are very few lateral, periphery-periphery links, and such links are of relatively minor significance in narrative terms. This constitutes visual confirmation of Ramón's emphatic centrality in the character network and is consistent with close reading observation.

The visualisation in Figure 2.2 also raises two other questions: why are there so many minor characters? and what is their function? Of the 87 characters, 60 (69%) appear in only one chapter, and only 6 characters (7%) appear in more than 5 out of 15 chapters. Only 10 characters (11%) have more than 40 references. I would suggest that the majority of characters fulfil one or both of two functions, both of which relate to the two central characters. The first is their role as representations of an idea, a principle or a point of view. In relation to Edmundo, for example, only three characters have the courage to stand up to him, at great personal cost: Larralde, the journalist who tries to expose his corrupt dealings, despite the threat of dismissal (which is carried out); Gloria, who finds the courage to abandon Edmundo at the end of the novel; and Villalba, the trade union leader at Edmundo's factory. For example, in Chapter 4 Hugo plays Ramón a tape recording he has been given by mistake of a meeting between Edmundo and Villalba at which Edmundo puts pressure on the trade union leader to betray two of his fellow strike leaders for money, making it clear that he will also lose his job if he does not do so. Villalba stands his ground:

> —¿Usted cree que por unos mugrientos quinientos pesos o los que sean, yo voy a hundir a dos amigos, a dos buenos tipos que lo único malo que han hecho es privarle a usted, señor, de dos meses de su podrida ganancia? Claro, usted tiene la plata y basta. Pues métasela donde le quepa, señor.
>
> (pp. 99–100)

> [D'you think that for five hundred dirty pesos or whatever, I'm going to betray two friends, two good guys whose only crime has been to deprive you, señor, of two months of your rotten profit? Of course, you've got money and you think that's all there is to it. Well, you can stick it where the sun don't shine, señor.]

The second function is that of helping to fill out the portrait of either Ramón's or Edmundo's character through their interactions with them. For example, Ramón's sensitive and respectful treatment of the terminally ill señor Ríos and his granddaughter in Chapters 9 and 10 helps to portray him as a more rounded character with positive qualities, in contrast to the dominant image of him as weak, indecisive and self-deluding.

68 Analysing the Source Text

The three thugs whom Edmundo hires as agent provocateurs to disrupt a left-wing demonstration in Chapter 4 (pp. 78–79) function as an illustration of the depths to which he will sink to pervert democratic opposition to the status quo.

Figure 2.3 Relationships between the five principal characters: This visualisation shows how a subset of the network can be isolated to show its relationship to the whole. Gloria, Gustavo and Dolly link almost exclusively to Ramón and Edmundo, forming a kind of nucleus within the network. They are defined in relation to the two central characters, and in turn help to define them through their interactions. Gustavo represents an idealistic and somewhat simplistic Marxist political viewpoint, and also provides a foil for Ramón, aka Benedetti, to express his moral and political beliefs in Chapter 8. He also has a political argument with Edmundo in Chapter 6, which serves to reinforce our view of Edmundo as a cynical hypocrite. Dolly's interactions with Ramón show that he is capable of a sincere and loving relationship with a woman, in contrast to both his transient sexual encounters and his loveless marriage to Susana.

Figure 2.4 Character relationships in chapter 9: This visualisation attempts in a limited way to turn space back into time, to represent a sequence of scenes in a chapter by showing which characters are involved, who they interact with and the flow of that set of interactions. Chapter 9 contains 40 pages and 8 separate scenes interspersed with 7 interior monologues of varying length by Ramón. In other words, this is a complex, information-rich chapter, the detail of which is difficult to retain as one reads. The visualisation, when coupled with further close reading of each scene and linking monologue, allows the reader-as-translator to stand back from the detail and see the major themes in the chapter: entrapment and death.

Ramón is trapped by having accepted his father's dirty money, as he acknowledges: 'aunque le devuelva la plata en su totalidad, siempre queda vigente el hecho de que usted me dio la oportunidad gracias a ese dinero' (pp. 164–165) [even if I repay you all the money, it will always be true that you gave me my opportunity with that money]. He is physically trapped in the flashback of the time when his foot was caught in a set of railway points and a train was approaching, and he is trapped by the dawning realisation that the only way out of his problems is to kill Edmundo: 'No hay solución. La única solución sería, quizá, matar al Viejo' (p. 173) [There's no solution. The only solution would be, maybe, to kill The Old Man].

Death and the manner in which it is faced feature in Ramón's conversation with his client Sr. Ríos, who confronts his certain death from cancer with calmness and fortitude; in his own near-death experience on the railway as the train bears down on him; and in the contemplation of the likely reaction of his family and society when he murders Edmundo. The scene analysis of Chapter 9 also visually reveals another structural

Analysing the Source Text 69

narrative feature, the fact that Ramón almost exclusively interacts with only one character at a time, in scenes in which there are almost always only two characters present.[16] This applies to 11 chapters and points to one-to-one dialogues as a narrative building block.

It is important to acknowledge that these visualisations only provide limited information about characterisation. The links shown are not weighted and do not indicate the nature, extent or duration of the relationships between characters. They do not give any clue as to how the relationships change over time,[17] and even when considered in the light of the reference figures in brackets, give only approximate indications of relative narrative importance. Ramón's brother Hugo, for instance, is referred to 73 times, but emerges as a rather stereotypical and two-dimensional character. Gloria, by contrast, is only referred to 45 times but occupies every page of two complete chapters, 7 and 15 (totalling 28% of the novel's page count), and her portrayal is both more nuanced and in plot terms far more important. The value of the visualisations lies in their role as part of a process of analysis which involves alternately looking up close at the text and then standing back, of a recursive dialogue between close reading and quantitative analysis.

I have argued that the CDR approach is capable of producing a deeper and more rounded appreciation of character portrayal which has both direct and indirect implications for translation. As Jane Johnson observes in the context of corpus stylistics and translation,

> queries involving character names may be used to 'Plot' the appearance of the characters through the text, while a closer examination of the collocates associated with the names themselves can help to provide more information of how the character is presented in the story, or what features are associated with him/her.
>
> (2008:5)

At an indirect level, character analysis can help when trying to find and develop an appropriate voice for each character, both in general terms and in the context of particular situations and relationships. Ramón, for example, has one voice – weak, resentful and frustrated – when he speaks to Edmundo after the latter has become *el Viejo*. He has a very different voice – strong, confident and full of conviction – when he discusses the need for social change with Gustavo. He has yet others in his many interior monologues.

At a direct level, translation decisions relating to register, dialect and idiolect may all be affected by the subtleties of character assessment. The translation of the appellation of Edmundo as *el Viejo* is a good example. My initial choice of translation for the term was *Father*, which retains the element of formality implied by Edmundo always being addressed as *usted*, but is too neutral. An understanding of the depths of ill feeling

70 *Analysing the Source Text*

which Ramón harbours for his father, and a knowledge of the extent of the repetition of this phrase across the novel, suggested rejecting the obvious translation of the phrase as *the Old Man* as having too many positive overtones in English, despite the capitalisation which indicates that the phrase is marked. The result of CDR character analysis was to opt for *The Old Man* as a consistent translation.

Undertaking the kinds of analyses described in this section was for the most part a fairly quick and easy process. For example, it took less than an hour to copy and paste all of Edmundo's direct speech in the novel into a new Word document and upload it to Sketch Engine. The entire process of creating the corpus, uploading and analysing it – including the assessment of the results – took half a day. Producing the network visualisations, by contrast, took several days. The value of undertaking this kind of analysis would need to be assessed on a case-by-case basis, but the initial stage of identifying a set of character names from a list of proper nouns would give the translator an idea of the number and range of characters in a text and is relatively quick to perform.

Notes

1 This information has been taken from Ruffinelli (1973:193–195); Beberfall (1981:360–376); Paoletti (1995:233–235); the front matter of Harry Morales' translation of *The Truce* (Benedetti 2015); and obituaries in the Uruguayan, Spanish and British press.

2 A name given to a period from the late 1950s to the early 1970s during which a number of Latin American writers were brought to literary prominence through translation and publication, the most well-known being Julio Cortázar (Argentina), Carlos Fuentes (Mexico), Mario Vargas-Llosa (Peru) and Gabriel García Márquez (Colombia) (Martin 1989; King 2005).

3 All source text page references are taken from the 2014 Alianza Editiorial (Madrid) third edition.

4 'Las entrevistas de El Informante': Selección del archivo del periodista Leonardo Haberkorn, 16 de marzo de 2016. Available at: http://leonardohaberkorn2.blogspot.co.uk/2015/03/mario-benedetti-la-terquedad-del-poeta.html

5 Mathieu cites this as a quotation from an article by Ariel Dorfman (1966), 'Edipo en Uruguay', *Ercilla*, 15 de junio, p. 35, which I have been unable to obtain.

6 As explained at the end of the Introduction, I had already completed a draft translation of the novel before developing the CDR methodology, so I am doing this analysis retrospectively and arguably with the benefit of hindsight. However, the examples given relate either to stylistic features which I had noted during initial reading or which had become noteworthy during translation, and so are appropriate for the purposes of the model.

7 A cautionary note is in order here. 'Tokens' sometimes refers to words, but in CATMA, Sketch Engine and Voyant Tools this term also includes punctuation marks, brackets, etc. Sketch Engine and Voyant Tools automatically deduct these from their total word count, but CATMA does not. There are also variations in the way words are counted. Contractions such as "it's", for example, can be counted as one word or two. CATMA also separates upper

and lower case words, whereas Voyant Tools is case insensitive by default and Sketch Engine offers users the choice of either. This does not affect the total word count, but it does affect the frequency counts of individual words.

8 'Lady Weare and the Bodhisattva' (1969) by Kylie Tennant.

9 There are different ways of defining the term 'lexical'. Some scholars exclude auxiliary verbs, for example, while others exclude certain adverbs (Johansson 2008:65–67).

10 I have not included the Portuguese title as it is identical to the Spanish, nor the Bulgarian, Hungarian or Polish titles as I have not been able to access their meanings.

11 I am indebted to Dr. Rajendra Chitnis, University of Bristol, for help with the Czech and Russian translations, and to Elena Gerola West for help with the Italian translation.

12 Benedetti, M., 1965. *Gracias por el Fuego*, Montevideo: Alfa.

13 Benedetto, U., 1977. *EDAF nuevo diccionario general inglés-español: new-comprehensive English-Spanish dictionary.* Madrid: EDAF; Oxford English Living Dictionaries: https://en.oxforddictionaries.com/; Merriam-Webster Dictionary: www.merriam-webster.com/; Theasurus.com: www.thesaurus.com/.

14 I actually did this manually as this analysis pre-dated my use of CDR, but I would have used Sketch Engine had I known about it.

15 There are named entity recognition (NER) programmes, such as the Stanford Named Entity Recognizer (available free at: https://nlp.stanford.edu/software/CRF-NER.shtml) which use Java, but these require specialist knowledge to implement.

16 Edmundo's secretary Javier's involvement in Scene 5 is confined to two lines of dialogue on p. 160, and his appearance is of no narrative significance.

17 Aris Xanthos et al. are developing software designed to allow the user to benefit from an interactive character network visualisation of a play or a narrative text, which will show how relationships change at different points. They argue that 'by allowing the user to browse the content of the narrative and manipulate an interactive character network, our motivation is ultimately to contribute to a better integration of distant and close reading practice' (2016:419).

3 CDR, Translation Theory and the Attempt to Create an 'English Benedetti'

This is not a book about translation theory, but about a proposed translation methodology. However, translation methodologies do not exist in a vacuum and must be related in some way to theoretical perspectives on translation. Before an act of translation takes place, there has already been an act of interpretation and choice in the selection of the text to translate, and a view of why the text is worth translating. The theoretical hypothesis underlying the close and distant reading (CDR) approach is that it can result in a better informed literary translation than one which relies on close reading alone, and that information maximisation is beneficial to the translation process as it can help to inform translation decision-making. But the way in which the tools and techniques are used is not value-free, as they will be put to work in the service of a particular model of translation, with a particular set of translation goals and in a particular social, cultural, political and historical context. In this chapter, I will spell out the set of choices I made and the interpretations I arrived at as a translator prior to developing and using the CDR approach to translate *Gracias por el Fuego*.

The methodology is in principle independent of any specific translation theory, and could, for example, be applied within the framework of foreignisation or domestication, Bourdieu, skopos theory, postcolonial or feminist translation.[1] It is also in principle independent of language-pair, literary genre or historical period. Having said that, and as I acknowledged in the Introduction, the methodology as applied to literary style is more likely to produce beneficial results in certain types of translation as opposed to others.

One of the most fundamental of differences between literary forms is that between poetry and prose. Poems are in general much shorter than prose works; they often stretch and even break traditional grammatical and linguistic conventions and are frequently full of deliberate ambiguity. The relatively short length of most poems means that it is more likely that linguistic patterns such as repetition will be more easily picked up by close reading than in longer texts where it is much easier for such patterns to be hidden. However, as O'Halloran notes, 'In the last few years, corpus analysis has begun to be used to help support interpretation (and evaluation) of poetry' (2012:178) through analysis of linguistic

CDR and Creating an 'English Benedetti' 73

patterns such as collocations and links between particular grammatical and lexical words (2012:178–179). Since the translator needs to have an interpretation of some kind in order to translate poetry, the CDR approach can still be of use, even more so if the translator is dealing with collections of poems (McIntyre and Walker 2010).

Another factor that affects the potential usefulness of the CDR approach is whereabouts on the literal-free continuum a translation strategy is located (Hervey, Higgins and Haywood 2004:13). As I will argue in this and the following three chapters, the methodology really comes into its own where the translation goal is to mirror as closely as possible the style of the source text (ST) in the target text (TT). Where the aim of the translation is to produce a much freer version, such as a highly domesticated rendering or an adaptation, some uses of the methodology may be less applicable. While ST analysis and information gathering during translation will still be useful, comparison of ST and draft TT may be less relevant.

In the first section of this chapter I put forward my approach to the translation of *Gracias por el Fuego*, which is informed by two main considerations. Like Antoine Berman ([1985] 2004) and Lawrence Venuti (2004) I believe that Anglophone readers benefit from the opportunity to confront the otherness of different cultures, so that, as Chantal Wright suggests, 'they come to think of themselves as only one culture among many, rather than as an imperial one' (2016:42). This means that in translating I adopt a broadly foreignising approach, a term which I explore critically, arguing that foreignisation is more usefully applied to translation as an ethical principle rather than as a specific set of linguistic strategies. My application of this principle manifests itself in the choice of author and text to translate, in the retention of as much of the source language and culture-specific references as possible, and in the attempted reproduction of ST style.

The eminent translator Anthea Bell classified herself as

> an unrepentant, unreconstructed adherent of the school of invisible translation... all my professional life, I have felt that translators are in the business of spinning an illusion: the illusion is that the reader is reading not a translation but the real thing.
>
> (2004:14)

While respecting her opinion, I take a very different view, that put forward by the translation scholar Rachel May, who argues that

> if we persist in believing that a reader should not be able to tell she is reading a translation, then we devalue the translator's art and remove one of the main reasons to produce or read translations in the first place: the chance to glimpse another culture.
>
> (1994:109)

74   CDR *and Creating an 'English Benedetti'*

This view is echoed by Venuti when he argues that 'A translated text should be the site where a different culture emerges, where a reader gets a glimpse of a cultural other' (2004:306).

Second, I espouse what Wright terms 'a textual ethics of respect for literary integrity' (2016:43). This means that I treat the ST as a whole 'package', whose literary integrity or wholeness consists in content which is inextricably bound up with a particular and marked mode of stylistic expression, the 'what' and the 'how' I referred to in the Introduction. My analysis of Benedetti's style is that it was designed to encourage his readers to see themselves in the character of Ramón, and to stop and think about the moral and political unacceptability of the society in which they lived. Therefore, my principal translation strategy at the linguistic level involves the attempt to achieve equivalence of style as far as possible in the hope that this will have similar effects on my readers to those I experienced when reading the original, although I acknowledge that I will never be able to claim that I have achieved this.

In Section 3.2, I explore this concept, relating it to Eugene Nida's concepts of 'formal' and 'dynamic' equivalence ([1964] 2004), but argue that my approach incorporates elements of both. I use examples from my draft translation, and a comparison with the 1983 French translation, to illustrate what an 'English Benedetti', based on a search for potential equivalence of stylistic effect, looks like in practice, how it differs from a more fluent and idiomatic version, and what I consider to be lost as a result of the latter approach.

In Section 3.3, I undertake a limited comparative analysis of the multiple translations into English of 'Familia Iriarte' (1956), a Benedetti short story included in the *Montevideanos* collection of 1959, and *La Tregua* (1960), Benedetti's most internationally successful novel. The aim is to take account of the way that existing translations of Benedetti into English have been done, and to analyse the effects on me of altering or preserving certain of his stylistic features, which are also present in *Gracias por el Fuego*, such as sentence rhythm.

3.1 CDR and Translation Philosophy

In undertaking any literary translation, the translator has to take account of a number of factors and make a number of choices. The factors include the context of production and reception of the ST; their attitude to the author, text and culture, and their role as an intercultural mediator; their own moral and political beliefs; their own translatorial style, to the extent that they are aware of it; the purpose of the translation, its target readership and any constraints imposed by publication. Of these factors the translator's attitude to what they translate is perhaps one of the most important and least often discussed.

CDR and Creating an 'English Benedetti' 75

It has been cogently argued by translation scholars that a translator almost inevitably reveals their attitude towards what they translate, consciously or unconsciously, and that therefore no translation can be said to be completely 'neutral' (Schiavi 1996; Hermans 1996, 2014; Munday 2007a, 2007b, 2008a). I locate myself as a broadly foreignising translator, but agree with the criticism of the idea that foreignisation and domestication can be seen as simple binary choices (Tymoczko 2000; Birdwood-Hedger 2006), and support the view that both can take a variety of forms and be productively combined in the same translation (Harker 1999; Mattar 2014). One of the key choices a literary translator has to make is that posed by Friedrich Schleiermacher: 'Either the translator leaves the writer in peace as much as possible and moves the reader towards him; or he leaves the reader in peace as much as possible and moves the writer towards him' ([1813] 2004:49). Anthony Pym has argued that in championing the first option Schleiermacher was not so much declaring a universal ethical principle as aiming 'to make the German language a platform for world literature, one that would eventually attract foreign intellectuals in the way that France had been doing' (2012:27). It was the French theorist and translator Antoine Berman who argued that Schleiermacher's approach should be seen as a general principle, and that 'the properly *ethical* aim of the translation act [involves] ... receiving the Foreign as Foreign' ([1985] 2004:285–286, emphasis in original). He suggests that a number of tendencies operate in such a way as to 'deform' translation and make it 'deviate from its essential aim' (ibidem). He defines 12 'deforming tendencies' which he collectively calls 'the negative analytic' of translation (ibidem), and to which I refer in relation to specific examples in Chapters 4 and 5.

It is, however, the translation theorist and translator Lawrence Venuti who has probably done the most to raise the profile of the principle of foreignisation in literary translation by effectively coining the term, with specific reference to translation into English. In *The Translator's Invisibility* Venuti argues that in contemporary Anglo-American culture

> a translated text, whether prose or poetry, fiction or nonfiction, is judged acceptable by most publishers, reviewers, and readers when it reads fluently, when the absence of any linguistic or stylistic peculiarities makes it seem transparent, giving the appearance that it reflects the foreign writer's personality or intention or the essential meaning of the foreign text—the appearance, in other words, that the translation is not in fact a translation, but the "original".
>
> (2004:1)

An example of this is provided by Anthea Bell in relation to her translation of the French comic Astérix. On the one hand, as a proponent of translator invisibility, she argues 'I like a translation to read as easily as if

76 CDR and Creating an 'English Benedetti'

it had been originally written in English' (2004:16); yet on the other, she admits to being 'absolutely amazed to find that some people – perfectly intelligent and well-educated people – didn't actually realise that Astérix was translated from French' (2004:22), as if the two phenomena were not intimately linked. Invisibility of translation can and often does lead in practice to the invisibility of a text as foreign. Venuti goes on to assert that this view of translation has led to the translator's invisibility, which 'at once enacts and masks an insidious domestication of foreign texts, rewriting them in the transparent discourse that prevails in English and that selects precisely those foreign texts amenable to fluent translating' (2004:17). He also suggests that 'The translator's invisibility is symptomatic of a complacency in Anglo-American relations with cultural others, a complacency that can be described—without too much exaggeration—as imperialistic abroad and xenophobic at home' (ibidem).

His work on foreignisation and domestication in the 1990s coincided with the 'cultural turn' in translation studies, a move away from the detailed comparison of individual STs and their translations to a consideration of the social, political and cultural contexts in which both ST and TT are produced and received. It struck a chord with a number of translation scholars (Boll 2013:90–92), and Jean Boase-Beier articulates the political and ethical sympathy which Venuti's critique of Anglophone translation evoked amongst some scholars when she argues that 'Venuti has done an enormous service to translation theory by linking the notion of 'transparency'... to ethics' (2010b:28). However, a number of criticisms have been levelled at the application of his ideas in practice. These can be divided into two groups: criticism of how his approach can be used to assess whether a specific translation can be considered to be foreignising or domesticating, and criticism of how he suggests a foreignising translation should be performed at a linguistic level.

In relation to the first group Maria Tymoczko argues that Venuti does not define his terms clearly enough for them to be useful:

> He [Venuti] suggests that he is offering a conceptual tool for analyzing translations, a kind of absolute or universal standard of valuation, with a sort of on/off quality rather than a sliding scale, but where and how the lines are to be drawn in applying his concepts are nowhere articulated for the scholarly community.
>
> (2000:38)

Taking a slightly different approach to the problem of classification of translations, Maya Birdwood-Hedger argues that 'Rather than describe translations as domesticating and foreignising, I will try to distinguish between domesticating and foreignising strategies present in different translations' (2006:65). In other words, within the overall framework of a foreignising approach, for example, some translation strategies such

CDR and Creating an 'English Benedetti'   77

as explanations of cultural references could be seen as domesticating in that they conform to target culture expectations. Yet at the same time they fulfil the foreignising function of introducing the reader to aspects of another culture. It is this more nuanced approach that I apply to my translation, seeing foreignisation as a principle which can be implemented in a variety of ways at different levels, rather than as a set of rigid prescriptions.

In terms of foreignising translation strategies at a linguistic level, Venuti advocates what he terms 'resistancy' (2004:24), a policy of challenging what he sees as Anglophone norms of fluency, transparency and invisibility of translation, in an attempt to 'restrain the ethnocentric violence of translation' (2004:20). Some examples of practical strategies are given, and he suggests that 'contemporary translators of literary texts can introduce discursive variations, experimenting with archaism, slang, literary allusion and convention to call attention to the secondary status of the translation and signal the linguistic and cultural differences of the foreign text' (2004:310–311). He also, however, warns that this approach must be applied within the practical constraints of the translator's contractual obligations to produce 'faithful' translations which are also readable: 'This means limiting discursive experiments to perceptible deviations that may risk but stop short of the parodic or incomprehensible' (2004:311). But as Tymoczko asks,

> how do we distinguish resistant translations from translations that are unreadable? Where in language does ideological tyranny end and grammar begin?... There is nothing in Venuti's definitions of his concepts or articulation of them that helps us to answer such questions.
>
> (2000:37)

In this context his critics make various charges. Anthony Pym argues that foreignising translations are open to the accusation of being elitist in that they only appeal to a small number of readers, and that Venuti 'makes no attempt to counter the quantitative argument that the more difficult a translation is to read, the less impact it will have on the wider target communities' (2012:35). But all difficult literature, whether original or in translation, tends to begin by only reaching a small number of readers – just think of James Joyce's *Ulysses*, for example – and it is only by introducing new ideas, styles and authors into a language that it changes, develops and is enriched. Spanish is no stranger to challenging innovation, either, as John McCaw notes in his assessment of the impact on the language of the poet Luis de Góngora (1561–1627): 'characterized by intense erudition, densely packed tropes, and convoluted, latinized syntax, Góngora's innovative style sparked a literary firestorm the likes of which had never been seen before in Castilian culture' (2013:3).

78   CDR *and Creating an 'English Benedetti'*

Literary difficulty is also, of course, a matter of degree. In my view *Gracias por el Fuego*, which was after all a popular novel, is mostly not difficult to read, its frequent markedness in Spanish still being idiomatic, and my translation is only very occasionally unidiomatic in its attempt to mirror this markedness. The difficult passages tend to relate to two particular kinds of sentences: short and condensed, and very long.

There is also the charge, which I find persuasive, that at a linguistic level it is often difficult to make a coherent distinction between foreignising and domesticating strategies and effects. In his article on how the concept of foreignisation can be applied to the analysis of two English translations of *The Black Book* by the Nobel-prizewinning Turkish author Orhan Pamuk,[2] Karim Mattar analyses the two translations of the novel's opening sentence, and shows how each can be argued to contain elements of both domestication and foreignization. He shows how fluency does not necessarily indicate domestication, because it can accurately replicate the flow of the original in certain ways; and how a more halting, awkward rendition may not foreignise, but actually obscure or distort important linguistic features of the source language. He concludes that 'domestication and foreignization are in themselves not the most coherent categories when it comes to the language of translation: they bleed into one another and fail clearly to define the political effects of a given translating strategy' (2014:49). Jaime Harker, in his article on 'middlebrow' translation, goes even further when he argues that 'all translations are, to varying degrees, *both* domesticating and foreignizing, and "dominant cultural values" are often varied and contradictory' (1999:30, emphasis in original).

Foreignisation and the Translation of Gracias por el Fuego

In the second edition of *The Translator's Invisibility*, and in response to some of the criticisms levelled against him since the book's first publication in 1995, Venuti refines his original position somewhat by arguing that

> the terms 'domestication' and 'foreignization' do not establish a neat binary opposition that can simply be superimposed on 'fluent' or 'resistant' discursive strategies, nor can these two sets of terms be reduced to the true binaries that have proliferated in the history of translation commentary.... The terms 'domestication' and 'foreignisation' indicate fundamentally *ethical* attitudes towards a foreign text and culture, ethical effects produced by the choice of a text for translation and by the strategy devised to translate it.
>
> (2008:19, emphasis in original)

The foreignising dimension of my translation consists of three elements: the choice of author and text, the creation of a visible translation through strategies such as source language and cultural reference retention, and a challenge to the dominant norm of smooth and idiomatic English at times.

The choice to translate Benedetti and *Gracias por el Fuego* can be seen as making a potential contribution to broadening the range of twentieth-century Latin American fiction available in translation and challenging the existing canon. He published over 100 books encompassing almost every literary genre and was awarded literary prizes in seven countries. To date, according to an estimate by his literary agent in Barcelona, Guillermo Schavelzon, he has sold some 500 million books worldwide.[3] Of this large body of work only two novels, three collections of poems, two collections of short stories and one play have been translated into English, amounting to less than 8% of titles.[4] *Gracias por el Fuego* itself has been translated into ten European languages, but not English. Every literary translation is an act of intercultural intervention, and as Esther Allen observes, 'the *political gesture* enacted by a translator is entirely separate from that enacted by the writer of the work translated' (2013:101, emphasis in original).

A number of writers and scholars, including both of Benedetti's biographers (Paoletti 1995; Campanella 2009), concur in viewing the political subtext of the novel as an appeal by the author to the Montevidean middle class to stop acquiescing in the perpetuation of a corrupt political system, with its insidious effects on their own morality and relationships (Fornet 1975; Céspedes 1976; Fernández Retamar 1976; Lewis 1982; Soubeyroux 1986; Paoletti 1995; Campanella 2009; Lagos 2013). Novels such as *Gracias por el Fuego* thus become socio-historic documents in a country whose literature, in relation to many Latin American nations, can be considered understudied.[5] Benedetti was in many ways an urban chronicler of twentieth-century Montevideo, a city of which he often said he was very fond.

The second foreignising element of my translation approach concerns its 'visibility'. I argue in Chapter 4 that there is some evidence to suggest that there was a tendency in twentieth-century translation of Latin American fiction into English towards the normalisation of cultural references, involving the removal or replacement of source language words, expressions, forms of address and dialect. While it is by no means always possible to retain or reproduce all of these features in a translation, my starting point is a desire to do so wherever possible. This is in order to offer my readers information and insights into another culture, and to actively remind them that they are reading a translation and not a pseudo-original.

In addition to translator visibility in the text itself, in preparing the translation for possible publication I chose to include three paratextual devices to emphasise the fact of translation and also to assist the reader to understand and explore aspects of the Montevideo of the 1960s. The

80 CDR and Creating an 'English Benedetti'

first is a map of Montevideo, showing 23 streets and landmarks mentioned in the novel, and also Montevideo's location within Uruguay. The second is a glossary containing a brief explanation of key political and cultural terms and references left untranslated in the text. The third is a translator's preface.

One reason I want to include a preface to the translation is because, as Marella Feltrin-Morris notes, 'It is an opportunity for translators to declare their visibility and remind readers... that every word, construction, stylistic element, and even the illusion of transparency, is the result of an interpretative choice' (2016:1). It will also make a contribution towards changing what Andrew Chesterman calls the 'expectancy norms' of Anglophone readers with regard to fluent and transparent translations (Chesterman 1997:64). But there are other reasons for wanting to provide a preface. Gerard Genette describes the paratext as a '*threshold* [...] It is an "undefined zone" between the inside and the outside' of the text (1997:1–2). It provides a space for the translator to speak to the reader directly, with a view to enhancing their understanding and enjoyment of the text. In my case the aim of the preface is therefore mainly to perform the first three of five principal functions which McRae suggests are fulfilled by such prefaces:

1   foregrounding differences of cultures and languages;
2   promoting understanding of the source culture;
3   promoting understanding of the translator's role and intervention;
4   helping critics assess the quality of the translation; and
5   useful as process documentation.

(2010:20)

While the last two of these are also useful, my prime concern is to communicate with the general reader. Like McRae, I concur with Peter Newmark's comment that 'a [literary] translation without a preface ought to be a thing of the past' (Newmark 1983:17).[6]

The final aspect of foreignisation relates to literary style. In her review of the development of the concept of foreignisation Wright suggests that 'the "foreign" in Berman's essay [1985/2004] is as much the stylistic otherness of the individual literary text as the fact of its existence in a foreign language' (2016:38). My attempt to create the potential for equivalence of stylistic effect in the translation is based on two premises. First, that Benedetti's style in the novel is marked in Spanish and that this should be reflected in English rather than smoothed out and normalised. Second, as I have argued, his style is integral to his communicative intention. While this close bond between form and content is by no means unique to *Gracias por el Fuego*, it is nevertheless important, and comparisons between my draft translation and the published French translation provide evidence of the possible effects both of preserving and of altering these stylistic features.

CDR and Creating an 'English Benedetti' 81

Before developing the concept of equivalence of stylistic effect in Section 3.2, I want to address the question of my attitude towards the author and the text and its potential influence on the translation and my use of the CDR approach. Instinctively, I would say that a translator who liked or admired a text and its author would be more likely to produce a more carefully considered and more painstaking translation than one who did not. It is generally harder, I would suggest, to bring such an attitude to a task which is disliked or resented.[7] In the 'Simpatico' chapter of *The Translator's Invisibility*, Venuti opposes the idea that 'the translator works better when he [sic] and the author are simpatico... not just "agreeable," or "congenial," meanings which this Italian word is often used to signify, but also "possessing an underlying sympathy"' (2004:273). He does not, however, produce any evidence to support his opposition to this idea beyond the assertion that 'the notion of *simpatico* actually mystifies what happens in the translation process' and an implication that the translator who identifies with the ST author will automatically want to produce a fluent, transparent translation (2004:286–287, italics in original). However, I do not see any inherent incompatibility in liking an author and attempting to recreate one of their texts in another language in a way which may not always result in a fluent or transparent translation.

While an admirer of Benedetti and his work, I am also, however, aware of the dangers of an uncritical approach to a text. I view *Gracias por el Fuego* as being worth translating and possessing qualities which make it immersive, interesting and distinctive. But I also agree, for example, with those critics who suggested that the characterisation of Edmundo borders on the stereotypical at times (Lewald 1966:148; Paoletti 1995:107–108), and that his apparent desire to be assassinated is hardly consistent with the reality of the class he represents. But my central contention is that respecting an author involves respecting both the 'what' and the 'how' of their writing, the content and the style, meaning and form, and in the following section I explain exactly what I mean by this and how I try to put it into practice.

3.2 Equivalence of Stylistic Effect and the Creation of an 'English Benedetti'

My approach to the translation of style accords with Chantal Wright's description of the cognitive stylistic approach to translation:

> This involves considering the effects of the source text's stylistic features upon its readers and creating a text that has a similar range of effects on the reader of the translation; ensuring that the translator has enough evidence, both textual and extra-textual, to support their assumptions of what the inferred author 'meant'; and, a moving

82   CDR and Creating an 'English Benedetti'

back and forth between style and text so as not to lose sight of the wider textual context of individual linguistic features and patterns.

(2007:260)

The clear implications of the idea of 'creating a text that has a similar range of effects on the reader of the translation' as the original had on its readers are that the translator-as-reader can experience the same effects as those experienced by other ST readers, that s/he can then recreate similar effects in the TT and that s/he can reasonably expect other target language (TL) readers to experience the same effects of the TT that s/he experiences. All three of these are problematic assumptions. Can a non-native speaker of a language, for example, who is also separated by distance, time and culture from the original readers of a ST, be confident that s/he can experience similar effects to those experienced by such readers? And can s/he be confident that the effects of the TT will be similar to those of the ST, and shared by other TT readers?

From an evidential point of view, it is very difficult to answer these questions in the affirmative, and yet one of the paradoxes of literary translation seems to me to be that this is how translators operate, and actually how they *have* to operate if they are to do their job. As translators we need to believe that we have the capacity to take not only words from one language, but also their effects, and recreate both in another language. Boase-Beier, a translator and translation scholar, makes this point when she argues that 'for the literary translator, understanding the style of the source text *and being able to recreate similar stylistic effects in the target text* are essential' (2011:73, my emphasis). The assumption here seems to be that not only is the recreation of stylistic effects desirable, but that with the exercise of care it is quite achievable.

Umberto Eco, a translator and also an author who has been translated into several languages, and who has discussed these translations with the translators involved, argues in *Experiences in Translation* that

> instead of speaking of equivalence of meaning, we can speak of *functional equivalence*: a good translation must generate the same effect aimed at by the original... Obviously this means that translators have to make an interpretative hypothesis about the effect programmed by the original text.
>
> (2001:44–45, emphasis in original)

and presumably about the effect 'programmed' by the translation. The assumption underlying this statement appears to be that it is possible for translators to make a confident judgement about whether functional equivalence has been achieved by a translation. My own view is that the only aspects of a translation I can talk about with real confidence are the effects which the ST and TT have on me. As Peter Bush suggests, 'although the translator will inevitably think about the eventual

CDR and Creating an 'English Benedetti' 83

readerships for his [sic] translation, the reader he must translate for is himself, as no one else will be so embedded in the struggle between original and nascent texts' (2003:123). As the translator I can only hope that the TT effects that I experience and attempt to recreate will be shared by my readers, but without carrying out a survey of all of them I will never be in a position to claim that I have actually achieved this. So, when I say that I am trying to create equivalence of stylistic effect in my translation, this can only ever be an aspiration, supported by argument and subjective evidence in relation to examples of specific effects on me which I discuss in this and the following two chapters.

In relation to the translation of *Gracias por el Fuego*, the rationale for this approach can be summarised as follows. A qualitative and quantitative stylistic analysis of the ST reveals distinctive linguistic patterning – marked, for example, by the repetition of words, phrases and syntactic structures at all levels of the text – which creates a block-like structure, as illustrated in the passage below taken from Chapter 13, where I have used bold, italics, underlining and grey highlighting to show the linguistic patterning.

> También está Dolores, pero ella sí comprenderá, aunque *en el primer* instante permanezca aterida e inmóvil, y *en el segundo* convenza a todos de que está llorando por el trágico destino de su pobre suegro, y *en el tercero* arribe casi enloquecida a su huidiza soledad, y *en el cuarto* se sumerja en el bienvenido arrepentimiento, porque mi acto, que será de amor <u>hacia</u> Papá, <u>hacia</u> el recuerdo de Mamá, <u>hacia</u> el país inclusive, será también y sobre todo un acto de amor <u>hacia</u> ella, ya que, pese **a toda su** magnitud, **a toda su** importancia, hubiera sido sin embargo el acto que yo habría sacrificado **nada más que** por ella, **nada más que** por el derecho de tenerla conmigo, de mirarla dormir, de penetrar en ella, de verla sonreír, de llamarla, de ser llamado, de tender mi mano en mitad del sueño y saberla ahí, de ver sus ojos, por Dios, cómo podré vivir sin ver sus ojos, pero también, cómo podría vivir viendo sus ojos y no tenerlos, no poder tildarlos al hacer un inventario de lo que es mío.
>
> (p. 270)

> [There's Dolores, too, but she will surely understand, even if *in the first* moment she remains stiff and unmoving, and *in the second* convinces everyone that she's crying about the tragic fate of her poor father-in-law, and *in the third* reaches, almost crazed, her evasive loneliness, and *in the fourth* buries herself in welcome repentance, because my act, which will be of love <u>for</u> Papá, <u>for</u> the memory of Mamá, even <u>for</u> the country, will also and above all be an act of love <u>for</u> her, since, in spite of **all its** magnitude, **all its** importance, it would still have been the act which I would have sacrificed **just for** her, **just for** the right to have her with me, to watch her sleep, to

84 CDR and Creating an 'English Benedetti'

penetrate her, to see her smile, to call her, to be called, to stretch out my hand in the midst of sleep and know that she was there, to see her eyes, my God, how will I be able to live without seeing her eyes, but also, how could I live seeing her eyes and not having them, not being able to tick them off when making an inventory of what's mine.]

Ramón is speculating about how the various members of his family will react when they discover that he has murdered Edmundo, and this part is dedicated to Dolores/Dolly. The entire long sentence forms a block, composed of six smaller blocks, represented by different forms of emphasis. These are defined by the repetition of prepositional, adjectival and verbal phrases. If this patterning were to be smoothed out in the TT, the effect of the text on me would be significantly changed and the distinctive stylistic quality of the ST would in my view be lost. While Spanish and English are different in a number of respects, they are similar in others. My assessment of Benedetti's style is that key features such as sentence length are marked in Spanish, for which I provide evidence in Chapter 5, and that their recreation in English is also marked, producing similar textual effects on me. The attempt to preserve this patterning in the TT at times places a strain on the English language, partly because of the contrastive grammar, syntax and lexis of Spanish and English. The resulting TT is an attempt to create what I call an 'English Benedetti', a stylistically faithful recreation of the ST in English, which at times involves an 'abusive fidelity' to the ST.

The term 'abusive fidelity' was coined by Philip Lewis ([1985] 2004), but I am using it in a more restricted sense. His concept of 'abuse' was a dual one: abuse of the TL through its attempt to reproduce the abuse of the SL present in the ST, and abuse of the ST by creating distortions of it in the TT, needed 'to make it comply with the discursive and referential structures of English' (2004:267).[8] I use the term solely to refer to my willingness to 'abuse' English, in the sense of occasionally stretching it beyond grammatical conventions, in an effort to recreate a stylistic effect I experienced in the ST.

In the Introduction, I referred to the work of Jean Boase-Beier on style in translation (Boase-Beier 2010a), and in particular her idea of style as the expression of authorial choices; and to Ernst-August Gutt, who argued that the value of recreating stylistic properties in translation lies 'in the fact that they provide *clues* that guide the audience to the interpretation intended by the communicator' (1991:127, emphasis in original). This raises the question of whether all stylistic properties can be preserved, and if not, which ones are more important and why. In this context Boase-Beier addresses the question of stylistic equivalence and suggests that it means

"having the same stylistic value". It is the task of the translator to assess the value – in terms of contribution to the text as a whole – of particular stylistic aspects of the text, in order to choose whether and how to preserve them.

(2002:15)

This idea of stylistic equivalence as involving assessments of 'stylistic value' can be related to the work of Werner Koller ([1979] 1989) on equivalence in translation. After describing five types of equivalence (denotative, connotative, text-normative, pragmatic and formal), he suggests that in approaching both segments and whole texts 'the translator must set up a hierarchy of values to be preserved in translation; from this he [sic] can derive a hierarchy of equivalence requirements for the text or segment in question' (Chesterman 1989:104).[9] In my translation the main priority relates to the preservation of the overall linguistic patterning because my interpretation of the novel is that this patterning is integral to the twin authorial aims of capturing and holding the reader's attention, and thus of maximising the possibilities of successfully conveying his message. This entails prioritising the maintenance, in many cases, of formal features such as sentence length and structure, punctuation and consistency of translation of key words and phrases within segments and across the text as a whole.

Difficulties with the Concept of Equivalence of Effect in Translation

At first sight my approach would seem to equate to Eugene Nida's concept of 'dynamic equivalence' in translation, which is 'based upon "the principle of equivalent effect"' ([1964] 2004:129) and is TT-oriented. He defines dynamic equivalence as the principle that 'the relationship between receptor and message should be substantially the same as that which existed between the original receptors and the message' (ibidem). However, Nida goes on to say that 'a translation of dynamic equivalence aims at complete naturalness of expression... it does not insist that he [the TT reader] understand the cultural patterns of the source-language context in order to comprehend the message' ([1964] 2004:129). The problem here is the word 'message', which Nida often uses but never defines. Does it refer to the message of a particular word or phrase, the message of a cultural reference, the message of the text as a whole or all of these? My emphasis on linguistic patterning could be seen as closer in spirit to Nida's concept of 'formal equivalence', which is ST-oriented, where 'one is concerned that the message in the receptor language should match as closely as possible the different elements in the source language' ([1964] 2004:129). So, paradoxically, I am arguing that in attempting to recreate an 'equivalent effect' in the TT (dynamic equivalence in Nida's terms) I also need to attempt to recreate formal equivalence, which I view as vital to the possible recreation of the overall stylistic and communicative effect of this particular text.

One of the central problems of any theory of equivalence in translation is how it is defined and measured. This applies as much to the idea of equivalence of stylistic effect as it does to equivalence of meaning. Jeremy Munday refers to criticism of the concept of equivalence of effect

86   CDR and Creating an 'English Benedetti'

by Raymond van den Broeck and Robert Larose, and summarises their objections: 'How is the "effect" to be measured and on whom? How can a text possibly have the same effect and elicit the same response in two different cultures and times?' (Munday 2008b:43). As I acknowledged earlier, this is a particularly relevant question for the translation of a novel written over 50 years ago in Latin America which is aimed at a contemporary British readership.

My answer to the first question is that I am primarily measuring the effect of the ST on myself as reader-then-translator. I can only attempt to reproduce an effect that I have experienced myself. However, I try to explain with examples how I think the narrative and linguistic style of the ST actually creates these cognitive effects in me, and how I have attempted to recreate effects in English that I experience as similar. While it is clearly the case that different readers will react to and interpret literary texts differently, I agree with Geoffrey Leech when he argues that

> it is common, in literary studies, to overestimate the extent to which texts are ambiguous, and hence to overstate the extent to which different readers (or one reader on different occasions) can vary in the way they make sense of the text... Shared responses between readers are far more substantial than has been thought, and rely on the meanings and formal characteristics which reside in the text.
>
> (2008:190, 194)

His rationale for this statement is that readers share 'linguistic common ground' and 'the common ground of shared assumptions about background which guide their interpretation of the text' (2008:198).

Another reason for suggesting that it may be possible to generalise about the effects of a text on readers is the development of an area which Leech refers to as 'empirical stylistics' (2008:183). The overlapping fields of cognitive linguistics, psycholinguistics, cognitive stylistics (or cognitive poetics as it is sometimes called), cognitive and psycho-narratology are attempting to empirically test the links between language use in texts and cognitive reader response, with interesting results. In *Mind, Brain and Narrative* (2012) Sanford and Emmott set out 'to show, by reference to relevant empirical work, how various stylistic devices employed by writers for rhetorical purposes serve to influence processing in ways that correspond to certain of the intuitions of analysts in the humanities' (2012:5). In earlier empirical work on reader reaction in text-change experiments, for example, they conclude that

> The stylistic features which we felt intuitively to be attention-capturing were confirmed to be so, in terms of increasing the amount that the readers noticed... Also the fact that attention increased when information was split off into short sentences or sentence fragments

makes sense in the context of the anomaly researchers' finding that information embedded in more complex structures is less detectable.
(Emmott, Sanford and Dawydiak 2007:7)

Although the context of their research is monolingual, and there is no suggestion that what they have found in relation to English would automatically be transferable to other languages, their findings are of direct relevance to translation since, as Reuven Tsur argues, 'Cognitive poetics... offers cognitive theories that systematically account for the relationship between the structure of literary texts and their perceived effects' (2002:279).

In answer to the second question about equivalence of response in different cultures and times, I fully accept that it is not possible to achieve the same effect. I cannot recreate the popularity and direct sociopolitical appeal of a novel written and read in the context of a very specific economic and political crisis, in a country which, while heavily influenced by its history of European immigration, was nevertheless very different from twenty-first-century Britain. However, despite the clear differences, there are some important parallels between 1960s Montevideo and late-2010s Britain which relate to the potential impact of Benedetti's call to his readers to reflect on the state of society and the need for change. Both societies share a number of features, including a well-established welfare state, a large public sector, a lengthy period of stable parliamentary government and a political class dominated by two parties which, while apparently opposed, in practice often share a great many assumptions and attitudes which seriously limit the opportunities for radical social change. In other words, I am suggesting that readers of my translation might find enough parallels between its setting and their own society for a number of aspects of the novel to resonate with them, allowing for the possibility of a degree of similarity or comparability of effect.

There is also much in the novel which I believe is capable of evoking a response in contemporary Anglophone readers. The themes of intergenerational conflict, unhappy sexual relationships, existential dilemmas and the challenges of trying to live according to one's principles, and of confronting mortality, for example, are all present in depth. It is in relation to how a reader can be encouraged to engage with these themes that literary style becomes central.

Examples of an English Benedetti in Practice

Two examples will help to illustrate how my theoretical approach is applied to the translation. The first is from Chapter 9 and illustrates the contrast between my approach and the kind of translation which privileges fluency and 'naturalness of expression' over close adherence to

88   CDR and Creating an 'English Benedetti'

ST style. Ramón is in his office and has just finished talking to Sr. Ríos, a client who has told him that he has only five months to live due to cancer, but who wants to arrange a trip to Europe with his granddaughter. Ramón is reflecting on the calmness with which his client is facing certain death.

ST	TT2 *(November 2016)*
[1]Este hombre. [2]Y aparentemente tan **tranquilo**. [3]Me impresionó más que cuando vi aquel <u>muerto</u> en la Rambla. [4] Es peor que ver un <u>muerto</u>. [5]Mucho peor. [6]Porque Ríos está *decretadamente* <u>muerto</u>, pero a la vez lo suficientemente vivo como para darse cuenta de que está condenado. [7]No entiendo cómo puede mirar su futuro, su escasísimo futuro, con tanta **tranquilidad**. [8]Y además tengo la impresión de que no tiene religión. [9]Se burló tenuemente de Dios. [10]No acabo de entender. [11]Debe de haber algo no totalmente limpio **en ese** sosiego un poco absurdo, **en esa** ternura hacia la nieta, **en esa** conformidad tan lúcida, **en ese** acatamiento <u>frente al</u> dictamen de Rómulo, **en ese** desapego <u>frente a la</u> probable compasión de sus hijos. [12] No obstante, tiene buena cara, ojos sin rencor. (p. 155)	[1]This man. [2]And seemingly so **serene**. [3]He made more of an impression on me than when I saw that <u>corpse</u> in the Rambla. [4]It's worse than seeing a <u>corpse</u>. [5]Much worse. [6]Because Ríos is *pronouncedly* a <u>corpse</u>, yet at the same time sufficiently alive to realise that he's condemned. [7]I don't understand how he can view his future, his very limited future, with such **serenity**. [8] And I don't think he's religious either. [9]He gently mocked God. [10]I don't get it. [11]There must be something not completely honest **in that** slightly absurd calmness, **in that** tenderness towards his granddaughter, **in that** clear sighted acceptance, **in that** resignation <u>in the face of</u> Rómulo's sentence, **in that** detachment <u>in the face of</u> the likely compassion of his children. [12]Nevertheless, he looks well, eyes content.

Bold and <u>underlining</u>: repetitions of words and phrases
Grey highlighting: compressed noun phrase
Italics: unusual word
[1]: sentence number

In the ST there are 130 words and 12 sentences. Sentence [11] contains 43 words, while the other 11 sentences contain an average of only 8 words each. There is a clear contrast between the earlier short sentences, which all suggest loosely connected thoughts and in which grammatical completeness is not required, and the single long, co-ordinated sentence, whose subclauses all start with the prepositional phrase *en ese/a* [in that]. Each of these subclauses relates to an aspect of the way Sr. Ríos is facing his death, and all are modified by the doubt implied by the phrase *no totalmente limpio* [not completely honest] which precedes them. The passage first invites the reader to follow Ramón's loose thoughts, and then his more considered reflection, and this requires a little effort because the rhythm of the first 10 sentences is one of stop-start. There are four sets of repetitions, constituting blocks within the passage, one

CDR and Creating an 'English Benedetti' 89

highly compressed noun phrase, and an unusual word which Benedetti may have created, *decretadamente* [pronouncedly]. The passage exhibits distinctive linguistic patterning, which presents several translation challenges.

In the TT I have preserved the sentence total and in most cases sentence length. In doing so I have had to solve three translation problems. The repetition of *tranquilo* and *tranquilidad* in sentences [2] and [7] appeared easy to deal with, and my original translation was *calm* and *calmness*. However, a closer reading of sentence [2], confirmed by reading it aloud, showed that there was an assonantal alliterative rhythm which I wanted to preserve because it seemed to me to emphasise the idea of the outward appearance of calmness: *aparentemente tan tranquilo*. This prompted me to change *calm* to *serene*, producing *seemingly so serene*. This is the sort of feature which is easy to miss, but given my analysis of the ST as being distinctively patterned, I was primed to look for patterns, some of which then emerged clearly.

The triple use of *muerto* in sentences [3], [4] and [6] posed another problem. In Spanish *muerto* can be both a noun and an adjective. In the first two instances it is a noun, and in the third an adjective. Originally, I had translated the first instance as *dead body*, the second as *corpse* and the third as *condemned to die* in the context of the phrase *decretadamente muerto*. However, after reviewing the passage it seemed to me that preserving the continuity of a single word would increase the impact of Ramón's reflections on death on the reader. The first two instances were easy to render as *corpse*, but the third was complicated by the presence of the word *decretadamente*, an unusual and possibly invented form[10] which clearly means *sentenced* to death. The unusual word, which is marked but not unidiomatic, allows Benedetti to convey the idea of Ríos being both dead and alive at the same time in two short, symmetrical adverbial phrases: *decretadamente muerto* and *suficientemente vivo*. This use of compressed contrastive phrases is a feature that Benedetti uses throughout the novel to highlight comparisons. I considered trying to match *decretadamente* by inventing a word in English such as *judgedly*, but decided that this was too clumsy, and so have chosen to translate it as *pronouncedly*, which does exist, but is uncommon. This also allowed me to translate the third instance of *muerto* as *corpse*, thus achieving consistency of translation and the recreation of a 'block'. The consequence of adhering to the ST patterning is to produce slightly unusual, but still idiomatic English, and what I see as stylistic similarity.

The final challenge was posed by the last three words, *ojos sin rencor*. Not difficult in themselves, there was nevertheless a strong temptation to introduce a connective before them such as *and*, or *with*, since the rest of the sentence is grammatically normal in Spanish. My first two attempts were fairly literal: *his eyes free of bitterness*, and *his eyes unembittered*. However, as with the alliteration in sentence [2], a closer examination of sentence [12] revealed that the second and third clauses are rhythmically

90 CDR and Creating an 'English Benedetti'

similar, with almost equal syllable counts. This, too, I wanted to preserve, because it emphasises Ramón's difficulty in deciding whether Ríos' calmness is a mask or real, and his reluctance to believe that someone facing a death sentence can do so with equanimity. This also relates to the fact that Ramón's preoccupation with death is an important theme in the novel. There are 44 occurrences of *muerte* [death] and a further 20 of *muerto/a* and *muertos/as* in all. So my current version is *eyes content* which matches *he looks well* syllabically, thus recreating the very condensed but still idiomatic Spanish, rather than flattening it out, and in the process creating an unidiomatic English construction. I see the phrases *pronouncedly a corpse* and *eyes content* as examples of 'abusive fidelity' in Philip Lewis' sense, when he talks about 'translation that values experimentation, tampers with usage, seeks to match the... expressive stresses of the original by producing its own' (2004:270). In the second case idiomatic but marked Spanish has been rendered by unidiomatic and marked English, involving the use of a strategy of compensation.

By way of comparison, I set out the French translation of this passage next to the ST below, which exhibits a number of features which I would argue tend to domesticate, and in one instance distort, the ST. For ease of reference, I have used bold, italics, underlining and highlighting to show how the words and phrases in the French correspond to the Spanish.

ST	French TT (Benedetti 1983:126)
[1]Este hombre. [2]Y aparentemente tan **tranquilo**. [3]Me impresionó más que cuando vi aquel <u>muerto</u> en la Rambla. [4] Es peor que ver un <u>muerto</u>. [5]Mucho peor. [6]Porque Ríos está decretadamente <u>muerto</u>, pero a la vez lo suficientemente vivo como para darse cuenta de que está condenado. [7]No entiendo cómo puede mirar su futuro, su escasísimo futuro, con tanta **tranquilidad**. [8] Y además tengo la impresión de que no tiene religión. [9]Se burló tenuemente de Dios. [10]No acabo de entender. [11]Debe de haber algo no totalmente limpio **en ese** sosiego un poco absurdo, **en esa** ternura hacia la nieta, **en esa** conformidad tan lúcida, **en ese** acatamiento <u>frente al</u> dictamen de Rómulo, **en ese** desapego <u>frente a la</u> probable compasión de sus hijos. [12] No obstante, tiene buena cara, *ojos sin rencor.* (p. 155)	[1]Cet homme. [2]En apparence si **paisible**. [3]Il m'a bien plus impression que lorsque j'ai vu le <u>mort</u> de la Rambla. [4]C'est pire, bien pire que d'avoir vu un <u>mort</u>. [5] Parce que Ríos est un <u>mort</u> en sursis, mais il lui reste encore assez de vie pour se rendre compte qu'il est condamné. [6]Je ne vois pas comment il peut envisage son pauvre future avec une telle **sérénité** et j'ai l'impression qu'il n'est pas croyant. [7]Il s'est moqué subtilement de Dieu. [8]Je n'arrive pas à le comprendre. [9] Il doit y avoir quelque chose de trouble **dans ce** calme un peu absurde, cette tendresse pour sa petite-fille, cette résignation si lucide, cette acceptation du diagnostic de Rómulo, ce détachement <u>devant</u> l'éventuelle douleur de ses enfants. [10]Pourtant il n'a pas mauvaise mine *et je ne devine aucune trace de rancœur dans ses yeux.*

The number of sentences has been reduced from 12 to 10, while the total word count has risen from 130 to 142 (9% longer). Only one of the four blocks which I identified in the Spanish has been preserved. While *muerto* has been translated consistently, *tranquilo* and *tranquilidad* have not; nor have the repeated use of the preposition *en* in sentence [9], or of *frente a* in sentence [11], been preserved. The unusual nature of the word *decretadamente* and its place in a compressed, clause-balanced sentence have disappeared, but this may be due to differences between Spanish and French. In sentence [7] the strong ST emphasis on the limited nature of Ríos' future – *su futuro, su escasísimo futuro* – has been muted to *pauvre future*. Finally, the last sentence has doubled in length from 8 to 17 words and been subjected to two of Antoine Berman's 'deforming tendencies', 'ennoblement' – 'producing "elegant" sentences, while utilizing the source text, so to speak, as *raw material*' – and 'the destruction of linguistic patternings' ([1985] 2004:290,293, emphasis in original). It should be acknowledged, however, that all translations will suffer to some extent from one or other of Berman's deforming tendencies, since in many cases they are an inevitable consequence of the transplantation from one language into another.

3.3 Existing Benedetti Translations:
Comparison and Analysis

A translator wishing to bring an unknown Benedetti novel to an Anglophone readership would be wise to take account of the small body of existing English translations of his work, and the approaches taken by his translators. To that end I conducted a limited comparative analysis of the multiple translations into English of 'Familia Iriarte' (1956), a short story included in the *Montevideanos* collection of 1959, and *La Tregua* (1960), Benedetti's most internationally successful novel. The comparisons involved a combination of close reading and quantitative analysis, and for reasons of space I have limited their focus to sentence length and structure, and the stylistic effects of these features, since these are of particular importance in the translation of *Gracias por el Fuego*. My aim was to see how closely the translations related to the ST, and what effects both preservation and alteration of features of the original had on the resulting TTs. The conclusions support my decision to broadly preserve sentence length and boundaries in my translation, on the basis that not doing so can result in significant stylistic loss.

'Familia Iriarte' is set in a Montevideo office and revolves around the telephone voice of a woman who rings the boss regularly, and whose call is initially received by a male office worker who falls in love with the voice, and is convinced that he recognises it whilst on a seaside holiday. The style is clear, colloquial and light, with very few unusual linguistic devices, and is written entirely in the first person. My methodology

92 CDR and Creating an 'English Benedetti'

involved an initial close reading of three of the four published English translations[11] – those of Gregory Rabassa, translating under the pseudonym of George Rothenberg (Benedetti 1963);[12] Lynn Tricario and Suzanne Jill Levine (Benedetti 1976); and Harry Morales (Benedetti 2010) – followed by a quantitative analysis using Computer-Aided Textual Markup and Analysis (CATMA).

Close reading and occasional direct text comparison suggested that there were marked differences in translation style between the three translators, but that all three had altered sentence features to different degrees. A statistical comparison of the ST and all three TTs is set out in *Table 3.1*.

The sentence bands used in *Table 3.1* are the same as those used in Chapter 5 to analyse *Gracias por el Fuego*, and have thus been chosen for consistency of analysis. The choice to highlight divergences of over 10% in word count and sentence features is an arbitrary one, but the aim was to identify some meaningful differences. The table below shows that while the LT-SJL translation has retained sentence number and has attempted to respect the short sentence pattern of the ST, the other two translations have merged some sentences, reduced the number containing 9 words or less, in one case by a third, and increased the number of long (40–80 word) sentences, in one case more than doubling them. An example will illustrate some of the effects of this altering of sentence length and structure in translation.

ST (67 words)	GR translation (69 words)	LT-SJL translation (64 words)	HM translation (73 words)
Fue precisamente en el Balneario donde volví a oír su Voz. Yo bailaba entre las mesitas de una terraza, a la luz de una luna que a nadie le importaba. Mi mano derecha se había afirmado sobre una espalda parcialmente despellejada que aún no había perdido el calor de la tarde. La dueña de la espalda se reía y era una buena risa, no había que descartarla. (p.80)	It was at the resort that I heard her voice again. I was dancing between the little tables on a terrace, by the light of a moon no one cared about. My right hand had planted itself on a partly peeled back that had not yet lost the warmth of the afternoon. The back's owner was laughing and it was a good laughter, not to be passed up lightly. (pp. 202–203)	It was precisely there in the resort where I once again heard her voice. I danced between the tables of a terrace, in the light of a moon that didn't matter to anybody. My right hand gripped a partially bare back that still hadn't lost the afternoon's warmth. The back's owner laughed and it was a good laugh, I didn't have to discard her. (p. 13)	It was at that very spa where I heard her voice again. While I was dancing amongst the little tables on a terrace, by the light of a moon which no one cared about, my right hand came to rest firmly on a partially peeling back which still hadn't cooled from the heat of the afternoon. The back's owner was laughing and it was a good laugh, it didn't have to be repudiated. (pp. 160–161)

CDR and Creating an 'English Benedetti' 93

Table 3.1 Quantitative analysis of 'Familia Iriarte' and three English translations

Analysis	ST	GR translation (1963)	LT-SJL translation (1976)	HM translation (2010)
Word count	3,085	3,221 (4% longer)	3,134 (1.5% longer)	3,396 (10% longer)
Sentence total	150	143 (4% fewer)	150	142 (5% fewer)
Sentences <9 words	48 (32%)	37 (23% fewer)	43 (10% fewer)	32 (33% fewer)
Sentences of 10–19 words	52 (35%)	51 (1.9% fewer)	57 (11.7% more)	51 (1.9% fewer)
Sentences of 20–29 words	31 (20.1%)	34 (9.7% more)	33 (6.5% more)	35 (12.9% more)
Sentences of 30–39 words	13 (8.7%)	12 (7.7% fewer)	10 (23% fewer)	11 (15.4% fewer)
Sentences of 40–80 words	6 (4%)	9 (50% more)	7 (16.7% more)	13 (116% more)
Average sentence length	20.5 words	22.5 words (10% longer)	20.9 words (1.9% longer)	23.9 words (16% longer)

GR: George Rothenberg/Gregory Rabassa
LT-SJL: Lynn Tricario and Suzanne Jill Levine
HM: Harry Morales
Number: those features differing by 10% or more from the original

The highlighting and underlining indicate the sentence boundaries for sentences [2] and [3] in two translations, and sentence [2] in the third.

There is a narrative rhythm to the first three ST sentences. As in the opening of Chapter 1 in *Gracias por el Fuego*, this involves a form of cinematic zooming in from the level of the resort down to the tables on the terrace, and finally to a hand on a bare back. Each sentence forms a distinct step in this zooming process, and each involves an increase in sentence length and depth of description, and in degree of personal intimacy. While Rabassa and Tricario and Levine have chosen to preserve this rhythm, Morales has merged sentences [2] and [3], and introduced the conjunction 'while' at the beginning, which immediately shifts the attention to the end of the sentence and increases the disruption of the step-by-step rhythm caused by merging sentences.

La Tregua is also set in a Montevideo office and describes how a middle-aged widower on the eve of retirement at 50 finds love with a new employee in his office who is half his age. The style is very similar to that of 'Familia Iriarte', and is also entirely written in the first person, but the interior monologues are more introspective and there are portrayals of office and family life, intergenerational conflict and social mores. The novel also contains a moral, and occasionally a political, critique which foreshadows that developed in *Gracias por el Fuego*. The two published

94 CDR *and Creating an 'English Benedetti'*

translations, both entitled *The Truce*, were done by Benjamin Graham (Benedetti 1969b) and Harry Morales (Benedetti 2015).

In the case of *La Tregua*, I only had paper copies of the two translations. As it would have required a disproportionate amount of work to digitise both texts in their entirety, I chose to work with a randomised 10% sample in each case, which I believe to be indicative of the novel's overall style. The novel consists of 178 chronologically linear, but not consecutive, diary entries, varying in length from a sentence to three pages. I digitised every tenth entry,[13] giving me a total of 18, and by measuring their collective page count manually determined that the sample contained almost exactly 10% of the novel's overall length. I thus compared the ST and both TTs for the 18 diary entries selected, and the results are shown in *Table 3.2*.

The increases in word count and average sentence length are higher than for 'Familia Iriarte'. Both translators have increased text length by over 10%, reduced the number of sentences of 9 words or less, and increased average sentence length by up to 18%. In Graham's translation there has been a marked increase in sentences of 10–19, 20–29 and 40–80 words. In Morales' translation, the increase has come in the 20–29 and 30–39 word bands. The pattern of translation shift in both sets of translations is broadly similar, and also shows that Morales has produced longer texts comprised of fewer, longer sentences than the other translators, which may indicate a particular translation style.

With 'Familia Iriarte' I started with close reading and moved to quantitative analysis. With *La Tregua* the process was reversed, and

Table 3.2 Quantitative analysis of *La Tregua* and two English translations

Analysis	ST	BG translation (1969)	HM translation (2015)
Word count	6,816	**7,618 (11% longer)**	7,736 (13% longer)
Sentence total	411	414 (0.7% more)	395 (3.9% fewer)
Sentences < 9 words	197 (48%)	**166 (15% fewer)**	**151 (23% fewer)**
Sentences of 10–19 words	136 (33.1%)	**155 (14% more)**	147 (8.1% more)
Sentences of 20–29 words	49 (12%)	**60 (22% more)**	**61 (24% more)**
Sentences of 30–39 words	14 (3.4%)	15 (7.1% more)	**23 (64% more)**
Sentences of 40–80 words	13 (3.2%)	**17 (30% more)**	**11 (15.4% fewer)**
Average sentence length	16.6 words	**18.4 words (13% longer)**	**19.6 words (18% longer)**

BG: Benjamin Graham
HM: Harry Morales
Number: those features differing by 10% or more from the original

the close reading was designed to help explain the quantitative results, which showed a willingness on the part of the translators to merge – and occasionally split – sentences, and to increase sentence length. Such increases can partly be explained by the frequently quoted general tendency for translations to be longer than their STs (Blum-Kulka 1986; Frankenberg-Garcia 2009; Toury 2012). Toury's 'law of growing standardisation' (Toury 2012) could also be relevant here, leading to fewer very short or very long sentences, although there is still debate about the extent to which this can be considered a 'law' of translation. Grammatical differences between Spanish and English also play a part in the explanation, in particular the normal requirement in English for verbs to have separate subjects, whereas in Spanish they are very frequently subsumed by the verb. However, my feeling is that translator willingness to elongate concise ST phrasing and sentence structure is rarely completely grammatically determined, and is often a matter of stylistic choice. One example from the entry for Monday 1st April in *La Tregua* will help to illustrate this point.

ST	BG translation (1969)	HM translation (2015)
Él me dejó con la mano tendida, me miró fijamente (una mirada bastante complicada, aunque creo que en ella el ingrediente principal era, a su vez, la lástima) y me dijo con ese desagradable acento de erres que suenan como ges: «Usted no compgende». Lo cual es rigurosamente cierto. No comprendo y basta. No quiero pensar más en todo esto. (p. 43)	He left me with my hand outstretched, looked at me fixedly (a pretty complicated look, though I think its principal ingredient was pity, in his turn), and said to me in that disagreeable accent, with its r's that sound like j's, "you don't compjehend." And that's entirely true. I don't understand; period. I don't want to think any more about all that. (p. 33)	He left me with my hand outstretched, stared at me (a very complicated look, although I think the main ingredient of it was, in turn, pity) and in that disagreeable accent of 'r's' that sound like 'g's' said to me: 'You don't understand.' Which is absolutely true. I don't understand and that's the end of it. I don't want to think about any of this any more. (p. 33)

The context of this entry is the regular visit to the office by a middle-aged German man, down on his luck, who always asks for a job, produces a tattered reference from Bolivia, and after begging to be given a practical typing test, fails it miserably. The highlighted sentence is blunt and abrupt in the ST, and suggests the narrator's sense of exasperation and lack of sympathy for the man, who never changes. In Graham's translation this is matched by translating *y basta* as *period*. Morales' version converts the two-word phrase into a six word one *and that's the end of it*. This has two effects: first it removes the abrupt force of the original, and in doing so softens the expression of exasperation, changing it into one which suggests philosophical acceptance. Given that nearly half of the sentences in the ST sample contain 9 words or less, if generalised this approach could result in noticeable shifts in stylistic effect. However, when comparing translations in this way it must be acknowledged that final decisions can often be made by publishers rather than translators, on the basis of 'what works' for them.

This comparative analytical exercise has led me to draw two conclusions which relate to my translation approach to *Gracias por el Fuego*. The first is that since, as I have suggested, short sentences often generate similar stylistic effects on me in both English and Spanish, and are clearly a prominent feature of Benedetti's style across at least two novels, his sentence boundaries generally need to be respected if I am to attempt to create any degree of equivalence of stylistic effect. The second is that for a translation to be both coherent and cohesive, the translator needs to be constantly moving from the micro- to the macro-level of the text and back again, a process which is aided and supported by the selective use of quantitative textual analysis. Christiane Nord sums up this way of translating in the following terms:

> In my opinion translation is not a linear, progressive process leading from a starting point S (=ST) to a target point T (=TT), but a circular, basically recursive process comprising an indefinite number of feedback loops, in which it is possible and even advisable to return to earlier stages of the analysis.
>
> (Nord 1991:34)

Simply moving from one word or phrase to the next without frequent regard to the wider context can often result not only in stylistic shifts, particularly in tone and register, but also in actual mistranslations.

Notes

1 For an introduction to these and other translation theories and approaches and further reading, see Munday 2008b.
2 *The Black Book*, translated by Gün Güneli (1994); and *The Black Book*, translated by Maureen Freely (2006).
3 'Las entrevistas de El Informante': Selección del archivo del periodista Leonardo Haberkorn, 16 de marzo de 2016. Available at: http://leonardohab erkorn2.blogspot.co.uk/2015/03/mario-benedetti-la-terquedad-del-poeta. html [accessed 13 February 2017].
4 Source: An unpublished bibliography compiled by Benedetti's US translator, Harry Morales, and sent to me in a personal communication [20 January 2014].
5 A Google Scholar search for 'twentieth-century Uruguayan literature' produces only a short list of directly relevant hits [19 September 2018].

6 Cited in McRae (2010:2).

7 Although a detailed discussion of the effects of translator attitude towards what they translate is beyond the scope of the present study, I would like to make a brief reference to the idea that it may correlate with translation quality. In a Think Aloud Protocol study of eight translators Riitta Jääskeläinen cautiously concluded that there was 'some evidence of the skilled use of knowledge and an involved attitude working together to produce high quality. In contrast, superficial processing and detached attitude seem to lead to poor results' (1999:244).

8 Lewis formulates the idea of abusive fidelity in the context of a discussion about his translation of an essay by Derrida from French into English.

9 This is quoted in Munday (2008b:47).

10 I have found no references to the use of the word in Spanish prior to 1965, although there are some subsequent examples of usage. It is also a word in Portuguese.

11 In a personal communication (2 July 2016) the translator of the fourth version declined to provide me with a copy, being unhappy with the translation.

12 At that time Rabassa was not known as a translator and was the editor of a small New York literary magazine, the *Odyssey Review*, dedicated to translations of Latin American literature. To give the impression that a number of different translators were being featured, Rabassa sometimes did the translations and wrote under this pseudonym, which used the same initials GR (Morales 2001:116-117).

13 The process involved scanning the page(s), running the scans through OCR software, copying and pasting the results into a Word document and then uploading the document to CATMA.

4 Applying the Methodology (Part 1)
The Translation of Culture

The literary critic Terry Eagleton argues that works which we call 'literary' cannot be 'tied to a specific context... All literary works are orphaned at birth... the poet cannot determine the situations in which his or her work will be read, or what sense we are likely to make of it' (2014:117). I both agree and disagree with this. I agree, because after the publication of a work of literature it can in principle be read, interpreted and translated at any point in the future. Walter Benjamin, referring to 'great works of art', speaks of 'their potentially eternal afterlife in succeeding generations', and suggests that in translations 'the life of the originals attains... its ever-renewed latest and most abundant flowering' ([1923] 2004:17). But I also disagree, because that 'afterlife' will be affected by the ability of subsequent generations to understand the context of the production and original reception of the work. In other words, in a real sense the understanding and appreciation of a work of literature *will* be 'tied to a specific context', that of its birth. An important part of that context is the culture within which it was produced, and it is to the way in which the dimension of another culture can be reproduced in a translation using the close and distant reading (CDR) approach that this chapter is devoted.

Specifically, I analyse the translation challenges presented by three particular cultural elements: culture-specific items (CSIs); the use of different languages in the source text (ST), including the target language (TL); and the use of *usted* and its formal interpersonal register. Although these features of the text vary in terms of their narrative and stylistic significance, my methodological approach to all three has been the same, namely the recursive use of CDR to inform and revise the translation. In all three cases the specific cultural elements in the ST were identified through reading and initial translation. The extent and location of their occurrence was quantified using a combination of manual counting and term searches in Computer-Aided Textual Markup and Analysis (CATMA) and MS Word. This data facilitated an assessment of the functions and narrative and stylistic importance of each element, carried out by close reading. On the basis of this assessment a review of scholarship in the field and examples of how translators of Latin American fiction had approached the problem are brought to bear in order to arrive at a number of possible translation strategies. Choices of strategy

The Translation of Culture 99

are explained and illustrated by example, their application frequently resulting in a revision of the initial draft translation.

In the light of my foreignising approach, these strategies tend to favour preservation of as much of the original language(s) as possible – and in the case of the translation of *usted*, the addition of source language (SL) words – complemented by a glossary where necessary. The main argument in Section 4.1 is that the translation of CSIs should not simply be a matter of choosing from the various taxonomies of available strategies on a case-by-case basis, but that it benefits from a consideration of the stylistic and narrative functions and importance of groups of CSIs in a text at a macro- and micro-level, as suggested by Eirlys Davies (2003). Furthermore, that decisions about CSI translation will also be informed by the translator's view of their readers' 'cognitive environment' and their view of their own role as intercultural mediators, as suggested by Gabriela Saldanha (2008). I give three examples of words and phrases which I leave untranslated in the text, but include in the glossary, and an example of how the three English translations of Benedetti's short story 'Familia Iriarte' treat one particular CSI in different ways.

In Section 4.2 my contention is that the use of different languages in *Gracias por el Fuego* fulfils several stylistic and narrative functions, including character portrayal and humour, both of which are illustrated by example, and that it is a marked feature of much modernist Anglophone literature. I argue that contextual considerations are important in deciding on a translation approach, in the light of which my main translation strategy is to leave the other languages untranslated, with an occasional glossary entry where no intratextual clue to meaning is provided in the ST. The challenge of representing the use of the TL in the TT is met by using another typeface to represent all the TL words in the text, and also by the use of the 'mirror-reflection translation' technique (Franco Arcia 2012), whereby in passages which mix English and Spanish together, the order of language use in the ST is reversed in the TT.

I argue in Section 3 that the use of the formal *usted* in *Gracias por el Fuego* fulfils both a stylistic and a narrative function, affecting both characterisation and plot development. I also suggest that while in translations of twentieth-century Latin American fiction there is some evidence for a tendency to erase this aspect of register through linguistic normalisation, it is possible to represent it in translation in different ways, in particular by the selective addition of *señor/a,* to indicate a polite form of address.

4.1 The Translation of CSIs: Flexible Foreignisation

The term 'culture-specific item' was coined by Javier Aixelá (1996:56–57), and his starting point was the observation that 'in general, when speaking about "cultural references", "socio-cultural terms", and the like, authors avoid any definition, attributing the meaning of the notion to a sort of collective intuition' (1996:57). He argues that what makes

100   *The Translation of Culture*

something a CSI is not its membership of a fixed category of linguistic items, but the fact that its translation is problematic due to the non-existence in the TL culture of an equivalent object, concept, custom, expression, etc. So, for example, a reference to the Spanish fish dish *paella* would not constitute a CSI in a Spanish to English translation because it is well known in the Anglophone world, but it might become one if the TL were Korean. This approach leads Aixelá to define CSIs as:

> Those textually actualized items whose function and connotations in a source text involve a translation problem in their transference to a target text, wherever this problem is a product of the nonexistence of the referred item or of its different intertextual status in the cultural system of the readers of the target text.
>
> (1996:58)

I find this approach convincing, but it raises the question of how to solve the translation problems they pose.

A number of translation scholars have devised taxonomies of translation strategies. Aixelá (1996:61–65) lists five strategies under the SL-oriented heading of 'conservation': repetition, orthographic adaptation, linguistic translation, extra- and intratextual gloss; and six strategies under the TL-oriented heading of 'substitution': synonymy, limited and absolute universalisation, naturalisation, deletion and autonomous creation. Davies (2003:72–88) lists seven 'individual procedures' at the micro-level of translation: preservation, addition, omission, globalisation, localisation, transformation and creation. Hervey, Higgins and Haywood (1995/2004:20–27) list five strategies along a continuum from SL to TL orientation: exoticism, cultural borrowing, calque, communicative translation and cultural transplantation. In short, there seems to be no agreed classification of CSI translation strategies and a significant degree of overlap between various terms. Aixelá's 'repetition', for example, seems very similar to Davies' 'preservation' and Hervey, Higgins and Haywood's 'exoticism', all of which refer to the conservation of ST terms.

I am in agreement with the view that decision-making about the translation of a CSI is not simply a matter of choosing from an array of possible strategies on a case-by-case basis, but is a process which benefits from framing at the macro-level. Eirlys Davies argues that:

> it may sometimes be helpful to adopt a macro perspective which looks at sets of culture-specific items in terms of their joint contribution to the development of the whole text. More reasoned and systematic decisions as to how to treat individual items may be made once they are seen as part of a network of references which work together to achieve a global impact.
>
> (2003:65)

The Translation of Culture   101

In other words, assessing both the importance of a particular CSI and an appropriate way of translating it can benefit from an approach which considers the different kinds of CSIs in a text and their narrative and stylistic function(s) in the text as a whole.

Another kind of macro-level framing is highlighted by Gabriela Saldanha who argues that, consciously or unconsciously, translators are influenced in their approach to explicitation – which CSI translation often, but not always, involves – by two factors. The first is the translator's view of their target readers' 'cognitive environment' (Saldanha 2008:30), a concept which embraces what Sperber and Wilson, whom she cites, refer to as their 'cognitive abilities and contextual resources' (Sperber and Wilson 1995:218). The second is their 'conceptions of their roles as intercultural mediators in relation to their audience' (Saldanha 2008:31). Both of these macro-level perspectives – narrative and stylistic textual function of CSIs, and translator attitude to TT readers and intercultural mediation – are relevant to my translation of CSIs in *Gracias por el Fuego*. Before looking at the novel, however, I want to briefly compare the three English translations of Benedetti's short story 'Familia Iriarte' cited in Chapter 3 in terms of their treatment of one specific CSI, as an example of different translator approaches to the same text.

There are three occurrences in the ST of the word *Este* [East], the first two in successive sentences and the third at the beginning of the following paragraph. The reference is to the location of a seaside resort to the east of Montevideo. In the ST the actual resort is not named, nor does its specific identity seem to have any importance, since the functional relevance of the seaside resort in the text is simply to act as a stereotypical setting where the narrator meets the woman he believes to be the owner of a particularly attractive telephone voice.

ST	GR translation (1963)	LT-SJL translation (1976)	HM translation (2010)
Unos meses después de esa variante me fui de vacaciones al Este. Desde hacía años, mis vacaciones en el Este habían constituido mi esperanza más firme desde un punto de vista sentimental. (p. 79)	Several months after things took that turn, I went East on my vacation. For some years my vacations in the East had inspired my strongest hopes from a sentimental point of view. (p. 202)	A few months after that development I went East for vacation. For years now, my vacations in the East had constituted my firmest hopes from a romantic point of view. (p. 13)	A few months later I went on vacation to Punta del Este. For years my vacations to this area had constituted, from a sentimental standpoint, my firmest hope. (p. 160)

102   The Translation of Culture

ST	GR translation (1963)	LT-SJL translation (1976)	HM translation (2010)
Ahora que en eso de encontrar la mujer en el Este, yo me he investigado mucho y he hallado otros motivos no tan sentimentales. (p. 80)	Now, I have questioned myself carefully about this matter of finding *the* woman in the East and have come up with other motives that aren't so sentimental. (p. 202)	Now about meeting women in the East, I've investigated the matter a lot and have found some other not so romantic motives. (p. 13)	As for that business of finding a woman in Punta del Este, I've done quite a bit of soul-searching and have found motives which aren't so sentimental. (p. 160)

GR: George Rothenberg (Gregory Rabassa)
LT-SJL: Lynn Tricario and Suzanne Jill Levine
HM: Harry Morales

Both the Rabassa and Tricario/Levine translations opt for preservation by direct linguistic translation, without further explicitation, in all three instances. Morales explicitates *Este* by translating it as *Punta del Este*, a fashionable coastal resort to the east of Montevideo, on the first and third occasions, while changing it to *this area* on the second. It would appear that he felt a need to disambiguate the text and name a specific resort – which, although the most well-known, is only one of a number to the east of Montevideo – despite the fact that Benedetti only uses the term *Este* and also refers to the resort on other occasions simply as *el Balneario*. I have not been able to find any reference suggesting that the phrase *el Este* was used as shorthand for *Punta del Este*. In *Gracias por el Fuego* there are four references to *Punta del Este*, but none to *el Este*, even though it would have been possible to use a shorthand reference in at least some of those cases. An analysis of the textual function of the two sets of ST references taken together suggests that ambiguity as regards the specific resort was intentional, and that its importance lay in its membership of a generalised category of place. Benedetti often uses capitalised nouns to indicate a general concept or type. For example, in his short story *Los Novios*, which also forms part of the *Montevideanos* collection, there is a reference to *el Banco* (Benedetti 1959b:99), the financial institution, which is never named. This analysis supports Davies' contention that looking at the textual function of CSIs, in this case supported by an intertextual perspective, can inform the translation of individual instances.

The Translation of CSIs in Gracias por el Fuego

My approach is framed by my translation goal of immersing readers in another culture as far as possible. This goal needs to take account of my

The Translation of Culture 103

target readership's cognitive environment and also of their prospective reading experience. My aim is to strike a balance between two contrasting approaches to intercultural mediation, summed up by Saldanha with reference to the views of two well-known translators of Spanish and Latin American fiction, Peter Bush and Margaret Jull Costa:

> Jull Costa wants her translations to be acceptable in the terms established by the target culture, her translations are driven by a desire to make their reading a pleasurable experience, which is not interrupted by encounters with information, such as source language words, that the readers cannot process in their own cognitive environment... However, when there is a cultural gap that would prevent the target text reader from making relevant assumptions, then she is likely to mediate, providing an intratextual gloss or adding contextual information.
>
> Bush, on the other hand, is driven by a desire to introduce new foreign authors to Britain's literary market... and is ready to challenge readers to shift out of their usual patterns to read them.
>
> (Saldanha 2008:31–32)

While my approach is closer to that of Bush than of Jull Costa, I see no reason not to provide some explanation of certain SL words left untranslated. My solution, therefore, is to preserve CSIs intact wherever possible, but where relevant to provide explicitation in the form of a glossary or an occasional intratextual gloss. The use of a glossary gives the reader the freedom to choose whether to interrupt their reading experience or not, and there is evidence that publishers are not unwilling to include them.[1]

In analysing and making translation decisions about CSIs, the CDR approach provides a way of assessing their textual function and relative narrative and stylistic importance. Drawing on Davies' suggestion that grouping CSIs and examining them at the macro-textual level can inform the translation of individual cases, and as a method of producing the translation glossary, I manually extracted CSI references, totalling 115 different items, and then grouped them into categories, quantifying their occurrences. These categories included Montevideo street names and landmarks (55), historical references (2), political references (24), literary references (4), idiomatic expressions (12), customs (18) and register (see Section 4.3). Historical references include *la degollada de la Rambla Wilson* (p. 54), the case of a headless woman found there on 29 April 1923; literary references include Baldomero Fernández Moreno (1886–1950) and his poem *Versos a Negrita* (p. 220); and references to customs include the *candombe*, a dance of African origin which is particular to Uruguay (p. 221) (Neto 1962). A detailed example from each of three other categories will serve to illustrate my approach and the use of the CDR methodology to arrive at translation solutions.

104 The Translation of Culture

A quantitative analysis of all the Montevideo street names facilitated an assessment of their function in the text, which I see as forming an important part of Benedetti's strategy for locating the storyworld in the real Montevideo of the time. The provision of a map of Montevideo showing the location of these streets (and the local landmarks referred to) as an appendix to the translation constitutes an attempt to provide the reader with a degree of familiarity with the novel's geographical setting.

Further quantitative analysis of the street names reveals that the most frequently mentioned one is *la Rambla*, the 22 km long wide coastal avenue that skirts the southern edge of the city.[2] This is mentioned 19 times, 17 times by Ramón and twice by Dolly. Four examples will help to indicate its significance. First, it is the daily route Ramón takes to and from his office and is often the highlight of his day:

> Lindo ir por la Rambla. El mejor momento del día. El único en que es un descanso manejar.
>
> (p. 54)

> [It's lovely going along the Rambla. The best moment of the day. The only time it's relaxing to drive.]

It is also a place of refuge for Ramón in time of crisis, the place to which he runs after witnessing his mother's rape. Third, it is the scene of a recent real-life murder which Ramón refers to, and which forms the start of a passage where he reflects on the deaths he has encountered. Lastly, it is the route he uses to take Dolly to the penthouse where they make love, a journey which she recalls in her desolation after his death, in Chapter 14. In his analysis of space and time in the novel Jacques Soubeyroux suggests that 'en efecto, al hablar de la Rambla, el texto alude varias veces al mar' [in effect, when talking about la Rambla, the text is often alluding to the sea] (1985:441), which in turn he argues represents 'los valores femeninos, sentimentales y maternales del agua' [the feminine, emotional and maternal values of water] thus constituting 'un conjunto de valores antitéticos del orden burgués' [a group of anti-bourgeois values] (1985:449–450). Added to this is the idea that the open spaces in the novel – including *la Rambla* – such as the streets, the beach at Portezuelo and the park, represent for Ramón places of refuge, evasion and a degree of freedom from his problems. By contrast, closed spaces, and in particular 'el triángulo Punta Gorda [Ramón's house]-Agencia-despacho del padre' [the Punta Gorda-Agency-his father's office triangle] represent 'el espacio de su enajenación' [where he feels alienated] (1985:446). Given the significance of *la Rambla* as a setting, I felt it important for the reader to know that it is a long coastal avenue and a major city landmark. Rather than using an intratextual gloss, I chose to include it in the map of Montevideo and highlight its length.

The Translation of Culture   105

In the category of idiomatic expressions, the adjective *falluto* is used for the first time in Chapter 1 in an exchange between Ramón and Marcela, who have recently introduced themselves at the Tequila Restaurant dinner and begun to tease each other a little. After one exchange Marcela asks Ramón if he is flirting with her, and he replies:

> —¿Sabés que no se me había ocurrido? Pero es una idea buenísima.
> Ahora es ella la que suelta la risa.
> —Falluto.

(p. 30)

> ["You know that hadn't occurred to me? But it's an excellent idea."
> This time it's she who laughs.
> "Falluto."]

Falluto is an adjective strongly associated with the River Plate dialect of Spanish spoken in Argentina and Uruguay, and has a range of meanings including hypocritical, untrustworthy, cowardly, false and treacherous. In this particular context it is being used in a gently mocking fashion, since the preceding text makes it clear that Ramón *was* flirting with Marcela and is only feigning innocence. Taken on its own the word appears to have little significance, and the most obvious translation would be *hypocrite*, which is how I initially translated it. However, when subjected to a combination of quantitative and text-functional analysis, it takes on greater significance as a CSI.

The word is used six times in all and is important for two reasons. Belonging to the local dialect, it forms part of Benedetti's identification of the novel's storyworld with his readers' real world. It also relates very directly to the novel's central theme, that of moral and political hypocrisy and the need for change. The adjective is used by Ramón to describe Montevidean middle-class morality (p. 141), and also to describe himself and his feeling of worthlessness just before he jumps to his death (p. 287). It is used by Edmundo to describe Ramón when the latter suggests that he can wipe the moral slate clean by paying back the loan his father gave him to set up the travel agency (p. 162). And it is used by Gloria to describe Edmundo just before she leaves him at the end of the novel:

> Es falluto, es deshonesto, pero ha perdido fuerza. Ya no inspira temor.

(p. 307)

> [He's *falluto*, he's dishonest, but he's lost his power. He no longer inspires fear.]

The implication for translation is that it needs to be treated consistently, so I decided to leave the word untranslated in the text on all six occasions, but to include it in the glossary.

106   *The Translation of Culture*

The third CSI example is a political reference from Chapter 4, repeated in Chapter 6, to *sociedades de padres demócratas*. These constituted one of a number of right-wing groups set up in Uruguay after the Cuban Revolution to fight 'communist infiltration' (Bucheli 2012:11–30). Again, taken on its own, this reference does not seem particularly important. A literal translation, *societies of democratic fathers* would leave the reader unclear as to the purpose or philosophy of the organisation, and the text provides no further clues since it is mentioned as part of a long list of disparate items. In these circumstances it would be tempting to employ the translation strategy Aixelá terms 'absolute universalization', whereby translators choose 'to delete any foreign connotations and choose a neutral reference for their readers' (1996:63). This would lead to a translation along the lines of 'anti-communist organisations'. However, the word *demócratas* is important when considered in the context of the novel. Edmundo, as the symbolic representation of the corrupt ruling elite, is a leading politician, industrialist and newspaper owner. He frequently trumpets the values of democracy in public and through his newspaper, but with surprising frankness explains his real opinion to Gustavo during their discussion of politics in Chapter 6:

> —En la democracia me hago caca, pero me sirve para ganar plata y entonces soy Demócrata con todas las mayúsculas que quieras.
>
> (p. 114)

> ["I crap on democracy, but it helps me make money, so I'm a Democrat with all the capital D's you want."]

Preservation of the idea of democracy is therefore important. As with *la Rambla* and *falluto*, my translation solution in this case is to leave the whole phrase intact in Spanish, particularly since its literal translation would be unproblematic for most readers, and to include it in the glossary. My aim with the translation of all three CSIs has been to go some way towards fulfilling Jull Costa's desire 'to reach out' to her readers (Saldanha 2008:31), while at the same time responding to Bush's enthusiastic injunction: 'Enjoy stoking up the otherness. Positively wallow in it' (Bush 1999:186).

4.2 Multilingualism: Preservation, a Glossary and Typography

Literary multilingualism can be defined as 'the co-presence of two or more languages in a text' (Meylaerts 2010:227). *Gracias por el Fuego* contains elements of English, French, German and Latin, used in different ways and in varying amounts. There are 7 instances of Latin and 10 of French spread across the novel, in the form of individual words or short phrases; while the 12 instances of German are contained in a span

The Translation of Culture 107

of 10 pages (Chapter 4, pp. 77–87), 11 of which form part of a flash-back relating to Ramón's time at the *Deutsche Schule* in Montevideo.[3] The most prominent language after Spanish is the TL, English, which appears in the text in various forms: the insertion of 30 instances of common or colloquial words and phrases in 11 chapters; in one side of three consecutive bilingual 'Spanglish' telephone conversations involving José, the Tequila Restaurant head waiter, in Chapter 1 (pp. 13–15); and in two conversations between Ramón and two US clients, Mr. and Mrs. Ransom, at the beginning of Chapter 3 (pp. 63–67). Manual quantitative analysis of the ST revealed the extent and location of the usage of the four languages, while close reading and contextual analysis suggested the narrative and stylistic functions of the various instances, both individually and collectively.

Benedetti spoke five languages: Spanish, Italian, German, French and English. By the time he wrote *Gracias por el Fuego* in 1962–1963 he had visited Europe twice – seeing 10 countries in 1947 and 13 in 1957 – and the US once, in 1959–1960. In his literary essays he also acknowledges the influence of Anglophone modernist writing, which is marked by its use of multilingualism (Taylor-Batty 2013). Joyce, Beckett, Eliot, Pound, Rhys, Lawrence, Mansfield and Richardson all used it, and as Taylor-Batty notes, 'the emblematically modernist themes of exile, travel and intercultural encounter lead inevitably, to the necessity of representing different languages' (2013:39). Both travel and intercultural encounter feature prominently in *Gracias por el Fuego*. In Chapters 1, 3, 9, 10 and 13 Ramón refers to his experiences in the US; in Chapter 4 he recalls an unpleasant episode during his time at the *Deutsche Schule* in Montevideo (pp. 83–88); and in Chapter 10 he reminisces about his time in Buenos Aires as a young man (pp. 213–220).

My contextual analysis of Benedetti's use of different languages suggests that it fulfils several functions. It forms an element of character portrayal; it serves to strengthen the identification of physical location in another country; it provides a vehicle for irony and humour; and it reinforces part of the novel's political subtext, namely the critique of US attitudes towards Latin America. Examples will illustrate two of these functions. The six instances of Latin phrases are used in relation to characterisation, political comment and plot development. In Chapter 1, during the Tequila Restaurant dinner, Pascual Berrutti bemoans the lack of religious education in Uruguay to Mirta Ventura, and praises what he sees as the pervasive religiosity of the US. He pompously quotes the adage "Errare humanum est" ['To err is human'] (p. 31) as part of a homily on original sin, while simultaneously ensuring that one of his feet makes contact with Mirta's leg under the table:

> Eso me gusta de este país: aquí sí está Dios en todo. En la enseñanza, en la Constitución, en la discriminación racial, en las fuerzas

108 *The Translation of Culture*

armadas. Estados Unidos es un país fundamentalmente religioso. Nosotros en cambio somos un país fundamentalmente laico. Por eso somos incoherentes. Dios une; el laicismo separa.

El piececito de Mirta se arrima, como por azar, al zapato número cuarenta y dos de Berrutti. Él no lo retira, y aunque todavía no tiene la absoluta certeza de que ella no lo está confundiendo con la pata de la mesa, igual prosigue con renovados bríos.

—Yo no pretendo que el ser humano deje de pecar. Errare humanum est. El error, el pecado, está en el ser mismo del hombre.

(p. 31, emphasis in the original)

[That's what I like about this country: here God's everywhere. In the education system, in the Constitution, in the racial discrimination, in the armed forces. The United States is a fundamentally religious country. We, however, are a fundamentally secular country. That's why we're incoherent. God unites; secularism divides.

As if by chance Mirta's dainty foot brushes Berrutti's size forty-two shoe. He does not withdraw it, and even though he is not completely sure that she isn't confusing it with the table leg, he presses on with renewed vigour.

"I don't expect human beings to stop sinning. Errare humanum est. The error, the sin, is in man's very being."]

The use of Latin here highlights Berrutti's pomposity and hypocrisy, and also forms part of Ramón's broader critique of the Catholic Church.

There are three instances of the pseudo-Latin phrase 'Mutus Nomen Dedit Cocis', which refers to a card trick involving the identification of a pair of cards chosen by the subject.[4] All three instances occur in Chapter 13, within the space of 12 pages (pp. 271, 280 and 283), and refer to Ramón's planned assassination of Edmundo. The first instance illustrates its narrative function:

Tengo la sensación de estar haciendo aquella vieja prueba de baraja basada en las palabras: Mutus, Nomen, Dedit, Cocis. Habré de pasar el día manteniendo conversaciones, realizando actos, haciendo gestos, que parecerán iguales a los cotidianos, a los opacos actos, palabras y gestos de todos los días, pero que en cambio serán un solo naipe de cada grupo. Sólo yo tengo el secreto de la prueba, sólo yo conozco dónde debo colocar el otro, es decir, sólo yo conozco el significado que esas conversaciones, esos actos, esos gestos, habrán de tener mañana, cuando yo tenga una muerte sobre mi espalda, y, a pesar de (o, mejor, a causa de) esa muerte, pueda echar mis hombros hacia atrás, en un gesto de buena respiración y libertad recuperada, y mirar sin rencores el prodigioso cielo vacío.

(p. 271)

The Translation of Culture 109

[I have the feeling that I'm doing the old card trick based on the words: Mutus, Nomen, Dedit, Cocis. I'll have to spend the day holding conversations, performing acts, making gestures, which will seem the same as the daily routine, the dull everyday acts, words and gestures, but which in fact will be only one card from each group. I alone hold the secret of the trick, I alone know where I must place the other one, in other words, I alone know the meaning that those conversations, those acts, those gestures will have tomorrow, when I have a death hanging around my neck, and, in spite of (or, rather, because of) that death, I can push my shoulders back, in a gesture of deep breathing and freedom regained, and look without bitterness at the wonderful empty sky.]

Here Ramón's actions are divided into how they will be seen by other people before and after he kills Edmundo, and the device of a card trick is used to emphasise the fact that he will have to appear to act normally, while keeping his terrible plan a secret.

Benedetti makes frequent use of humour and irony in both his short stories and novels, and in *Gracias por el Fuego* he uses English to do this on several occasions. For example, in Chapter 3 in the context of recounting his sexual conquests in the US, Ramón muses that:

Así como existe la notable Agencia de Viajes Ramón Budiño y Cía., debería existir una asesoría de turismo sexual. ¿Cómo iba a saber yo que la frase clave era *would you like to see my etchings*? Eso se llama un eufemismo.

(p. 71)

[Just as there's the well-known Agencia de Viajes Ramón Budiño y Cía., there should be a sexual tourism advice service. How was I to know that the key expression was *would you like to see my etchings*? That's called a euphemism.]

This highlights an encounter with a different set of cultural and linguistic codes, portrayed with accuracy and irony.

Research on the translation of multilingual texts seems to be a relatively recent phenomenon (Cincotta 1996; Pym 1996a; Eco 2001; Delabastita and Grutman 2005; Grutman 2005; Rosenwald 2008; Suchet 2009; Meylaerts 2010; Zabalbeascoa 2012). In some cases, it is dealt with as a subcategory of code-switching (Franco Arcia 2012; Gardner-Chloros and Weston 2015), which also embraces the translation of dialect and register. While there is disagreement about particular approaches, two broad ideas appear to command general support. Contextual considerations and an assessment of the function of other languages in a text should inform the choice of translation strategies. Target culture norms, and in particular publisher preferences, also play an important part in

110   *The Translation of Culture*

translation decisions, and override other considerations in some cases (Grutman 2005:23–26; Bush 2012). In Chapter 3, I positioned my translation philosophy as being broadly foreignising. In this context Berman lists 'the effacement of the superimposition of languages' as one of the 'twelve deforming tendencies' in translation ([1985] 2004:288). In this and the following subsection I explore various strategies for maximising the retention of this superimposition and its stylistic effects.

Madeleine Cincotta suggests that there are four possible translation solutions in this situation: translate everything into the TL, preserve the SL(s) in the TT, use a colloquial form of the TL and substitute another language or dialect for the foreign language(s) (1996:2–3). My preference is for the second option, since as Rosenwald argues, 'The representation of heterophone languages forces readers to confront and interpret the multiplicity of speech communities in the world' (2008:6), which are represented in the novel. The French and Latin phrases are mostly ones which an educated Uruguayan reader might reasonably have been expected to know or been able to decipher. Examples include words like 'troupe' and 'rouge' in French, and 'alma parens' in Latin. In the case of one Latin phrase, and also the German song lyric quotations, Benedetti adds an intratextual gloss to indicate the broad idea of what is being referred to. In these cases, I have followed his lead, leaving the Latin, German and French untranslated, and included the pseudo-Latin phrase – Mutus, Nomen, Dedit, Cocis – in the glossary.

The most difficult translation challenge is presented by the use of the TL in the ST. For José's 'Spanglish' telephone conversations I have decided to use a technique referred to by Franco Arcia as 'mirror-reflection translation' (2012:78). In his study he focuses on España, the main character in the novel *Killing Me Softly (Morir Amando*, 2004) by Francisco Ibáñez-Carrasco. España is gay and speaks in a mixture of English and Spanish, as in this example:

> *Mi nombre es España*, well that is not my real name, *es mi apodo, y la historia que les voy a contar* does not end today, it is, like they say, *el principio de un final feliz, como las canciones*, the songs with happy endings, even when it is my ending.
>
> (italics in original)[5]

The mirror-reflection translation from English into Spanish involves reversing the order of the languages in the ST:

> *I am* España, bueno, ése no es mi nombre verdadero, *it's my nickname, and the story I am about to tell you* no termina hoy, es, como dicen, *the beginning of a happy ending*, como el de las canciones con finales felices, aunque se trate de mi final.
>
> (Franco Arcia 2012:80, italics in original)

The Translation of Culture 111

This preserves the foreign language-TL order in the translation and retains the use of both languages. In the case of José's one-sided telephone conversations in *Gracias por el Fuego*, the bulk of the conversation is in Spanish, with the occasional English word or phrase thrown in. So reversing this in the translation preserves the effect of a sprinkling of a second language, as an example from his first conversation, with my translation, illustrates. The ST English and TT Spanish renderings are highlighted for ease of reference.

ST	TT (October 2016)
— *Aló.* Tequila Restaurant. Speaking. Ah, you speak *español. Sí, señora. No, señora. Sí, señora. Todo típico,* of course. *No, señora. Sí, señora. No, señora. Primera calidad. ¿Y cuántos gringos piensa traer? Sí, señora. No, señora. Sí, señora. Claro, cuando vienen gringos traemos las panderetas.* Typical, you know. *También las gaitas. ¿Gaitas nicaragüenses? Sí, por supuesto. Nuestras gaitas son para todo servicio. Quédese tranquila, señora, todo saldrá bien. ¿Y para cuándo?* Next Friday. *Okei, señora, aquí lo anoto.* (p. 13)	"Aló. Tequila Restaurant. Le habla. Ah, habla *español. Sí, señora. No, señora. Sí, señora. Everything typical,* naturalmente. *No, señora. Sí, señora. No, señora. Top quality. And how many gringos are you thinking of bringing? Sí, señora. No, señora. Sí, señora. Yes, of course, when gringos come we bring out the tambourines.* Típico, sabe. *And the bagpipes, too. Nicaraguan bagpipes? Yes, of course. Our bagpipes are all-purpose. Don't worry, señora, everything'll be fine. And when for?* El próximo viernes. *Okei, señora, I'll make a note of it.*

The bilingual feel of the passage is reinforced by the decision to leave all the instances of *No, señora. Sí, señora* untranslated. I have also used a different typeface for all the English words used in the novel, a decision I explain below.

Typography and Translation

The visual presentation of written text forms part of its communicative effect. As Saldanha argues, 'A text's visual organisation will inevitably have an impact on how it is understood and interpreted by readers' (2005:88). Theo van Leeuwen suggests, for example, that 'letter forms can become "signifiers in their own right"… they are a *resource* for meaning-making' (2005:139, emphasis in original), as evidenced by the typeface american uncial, often used to suggest an Irish or Celtic connection. Yet despite this, as Carol O'Sullivan notes, 'To date, typeface choice and other printing decisions have not been taken much into account by scholars of translation' (2013:4).

112 *The Translation of Culture*

The commonest typographical variation in literature that has been studied would seem to be the use of italics (Šlancarová 1999; Saldanha 2005, 2011b), and Benedetti uses them in six different ways in *Gracias por el Fuego*: for general emphasis; to highlight non-Spanish words and phrases; to indicate the verbatim content of a tape-recorded conversation (Chapter 4, pp. 99–102); for the titles of newspapers and institutions; for song lyrics; and to suggest to the reader that Chapter 1 is a preface to the novel, since the convention at the time in Uruguay was for prefaces to be printed in italics. I want to suggest that what Mick Short terms 'graphological deviation' (1999:305) can be used in a variety of other ways in translation, and in particular to convey the use of the TL in the ST.

The most prominent use of English in the novel comes at the beginning of Chapter 3 (pp. 63–67) in the form of a conversation between Ramón and two of his US clients, Mr. and Mrs. Ransom, whom he has taken to see the Montevideo carnival. I present part of it here as it appears on the printed page:

Debe hacer por lo menos diez años que no veo un carnaval. De chico iba a los tablados, y me gustaban. Ahora no soporto nada de esto. Pero hay que mostrárselo a los yanquis.

—Don't you think it's very beautiful?
—Marvelous,[6] it beats New Orleans.
—Oh no, I've been there.
—Really? When?
—Fifty-nine.

Ella tiene tantas pecas. ¿Cómo alguien puede tener tantas pecas? Él no tiene pecas, pero tiene Kodak. ¿Cómo alguien puede sacar tantas fotos? Cabezudos a la vista. Gran detalle folclórico.

—Look at those heads.
—How wonderful.
—How funny.

Lástima que no haya más Marqués de las Cabriolas. Lo encontrarían aún más folclórico.

—You think we are funny people?
—Of course you are.
—Sorry, we are not.
—Pardon.
—We are very sad people.
—Like the tango?
—Sure, like the tango.
—Oh, I love tango.
—El choclo, for instance?
—Pardon.

The Translation of Culture   113

—That means Kiss of Fire.
—Oh, yes, I love Kiss of Fire, d'you remember Tom?
—What?
—But, Tom, we used to dance Kiss of Fire at the Havana Hilton.
—I see, Mrs. Ransom, you have been at Havana.
—Every season B. C.
—B.C.?
—Yes, Before Castro.

(pp. 63–64)

Simply leaving the English as it is and translating the Spanish would erase the linguistic interplay. Substituting another language for English would not work, since the content of this and a subsequent conversation relate to the US and Latin America in what Hermans (1996) terms a 'self-referential' way. Since both the content and the language need to be preserved, some way needs to be found to visually highlight the inter-linguistic code-switching. My solution is to use another typeface for the English, Bookman Old Style, and to retain the use of the Spanish 'quotation dash' (Houston 2014:146), replacing the normal English inverted commas in a form of 'mirror-reflection punctuation':

It must be at least ten years since I saw a carnival. As a child I used to go to see the tableaux and I liked them. Now I can't bear any of that. But I have to show them to the yanks.

— Don't you think it's very beautiful?
— Marvelous, it beats New Orleans.
— Oh no, I've been there.
— Really? When?
— Fifty-nine.

She has so many freckles. How can someone have so many freckles? He hasn't got any freckles, but he's got Kodak. How can someone take so many photos? Huge Carnival heads in sight. Great folkloric detail.

— Look at those heads.
— How wonderful.
— How funny.

A pity there aren't any more Marqués de las Cabriolas. They would find it even more folkloric.

— You think we are funny people?
— Of course you are.
— Sorry, we are not.
— Pardon.
— We are very sad people.

114   *The Translation of Culture*

— Like the tango?
— Sure, like the tango.
— Oh, I love tango.
— El choclo, for instance?
— Pardon.
— That means Kiss of Fire.
— Oh, yes, I love Kiss of Fire, d'you remember Tom?
— What?
— But, Tom, we used to dance Kiss of Fire at the Havana Hilton.
— I see, Mrs. Ransom, you have been at Havana.
— Every season B. C.
— B.C.?
— Yes, Before Castro.

Bookman Old Style is a similar serif font to Times New Roman, but just different enough to be distinguishable. The aim is to draw attention to the fact that two languages are being used, rather than to the typeface itself. Typographical representation of another language being used is a technique employed by Yann Martel in the novel *Life of Pi* (2001), where the use of Japanese is indicated by italics and an in-text reference (cited in Stratton 2004). In my case the use of italics would be unhelpful in a text where it is already multifunctional. To help the reader appreciate the code-switching, I include a specific reference in the translator's preface to the fact that all English words and phrases appear in a different typeface.

4.3 *Usted* and the Translation of Tonal Register

Forms of interpersonal address such as *usted* constitute part of 'pragmatics', which Mona Baker defines as 'the study of language in use. It is the study of meaning, not as generated by the linguistic system but as conveyed and manipulated by participants in a communication situation' (2011:230). In the context of literary translation, it is important to bear in mind that, as Monika Fludernik points out,

> spoken language can never be faithfully represented in writing... Characters in novels and plays do not speak in the same way as real people do when they talk to each other. Recordings of genuine spoken exchanges show that written representations of these have been stylized or "purified".
>
> (2009:65)

Nevertheless, despite their acknowledged artificiality, dialogues in literature are very important and forms of address can often play a central role as markers of degrees of formality and of the relative status and power of speakers.

The Translation of Usted *in Latin American Fiction:* Examples and Options

The word *usted*, widely accepted as originating from a contraction of *vuestra merced*, whose first appearance in Spain is said to have been in the 1400s (Pearson 2003:1), is used as a standard form of polite address in both peninsular and Latin American Spanish. It is used between people who meet for the first time; as a standard form of mutual address in many workplaces; as a form of respect when people of perceived lower social status are talking to people of a perceived higher status; and within families, where younger members and sons-/daughters-in-law often address older members with respect, for example.

There are a number of options open to the translator for the translation of *usted* and its associated register. Alexandra Assis Rosa suggests that in relation to the translation of literary varieties of speech generally there are four main possibilities: 'omission, addition, maintenance or change of... linguistic features and their associated contextual information' (2015:214). I have not been able to find any studies which focus directly on the literary translation of *usted* into English, although there are a number in which it is mentioned (Hervey, Higgins and Haywood 2004; Saldanha 2005, 2008). However, I have carried out research which provides some evidence to suggest that there has been a tendency in translations of twentieth-century Latin American fiction to use the strategy of omission, translating *usted* as *you* without the addition of any register-defining intratextual elements. I looked at a sample of these translations, involving well-known writers and translators, which is listed in *Table 4.1*.

I analysed the complete texts of the short stories; the 10% random sample of *La Tregua* and its two English translations, referred to in Chapter 3; and the first 14 chapters of *Rayuela*. This is neither a systematic nor a comprehensive survey of the translation of *usted*, nor does it take into account the more frequent uses of the 'implied *usted*', where it forms the understood but unarticulated subject of a verb in the third-person singular. Yet in 47 out of the 50 instances I found that *usted* was normalised as *you*, without further contextualisation by the translator. Three examples will illustrate this.

'Familia Iriarte':

– ¿Y usted, qué refresco prefiere? (Benedetti 1959a:80)
"And what do you like to drink?" (Rabassa) (Benedetti 1963:203)
"And what do you like to drink?" (Morales) (Benedetti 2010:161)
"And which soda do you prefer?" (Tricario & Levine) (Benedetti 1976:13)

116   *The Translation of Culture*

Table 4.1 Sources used for an analysis of the translation of *usted*

ST	Author	Instances of usted	Translation and translator(s)
'Familia Iriarte' (1956) [SS]	Mario Benedetti	2	• 'The Iriarte Family' (1963), Gregory Rabassa under the pseudonym George Rothenberg • 'The Iriartes' (1976), Lynn Tricario and Suzanne Jill Levine • 'The Iriarte Family' (2010), Harry Morales
La Tregua (1960) [N]	Mario Benedetti	12	• *The Truce* (1969), Benjamin Graham • *The Truce* (2015), Harry Morales
Rayuela (1963) [N]	Julio Cortázar	10	*Hopscotch* (1967), Gregory Rabassa
'María dos Prazeres' (1992) [SS]	Gabriel García Márquez	2	'María dos Prazeres' (1993), Edith Grossman
'Las Amigas' (1995) [SS]	Carlos Fuentes	24	'Las Amigas' (1997), Alfred Mac Adam

[N] Novel [SS] Short story
Total instances of *usted*: 50

> ***Rayuela:***
> – ¿A usted le vuelve su papá? Quiero decir el fantasma? (Cortázar 2013:73)

> "Does your father ever come back to you? His ghost I mean?" (Rabassa) (Cortázar 1998:46)

> **'Las Amigas':**
> – Porque estaba convencido de que usted en realidad no quería a nadie. Por eso necesitaba que usted primero le diera una prueba de cariño. (Fuentes 1999a:136)

> "Because he was convinced you never loved anyone. He needed you to give him proof of your affection." (Mac Adam) (Fuentes 1999a:137)

Of the other three instances, two involved omission as in the following example:

> **'Las Amigas':**
> – Mire usted, tía. (Fuentes 1999a:136)

> "Listen to me now, Aunt Amy." (Mac Adam) (Fuentes 1999b: 137)

The other involved the use of 'one' instead of 'you':

La Tregua:
«Usted pasaba al atardecer...» (Benedetti 2015:152)

"In the evenings, one could pass by..." (Morales) (Benedetti 2015:131)

It is not my intention to attempt to evaluate this translation approach in these contexts, but simply to suggest that it provides some evidence to support Toury's 'law of growing standardization' with regard to the translation of *usted* by normalisation:

> in translation, textual relations obtaining in the original are often modified, sometimes to the point of being totally ignored, in favour of [more] habitual options offered by a target repertoire.
>
> (Toury 2012:304)

The Translation of usted *in* Gracias por el Fuego

In *Gracias por el Fuego* the word appears 189 times (every 1.6 pages on average), but is actually used as an implied *usted* far more often. Benedetti uses it in dialogue in different ways. It constitutes the standard form of address on first meeting. It is used self-referentially when two characters decide to change to the more familiar *tú*, whose usage is known as *tuteo*. It also emphasises the asymmetric power and status relationship between Edmundo and the rest of his family, especially Ramón. In this connection, its absence is used to highlight a significant change in the relationship between Gloria and Edmundo. In Chapter 7 Gloria is still the respectful, if increasingly unhappy mistress, while in Chapter 15, disgusted by Edmundo's self-centred reaction to Ramón's suicide, she addresses him in the familiar second person and has no hesitation in criticising him severely. And finally, *usted* is used as a stylistic and pragmatic framework for a workplace conversation in which both parties observe the outward forms, but have no respect for each other and are deeply at odds.

To sum up, the use of *usted* forms part of character and relationship portrayal – including relationship change – which is linked to plot development, as well as constituting a culture-specific dimension of spoken discourse. In my view, therefore, it needs to be translated, in some way, in order to minimise what Berman terms 'the destruction of linguistic patternings' and 'the destruction of networks of signification' ([1985] 2004:288). My translation approach involves a combination of all four of Rosa's strategies, and four examples will serve to illustrate this. The first example, from Chapter 1,[7] relates to one of the commonest uses of

118   *The Translation of Culture*

usted, which is in normal conversation between people on first meeting and before a more familiar form of address has been employed:

ST	TT
– ¿Usted es algo de Edmundo Budiño? – pregunta Ruth Amezua, a la izquierda de Ramón.(p. 17)	"Are you related to Edmundo Budiño, señor?" asks Ruth Amezua, to Ramón's left.

In this case the addition of an instance of *señor* serves to establish the tone of polite formality conveyed by *usted*.

The next example concerns the self-referential use of *usted* in the context of changing from this usage to the more familiar *tú*. In Chapter 1 at the Tequila Restaurant dinner, Ramón and Marcela are encouraged to address each other less formally. The way this is done forms part of the early development of Ramón's character and portrays him as a womaniser:

ST	TT
A la izquierda de Budiño, suena la voz nerviosa de Ruth: – ¿Por qué no se tutean, como nosotros?	To Budiño's left Ruth's nervous voice can be heard: "Why don't you use tú, like us?"
Ramón y Marcela cruzan una mirada inteligente y cómplice.	Ramón and Marcela exchange a knowing, conspiratorial look.
– Sucede que todavía no hemos considerado esa posibilidad – dice Budiño—. Pero a lo mejor la consideramos.	"It so happens that we haven't considered that possibility yet" says Budiño. "But we probably will."
– ¿Verdad? – dice Marcela, levantando las cejas.	"Really?" says Marcela, raising her eyebrows.
– Siempre y cuando estos pesados casi veinte años de diferencia no la cohíban a usted.	"As long as the weight of our nearly twenty year age difference doesn't inhibit the señora."
– ¿A usted?	"The señora?"
– Quiero decir: no te cohíban.	"I mean, doesn't inhibit you."
– No, te aseguro que no. (p. 21)	"No, I assure you it doesn't."

Here I have changed *usted* to '*the señora*' as an indication of formality, contrasting this with the translation of *te* as *you*.

The third example also involves overt self-reference to *usted*. When the character and the personality of Edmundo are introduced in Chapter 2, the fact that his entire family addresses him as *usted* is used to indicate his power and status:

The Translation of Culture   119

ST	TT
Por algo todos lo tratamos de *usted*. Todos: hijos, nietos, nueras. Un hábito anacrónico que él había sabido mantener, para dejar bien especificada la distancia. (p. 46)	It's for a reason that that we all address him as *usted*. All of us: children, grandchildren, daughters-in-law. An outdated habit which he's managed to maintain to make the social distance very clear.

Here I have used maintenance, preserving the word *usted*, on the basis that the context makes its implication clear, that its inclusion retains the Spanish feel of the text and that it is a sufficiently common Spanish word for most educated readers to be familiar with it.

The final example illustrates another cultural dimension, namely the way in which social convention can regulate the expression of hostility between two educated speakers. In Chapter 4 Hugo plays Ramón a tape recording of an argument between Edmundo and Villalba, a trade union leader at his factory, following a strike (pp. 99–102). Edmundo (who speaks first here) uses a combination of threats and bribery to try to force Villalba to reveal the names of two fellow strike organisers, which he refuses to do. Both speakers address each other as *usted*, while clearly having no respect for each other. The final line provides a powerful ironic contrast in what Hervey, Higgins and Haywood refer to as tonal registers (2004:123), between the formality of *usted* and the colloquial insult *hijo de puta* [son of a bitch].

ST	TT
—*Pero ¿por qué? No es malo ser ambicioso.* —*Claro que no.* —*No es malo ser cómodo.* —*Seguro que no. ¿Sabe qué es lo único malo?* —*No.* —*Ser un hijo de puta como usted, señor.* (p. 102, italics in original, to represent a tape recording)	"*But, why? It's not bad to be ambitious.*" "*Of course not.*" "*It's not bad to have an easy life.*" "*Certainly not. You know what the only bad thing is?*" "*No.*" "*To be a son of a bitch like you, señor.*"

In this case, since the context of the conversation and the asymmetric power relationship between the speakers have already been firmly established, and since the ST also contains the word *señor* which reinforces this, I have chosen to translate *usted* as *you*.

What I see as important in approaching the translation of *usted* as a form of address, which indicates a certain tonal register, is not the

120 *The Translation of Culture*

translation of every instance, which would draw attention to itself and become much more marked in the TT than in the ST. It is that the reader should be made aware of the nature of the social relationship this form of address indicates when used between speakers. In the case of *Gracias por el Fuego* a consistent strategy of omission, with the consequent erasure of tonal register, would involve stylistic and narrative translation loss, and would also veil an important culture-specific phenomenon which I want to convey to the reader. Once established early on, the tonal register of *usted* can be occasionally reinforced by any of the strategies Assis Rosa enumerates, depending on context, as I hope to have demonstrated.

Notes

1 At the 2016 International Translation Day conference in London, I asked a panel of publishers' representatives (from MacLehose Press, Scribe UK and Oneworld) whether they would be receptive to translator requests to include a preface. Their answer was a clear affirmative, and they added, without being asked, that they also favoured the inclusion of glossaries.

2 www.zonu.com/uruguay_maps/Montevideo_Rambla_Map_Uruguay.htm [accessed 8 March 2017].

3 This scene is partly autobiographical, as Benedetti spent four years at this school from the ages of 9 to 13.

4 The actual words were chosen not for meaning, but to create a kind of mathematical mnemonic, and there are other sets of words which can be used for this particular card trick, such as 'David Lovel In Yon Abbey', which is how I was taught to do it. What is important is that in the set of four words (in this case) any two words will have one letter in common, and that each word will contain one repeated letter. This is how the pairs are identified.

Twenty cards are laid face down in pairs and the subject is asked to pick up and memorise any pair of cards, then lay them face down again. While this is happening the magician turns away. After collecting and laying the cards face-up in a four by five matrix, the subject is asked to point out which row(s) they lie in, and the magician then correctly names the cards they chose.

5 Ibáñez-Carrasco, F., 2004. *Killing Me Softly. Morir Amando.* San Francisco: Suspect Thought Press, p. 13, cited in Franco Arcia (2012:77).

6 This is the US-American spelling.

7 Cited in Chapter 1 as part of the character portrayal of Ramón and Edmundo.

5 Applying the Methodology (Part 2)

The Translation of Punctuation

In his well-known study, *Pause and Effect: An Introduction to the History of Punctuation*, Malcolm Parkes argues that the primary function of punctuation is 'to resolve structural uncertainties in a text, and to signal nuances of semantic significance which might otherwise not be conveyed at all, or would at best be much more difficult for a reader to figure out' (1992:1). Clive Scott goes further by suggesting that punctuation is capable of much more than simple segmentation: 'punctuation has at its disposal the ability to register the temperamental and psychic landscape of the writer and reader, over and above the service it could render to a text's purely linguistic constitution' (2010:118). Several scholars have written about punctuation and translation (Newmark 1988; May 1994, 1997; Raffel 1994; Munday 1997, 2002; Baker 2011; Boll 2013), and three themes seem to emerge from their studies. First, punctuation is an important dimension of translation, but one which is often overlooked in favour of a concentration on meaning. In *A Textbook of Translation* Peter Newmark comments that 'Punctuation can be potent, but it is so easily overlooked that I advise translators to make a separate comparative punctuation check on their version and the original' (1988:58).

Second, altering punctuation in translation can lead to significant shifts in emphasis, cohesion and linguistic rhythm. This will be illustrated in Sections 5.2 and 5.3 of this chapter. The third theme is the fact that literary translators often seem to assume the right to alter sentence boundaries and punctuation at will. In her study, *The Translator in the Text: On Reading Russian Literature in English*, Rachel May suggests that:

> English translators regularly perform two types of transformations upon sentence boundaries in Russian prose... they show excessive devotion to the content of the sentence... but often ignoring features... such as idiosyncrasies of punctuation. Second, they often exhibit insensitivity to sentence boundaries as such, arbitrarily cutting up long sentences or combining several short ones.
>
> (1994:121)

122   *The Translation of Punctuation*

The sentence is such a basic and intuitive unit of writing that it is rarely given a second thought as an object of study or inquiry. As May argues,

> Although everyone agrees that the sentence is a fundamental unit, perhaps *the* fundamental unit of writing, not to mention of translating, sentences as such have received very little attention... the sentence has fallen through the cracks of linguistic, literary, and philosophical inquiry.
>
> (1994:120, emphasis in original)

Taking this as my starting point, I argue in this chapter that sentence length and structure are distinctive and important stylistic features of *Gracias por el Fuego*, and that assessing the extent of their stylistic importance benefits from a CDR approach.

In his well-known *Dictionary of Modern English Usage* (1926), Henry Fowler boldly defined a sentence as 'a set of words complete in itself, having either expressed or understood in it a subject and a predicate, and conveying a statement or question or command or explanation'.[1] Nearly a century later the *Oxford Dictionary of English Grammar* is more circumspect in its definition: '**sentence** The largest unit of analysis in grammar... Sentences usually have a subject and predicate, and (when they are written) begin with a capital letter and end with a full stop' (Aarts, Chalker and Weiner 2014:375, bold in original). It goes on to qualify this definition:

> Traditional definitions of the sentence are often formulated in notional terms, e.g. 'a set of words expressing a complete thought', but this is too vague to be useful. However, attempts at rigorous structural definitions (as above) are not entirely satisfactory either... modern grammarians often prefer to analyse syntactic structures in terms of clauses.
>
> (2014:376)

From a translator's point of view, the definition of a sentence in grammatical terms is less important than attempting to define the way in which sentence properties in a text work to produce particular effects. What a translator-as-reader first responds to is how the text affects her/him, only then analysing it to see how the creation of those effects may have been achieved. This is precisely how the methodology which this book sets out to apply and test was developed. Reading and then drafting an initial translation of Chapter 2 of *Gracias por el Fuego* gave me the impression that Benedetti had used a large number of short sentences. Also, that when combined with the use of the present tense within the narrative framework of an interior monologue, they had the effect of drawing me in as a reader and actively engaging me in Ramón's mental and emotional world, obliging me to follow a sequence of short steps each containing a thought. I then wanted to know how many short sentences there actually were, both in the chapter and in the novel as a whole; to define 'short' in numerical terms; and to look at the possible role played by both sentence length and structure in producing particular effects in the novel as a whole. From this analysis of sentence length and structure grew the realisation that a mutually beneficial and recursive use of close reading and quantitative analysis could constitute an approach to the translation of many aspects of literary style. But it all started with sentences.

It has been argued that sentences form a fundamental unit of reader engagement with a text. May argues that one thing the sentence does is 'organise the reader's active participation in the work' (1994:135), and Caryl Emerson suggests that 'the shape of a sentence governs the shape of the response. A translator is first of all and foremost a good reader, and must be sensitive to that shape' (1983:32). Short sentences do this in a different way from long sentences. A long sentence typically retains a wider, 'global' feel of uniting a series of ideas or topics, whereas breaking this up into shorter sentences focuses attention on a succession of new and often discrete ideas more than on their totality. Sentence length is therefore often an important aspect of authorial style, and in *Gracias por el Fuego* I argue that it is distinctive, but not unique.

Distinctiveness in literary style is often equated with frequency of occurrence in the work of an author or translator, but, as Gabriela Saldanha notes, frequency needs to be related to 'literary relevance'. She refers to an article by Halliday[2] which argues that

> the fact that a linguistic feature is prominent does not necessarily mean that it has literary relevance, since there are idiosyncrasies of style that have no discernible literary function... For a prominent feature of style to achieve literary relevance it has to form a coherent pattern of choice, together with other features of style, and impact on the meaning of the text as a whole.
>
> (Saldanha 2011a:240)

Where sentence length is distinctively different from a comparable average, the chances are that it represents 'a coherent pattern of choice', and that when combined with other aspects of punctuation and sentence structure it often has a significant impact on the way a text comes to have meaning, and what demands are made on the reader. Two contrasting examples will serve to illustrate this. The first is from Saul Bellow's 1964 novel *Herzog*:

> A city. In a century. In transition. In a mess. Under organized power. Subject to tremendous controls. In a condition caused by mechanization. After the late failure of radical hopes.
>
> (Bellow 1964/2007:201)

124 The Translation of Punctuation

The second is from the beginning of Molly Bloom's final interior monologue in James Joyce's *Ulysses*:

> YES BECAUSE HE NEVER DID A THING LIKE THAT before as ask to get his breakfast in bed with a couple of eggs since the *City Arms* hotel when he used to be pretending to be laid up with a sick voice doing his highness…
>
> (Joyce 1932/2010:640)

Both demand effort and active engagement on the part of the reader, but in wholly different ways. In the first example the reader needs to fill in the blanks left by the absence of main verbs and conjunctions, and even subjects. In the second, s/he needs to mentally create punctuation to make sense of the unsegmented stream of text. In both cases it is, as Tom Boll notes, 'only in the act of reading that it [the effect] can be understood, in the jolt that one experiences as grammatical expectation is confounded' (2013:81).

5.1 Sentence Length in *Gracias por el Fuego*

Sentence length is something which a translator-as-reader may well register impressionistically, but which requires computer-assisted analysis to quantify accurately. In Figures 5.1 and 5.2 I present a summary of the key findings of a quantitative analysis of sentence length in the novel as a whole, and by chapter. These, and all the statistics relating to the novel presented in this chapter, are drawn from more detailed analyses of word count and sentence length in both the source text (ST) and initial target text (TT), which are included in Appendix A, Tables A1 and A2. The methodology involved running three search queries using the

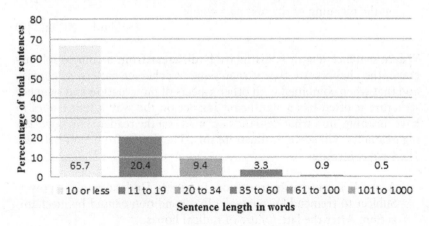

Figure 5.1 Proportions of sentences in *Gracias por el Fuego* by length.

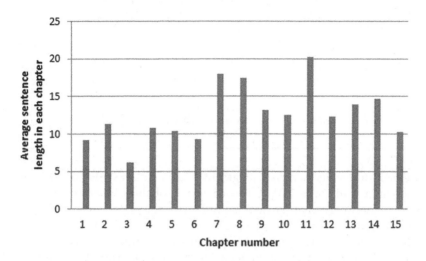

Figure 5.2 Average sentence length in *Gracias por el Fuego* by chapter.

CATMA web-based corpus linguistic programme. The Wordlist query gave the 'token' or word count for each chapter and for the novel as a whole. To arrive at figures for average sentence length, I used a query[3] to find the total number of sentences in each chapter and in the novel as a whole, then divided the word totals by the sentence totals. To arrive at more fine-grained sentence length statistics, by altering the regular expression search query I divided the sentence totals into seven different bands, ranging from 6 words or less to 101–1,000 words, and the results were aggregated to give banded totals for each chapter and the novel as a whole.

The salient feature that emerges from Figure 5.1 is that 65% of the novel's sentences contain 10 words or less. If we look at the number of sentences in the novel which contain 6 words or less, this, too, is very high: 45%. This confirms that short sentences are a key feature of the novel's linguistic structure. If we look at average sentence length by chapter in Figure 5.2, the picture that emerges is one of a range from 6.2 in Chapter 3 to 20.2 words in Chapter 11.

What also emerges from Figure 5.2 is that 12 out of 15 chapters have an average sentence length of under 15 words. In terms of the novel as a whole, the average sentence length is **11.8** words.

To put these findings in context, I compared overall average sentence length in *Gracias por el Fuego* with three Spanish reference corpora. The 5.7-million-word fiction content of the *Corpus del Español*, a 23-million-word corpus of twentieth-century Iberian and Latin American Spanish, was analysed using a similar procedure to that used in Computer-Aided Textual Markup and Analysis (CATMA),[4] and this

126   *The Translation of Punctuation*

Table 5.1 Average sentence length in four major Boom novels

Novel and year	Author	Average sentence length
La Ciudad y los Perros (1962)	Mario Vargas Llosa	12.0
La Muerte de Artemio Cruz (1963)	Carlos Fuentes	13.8
Rayuela (1963)	Julio Cortázar	17.4
Cien Años de Soledad (1967)	Gabriel García Márquez	24.7

yielded an average sentence length of **17.2** words. Estelle Irizarry carried out a study of 'a 150,000-word corpus of short stories by 30 well-known twentieth-century Spanish authors'[5] (1990:265) using 'random block samples of 5,000 continuous words' (ibid.:266) for each author. The average sentence length in the corpus was found to be **16.5** words. Lastly, I analysed average sentence length in four major Boom novels, using the same procedure as for the *Corpus del Español*, and the results are displayed in *Table 5.1*.

The evidence from these control corpora suggests that with the exception of *La Ciudad y los Perros*, *Gracias por el Fuego* has a shorter sentence length than the average for Spanish and Latin American twentieth-century fiction. In Sections 5.2 and 5.3, I examine the effects on me as reader-then-translator of the novel of both the dominant short sentences and the occasional contrasting long ones. I argue that the translation should generally attempt to preserve sentence length, boundaries and where possible, structure, because of the stylistic importance of these syntactic features and the way they relate to the presentation of the novel's message. In *Translation Studies* Susan Bassnett emphasises the importance of looking at sentences as part of the overall structure of a novel and argues that

> again and again translators of novels take pains to create *readable* TL texts, avoiding the stilted effect that can follow from adhering too closely to SL syntactical structures, but fail to consider the way in which individual sentences form part of the total structure.
>
> (1994:115, emphasis in original)

Sentence structure can also constitute an important aspect of authorial style. For example, in *Gracias por el Fuego* Benedetti uses a number of grammatical constructions throughout designed to emphasise and contrast ideas, judgements and descriptions. These include the use of symmetrical phrases, clauses and even whole short sentences, illustrated by the following underlined examples:

The Translation of Punctuation   127

A ellos tampoco les importa la democracia, a ellos también les inte-resa el negocio.

(p.114)

[They also don't care about democracy, they also care about business.]

(my translation)

Porque Ríos está decretadamente muerto, pero a la vez lo suficien-temente vivo....

(p.155)

[Because Ríos is pronouncedly a corpse, yet sufficiently alive...]

(my translation)

...tan famosamente libre y sin embargo tan irremediablemente estancado....

(p.142)

[...so famously free and yet so irremediably stagnant...]

(my translation)

While analysing occurrences of this contrastive construction pattern I noticed that phrases comprising *tan* [so] followed by an adjective fea-tured prominently. I therefore decided to analyse the latter in more de-tail, using a simple CQL query in Sketch Engine.[6] The results, including a comparison with the same four Boom novels used to analyse average sentence length earlier, are set out in *Table 5.2*.

They suggest that Benedetti's use of this adjectival phrase is distinc-tive. An analysis of the contexts of the 138 occurrences in *Gracias por el Fuego* – aided by a Sketch Engine visualisation of their distribution across the novel which identified particular instances of high frequency – indicates that he uses it both for general emphasis and to underline

Table 5.2 Raw and normalised frequency analysis of occurrences of 'tan' + adjective in *Gracias por el Fuego* and four major Boom novels

Title	Word total	Raw frequency	Normalised frequency (per 1,000 words)
Gracias por el Fuego	76,442	138	1.80
Cien Años de Soledad	137,918	175	1.26
Rayuela	172,818	186	1.07
La Muerte de Artemio Cruz	95,569	56	0.58
La Ciudad y los Perros	128,936	59	0.45

128 *The Translation of Punctuation*

contrasting descriptions, as in the short extract from Chapter 4 below, where Ramón's aunt Olga is first describing her deceased husband in somewhat deprecating terms:

> [Esteban] Era un pedazo de pan, lo reconozco, pero <u>tan apocado, tan reservado, tan modesto.</u>
>
> (p. 92, emphasis added)

> [He [Esteban] was an angel, I know, but <u>so unassuming, so reserved, so modest.</u>]
>
> (my translation, emphasis added)

and then Edmundo, with unbounded admiration:

> Es que hombres así ya no vienen más. <u>Tan seguros, tan elegantes, tan simpáticos, tan fuertes, tan vitales</u>.
>
> (p.93, emphasis added)

> [They don't make men like that anymore. <u>So confident, so elegant, so charming, so strong, so vital.</u>]
>
> (my translation, emphasis added)

The implication for translation is that in order to preserve the rhythm created by the repetition of *tan* – obligatory in Spanish, but not in English – and its emphatic effect, the word *so* should be repeated and not simply used once, followed by the list of adjectives.

5.2 Short Sentences and the Creation of an English Benedetti

Building on the idea that punctuation can be viewed as 'the author's visual tool for manipulating the reader's response' (May 1997:4), the focus in this section is on the impact of short sentences in *Gracias por el Fuego* and how their translation can pose challenges. In grammatical terms, short sentences involve greater segmentation of a text. They create a jerky, stop-start reading rhythm, forcing the reader to go more slowly and often to unpack meaning(s) which has/have been condensed into small 'blocks' of words that frequently flout general grammatical conventions. However, while such sentences will often share a number of formal properties, such as the lack of a verb, they can be employed by an author in different ways and can fulfil different stylistic functions. In the case of *Gracias por el Fuego* they are used in at least three different ways.

The 1,357 sentences (21% of the total) of 3 words or less are very largely to be found in passages of dialogue, where they form part of

The Translation of Punctuation   129

normal conversational exchange. Examples include *Si, señora, ¿Por qué?* [Why?], *todo depende* [It all depends], etc. In this context their brevity is unmarked and does not produce a disruptive effect. This has an important translation implication, namely that in at least some cases these short sentences can be merged with no loss of effect. It is important to stress that my translation approach does not involve a rigid and indiscriminate adherence to ST sentence boundaries and length. My concern is to reproduce them where they make an important contribution to stylistic effect, and it is primarily in the 4- to 10-word band of sentence length, numbering 2,952 sentences (46% of the total) that such effects are to be found.

The most common use of short sentences is as part of Ramón's interior monologue passages, which account for 57% of the novel's page count. The first use to highlight is that of the representation of a child's eye view of the world in Ramón's flashbacks, where sights, actions and interactions are experienced with great simplicity. The following example is taken from an interior monologue in Chapter 3 (pp. 60–61), where the 11-year-old Ramón recalls meeting a boy of his own age, Ángel, while watching the Montevideo carnival:

> El tablado en Capurro y Húsares. Y yo abajo, once años, sin amigos, mirando. Mamá me había dado diez pesos. Diez pesos en mil novecientos veintiocho. Una fortuna. Para comprar papelitos, serpentinas, caramelos, cualquier cosa. Vino la *troupe* Oxford y era un mundo de gente. Yo apretado contra un ángulo, trepado al cajoncito. Vino una máscara suelta y la gente aflojó. Vino otra *troupe* con un bailarín niño, más chico que yo. Bailaba jotas, tarantelas, milongas, malambos, bolero de Ravel. Cuando terminó, se arrimó a mi rincón. Tenía unos ojos grandes y unos bracitos flacos. ¿Te gusta?, dijo. Sí, contesté, ¿querés bajar? No puedo, dijo. Tengo diez pesos. Y se los mostré. Abrió los ojos desmesuradamente. Pediré permiso, dijo. Habló con un hombre de negro. Después volvió. Vamos, dijo. Bajó y nos fuimos.

> (p. 65)

> [The tableau at Capurro and Húsares. And me below, aged eleven, without friends, watching. Mamá had given me ten pesos. Ten pesos in 1928. A fortune. To buy confetti, streamers, sweets, anything. The Oxford *troupe* came past and they were a huge crowd. Me, squashed against a corner, perched on a little box. A masked performer passed by and people made way. Along came another *troupe* with a child dancer, younger than me. He was dancing jotas, tarantelas, milongas, malambos, Ravel's bolero. When he finished, he came over to my corner. He had large eyes and skinny little arms. D'you like it? he said. Yes I said. D'you want to get down? I can't, he

130   *The Translation of Punctuation*

said. I've got ten pesos. And I showed them to him. His eyes opened wide. I'll ask if I can, he said. He spoke to a man dressed in black. Then he came back. He got down and off we went.]

(my translation)

At the beginning of the passage the feeling is closer to that of a stream-of-consciousness narrative, with the first few sentences containing simple thoughts and images. Then the sentences become longer and more grammatically complete, but still comparatively short. The encounter with Ángel is portrayed through an elaborate sequence of actions, descriptions and verbal exchanges, whose overall effect, I would suggest, is highly cinematic.

Another use of short sentences involves the representation of imaginary newspaper headlines in Ramon's interior monologues. Edmundo is a newspaper proprietor, and Benedetti uses these headlines as a form of ironic description several times. For example, in the first description of Edmundo in the novel, in Chapter 2, there is a sentence containing a highly compressed pen portrait:

Desplantes principistas, encendida oratoria, figura prócer.

(p. 46)

[Pompous pronouncements, fiery speeches, heroic figure.]

(my translation)

It constitutes a six-word portrait of Edmundo's public image, suggesting a self-important and self-righteous man, a great orator and a heroic figure. The compressed effect is achieved, I would suggest, by the use of three separate but interlocking literary devices. First, there is the consonantal alliteration of the first two words, *Desplantes principistas*, which manages to lend bombast to the words. Then there is a symmetrically balanced phrase pattern consisting of the sequence noun+adjective/adjective+noun/noun+adjective. In the context of narratology Mieke Bal notes, in relation to a similar sentence, that 'the grammatical peculiarity that this "sentence" lacks a verb enforces its emotional effect' (1997:44). The last device is the use of linguistic rhythm, whereby the first two clauses have very similar stress patterns, while the last one, containing shorter words, culminates in the phonetically strong word *prócer*. This, above all, signals Edmundo's image and his apparent role in his family, in politics and in Uruguayan society: that of a hero.

A typical example of short sentence use in Ramón's adult interior monologues can be found in the opening paragraph of Chapter 2:

La ventana se abre a la calma chicha. Allá abajo, los plátanos. Por lo menos la mitad de las hojas están inmóviles, y el movimiento de

The Translation of Punctuation   131

las otras es apenas un estremecimiento. Como si alguien les hiciera cosquillas. Transpiro como un condenado. El aire está tenso, pero ya sé que nada se va a estallar. ¿Qué puedo decirme? Éste es el momento, estoy seguro.

(p. 45)

[The window opens onto a dead calm. Down below, the plane trees. At least half of the leaves are motionless, and the movement of the rest is barely a rustle. As if someone was tickling them. I sweat like a man condemned. The air is full of tension, yet I know that nothing is going to erupt. What can I tell myself? This is the moment, I'm certain of it.]

(my translation)

The average length of these eight sentences is eight words, and six of the eight sentences consist of eight words or less. Each sentence in the passage represents a description, a sensation, an idea, an association or a judgement. Ramón can be read as *talking* to himself, not just silently musing, and this idea is supported by the fact that Benedetti uses the sound of words as well as the cinematic images they create. For example, assonantal alliteration is frequently used: 'A̲llá a̲ba̲jo, los plá̲ta̲nos.' (p. 45), '¿Ta̲n a̲trás, ta̲n a̲trás?' (p. 47), 'Víctor abrió primero un ojo, después el otro, y dijo quejoso' (p. 233). The dominant narrative style rests upon the verbal representation of mental activity, both visually as words on the page and phonetically as their sound. The translation of this style, and its effect, involves not merely attempting to preserve sentence boundaries and length, but also incorporating other aspects of style which impinge upon them.

The Translation Challenges of Short Sentences

The central argument of this section is that the locus of the main translation challenge presented by the attempt to produce an English Benedetti lies in the short sentences contained in interior monologue passages, principally in the 4–10-word range. This is not only because there is a strong temptation to expand or merge a number of these sentences to produce smooth English, but also because the attempted recreation of Benedetti's style requires that other considerations which operate above the level of the sentence are brought to bear on the translation. For example, the verb *estallar* appears in this passage, and on the basis of the analysis of the ten occurrences of this verb in the novel I concluded that it needed to be translated consistently as 'erupt' (see Chapter 6, Section 6.3). These represent stylistic constraints on the translation, which supplement and influence localised semantic considerations. It is the ability of quantitative analysis to contribute to an understanding of this wider

132 *The Translation of Punctuation*

context, and to enter into a constructive dialogue with close reading, that makes the detailed recreation of literary style in relation to these short sentences more achievable.

The following pair of sentences constitutes a good example of the specific translation challenges posed by short sentences in the novel:

Hacia abajo es desprecio. Hacia arriba, admiración.

(p. 46)

[Literal translation: Towards down is contempt. Towards up, admiration.]

In addition to symmetrical contrast, these two sentences contain identical prepositional phrases; an identical syllable count (9); an absence of subject, object and in one case a verb; and they are very short. In other words, they represent very condensed, or compressed, sentences that do not need to be spelt out because their meaning is fairly clear and because Ramón is talking to himself, not to anyone else, and he knows what he means. This goes to the heart of the particular interior monologue style in this novel. It contains little full-blown stream-of-consciousness writing, with the exception of the passages describing a near-death experience in Chapter 9 and immediately preceding Ramón's suicide at the end of Chapter 13, but often resorts to very brief representations of sequences of thought, many of which rely for their intelligibility on the wider context of the paragraph, chapter or previous chapters.

Between December 2013 and September 2014, I translated this pair of sentences in three different ways.

TT1 (Dec 2013)	TT2 (July 2014)	TT3 (Sept 2014)
To look down implies contempt, to look up, admiration.	To look down is to despise; to look up, to admire.	Superiors despise. Inferiors admire.

The first two attempts ignored sentence boundaries, length and structure, although there was an attempt to maintain the effect of contrast. The emphasis was on meaning rather than effect, which bears out Hervey, Higgins and Haywood's observation that 'as a rule, *semantic* considerations override considerations of *grammatical* translation loss, priority being given almost automatically to the *mot juste* and to constructing grammatically well-formed, idiomatic TL sentences' (2004:63). In this case the foundation of the translation challenge lies in the contrastive linguistics of English and Spanish. In Spanish, the phrases *hacia abajo* and *hacia arriba* are unmarked, and here convey the idea of a person/

The Translation of Punctuation   133

people looking down on, or up to, other people, without the need to resort to an artificial construction.

Since the maintenance of the prepositional phrasing in English was impossible, I had to resort to the strategies of 'circumlocution' (Hervey, Higgins and Haywood 2004:63) and compensation, which involved the substitution of nouns for prepositions and verbs for nouns. In TT3 the focus of my translation, 'Superiors despise. Inferiors admire', also shifted from content to style and effect, grammatical form becoming almost as important as meaning. While clearly involving a degree of translation loss, this version meets several of the translation challenges. It preserves sentence boundaries and length; a two-element symmetrical phrase structure and linguistic rhythm; intrasentential topic order; stark semantic contrast; and syllabic symmetry, with seven syllables in each sentence. Like the Spanish, it is also grammatically unmarked. In other words, it represents an attempt to create an English Benedetti, whose form makes as important a contribution to message and style as semantic content. In her reflections on translating from Spanish into English in *The Subversive Scribe*, Suzanne Jill Levine argues that 'the good translator performs a balancing act... attempting to push language beyond its limits while at the same time maintaining a common ground of dialogue between writer and reader, speaker and listener' (2009:4).

Another example illustrates the ease with which punctuation can be altered to fit target language (TL) conventions, to the detriment of stylistic effect. The three short sentences I have chosen form part of the first of Ramón's childhood flashbacks, in this case recounting a visit to a toyshop with his father, a time when Edmundo was still *Papá* and had not yet become *The Old Man*, in Chapter 2. Ramón has been to the doctor, and his father promised him that if he did not cry when being given an injection, he could choose any toy he wanted from Oddone's toyshop.

Yo no he llorado y Papá cumple la promesa. Lo que más me gusta es la caja de soldados, pero me da mucha lástima que me guste precisamente eso, lo más barato. Qué problema, eh botija, dice Oddone. No me agrada la cara de Oddone. Hago fuerza para que el triciclo me guste más que ninguna otra cosa. Tengo noción exacta de que el triciclo es el juguete más lindo, el que será más codiciado por los otros chicos de mi calle. Lagunillas. Calle Lagunillas. ¿Y?, vuelve a preguntar Papá, esta vez consultando el reloj. Quiero los soldaditos. Lo digo en mi media lengua. Mucho tiempo después pude comprender que tanto Oddone como Papá, por distintas y comprensibles razones, se habían sentido defraudados. Pensalo bien, nene, me advierte Oddone. ¿No te gustaría más el monopatín? Tiene llantas de goma, freno y campanilla. Claro que el monopatín es estupendo, pero a mí me gustan más los soldados de plomo. Déjelo, interviene Papá, él sabe que puede llevarse lo que quiera. Respiro aliviado,

134　*The Translation of Punctuation*

sobre todo porque Oddone, al hacerme propaganda del monopatín, me ha hecho dudar. Y a esta altura yo no quiero dudas; quiero que me sigan gustando los soldados sobre toda otra novedad, por fabulosa que ésta pueda ser. Quiero los soldados, repito con una firmeza que no deja lugar a ninguna esperanza para Oddone. Papá sonríe. Me mira. Esos ojos azules y sin embargo cálidos. Se quita la boquilla antes de decir: Lo que vamos a hacer es llevarnos diez cajas de soldados.

(pp. 47–48)

Key text: the three sentences which are analysed in detail below.

[I didn't cry and Papá kept his promise. What I prefer is the box of soldiers, but it's a real shame I prefer them in particular, the cheapest thing. What a problem, eh son, says Oddone. I don't care for Oddone's face. I make an effort to prefer the tricycle to anything else. I understand clearly that the tricycle is the greatest looking toy, the one which will be most envied by the other boys in my street. Lagunillas. Lagunillas Street. Well? Papá asks again, this time looking at his watch. I want the little soldiers. I say it in my childish way. Much later I came to understand that both Oddone and Papá, for different and understandable reasons, had felt short-changed. Think carefully about it, my lad, Oddone warns me. Wouldn't you prefer the scooter? It's got rubber tyres, a brake and a little bell. Of course the scooter is fantastic, but I prefer the lead soldiers. Don't push him, Papá intervenes, he knows he can have whatever he wants. I breathe a sigh of relief, above all because Oddone, in talking up the scooter, has made me doubt. And at this point I don't want doubts; I want to carry on preferring the soldiers to any other novelty, however amazing it might be. I want the soldiers, I repeat with a confidence that leaves Oddone no room for hope. Papá smiles. Gazes at me. Those eyes blue and yet still warm. He takes the cigarette-holder from his mouth before saying: What we'll do is take ten boxes of soldiers.]

(my translation)

A number of effects are created by the extended use of short sentences. They lend a powerful sense of immediacy to the narrative, especially when combined with the use of the present tense. We witness the scene entirely through the child's eyes, moment by moment. This feels very cinematic, and in the 1984 film version of the novel the camera pans around the toyshop in point of view shots, encouraging us to enter the child's mind. They also create a sense of constant expectation in the reader, encouraging her/him to want to keep reading to find out what comes next.[7] As Wolfgang Iser notes, 'Every sentence contains a preview of the next and forms a kind of viewfinder for what is to come; and this in turn

The Translation of Punctuation   135

changes the 'preview' and so becomes a 'viewfinder' for what has been said' (1972:54). Lastly, they emphasise the importance of each thought and feeling. The space between two full stops intuitively feels like a complete thought, even where it consists of a single word. Full stops can be seen as 'linguistic boundary markers' which 'locate much of the interaction between narrator, author, reader, and translator' (May 1994:136).

The sequence of three very short sentences, highlighted in grey above, illustrates the translation challenges which can arise from this narrative format, as shown by a comparison of my first translation attempt (TT1) with the current version (TT2). This was the first version:

ST: Papá sonríe. Me mira. Esos ojos azules y sin embargo cálidos.
TT1: Papá smiles, and looks at me with those blue, yet warm eyes.

This is clearly a smooth translation which both domesticates and simplifies the ST. It involves sentence structure change; word count, syllable count and pattern change; arguably what Chesterman terms 'interpersonal change' in that 'the degree of emotiveness and involvement' (1997:110) has changed from being a stark montage of three elements of the description of a single action – each of which has significance – into an almost unremarkable aside of little narrative importance. In terms of Berman's 'deforming tendencies' this translation suffers from rationalisation, ennoblement, the destruction of rhythms and the destruction of underlying networks of signification and of linguistic patternings ([1985] 2004:285–297). The point about networks of signification is crucial here, and as so often with translation decisions, context is all important. If we look at the preceding text, clues emerge as to why all three sentences constitute separate but interrelated sets of signifiers, and need to be translated as such.

The young Ramón is in a difficult position. He knows he has to choose a toy, and is under pressure to choose something exotic and flashy from the shopkeeper Oddone because those are the expensive toys, and from Edmundo because he wants Ramón to show off his new toy to his friends:

el que será más codiciado por los otros chicos de mi calle.

[the one which will be most envied by the other boys in my street.]
(my translation)

and to be seen as a wealthy and generous father. Despite all the pressure, Ramón chooses the cheap lead soldiers,[8] at first hesitantly:

Quiero los soldaditos. Lo digo en mi media lengua.

[I want the little soldiers. I say it in my childish way.]
(my translation)

136   *The Translation of Punctuation*

and then decisively:

> Quiero los soldados, repito con una firmeza que no deja lugar a ninguna esperanza para Oddone.

> [I want the soldiers, I repeat with a confidence that leaves Oddone no room for hope.]
> (my translation)

This immediately precedes the three sentences under consideration and casts light on all three.

1   'Papá sonríe.' [Papá smiles.] This could well be a combination of normal parental affection, and pride because his son has stood up to the pressure from the two adults and stuck to his choice. The diminutive *soldaditos* used when Ramón first chooses has been replaced by the more adult *soldados* when he restates it.
2   'Me mira.' [Gazes at me.] This could well indicate that Edmundo is appraising his son and his decision, which brings him a mixture of pride and frustration:

> Mucho tiempo después pude comprender que tanto Oddone como Papá, por distintas y comprensibles razones, se habían sentido defraudados.

> [Much later I came to understand that both Oddone and Papá, for different and understandable reasons, had felt short-changed.]
> (my translation)

3   'Esos ojos azules y sin embargo cálidos.' [Those eyes blue and yet still warm.] (my translation). What is marked here is the separation of this clause, which would normally follow on – with the addition of the connective *con* – directly from *Me mira*, and its conversion into a separate sentence. This separation serves to highlight both the act of gazing and the nature of the gaze. *Ojos azules* is not simply a description of eye colour, it is often used in Latin America to refer to a gringo – usually a white man from the US – and also to someone who is not of indigenous descent. Many Latin Americans had, and still have, very mixed feelings about gringos. On the one hand, they represent wealth and power, to be emulated and envied, and even befriended in the hope of receiving money and favours. On the other, their historical behaviour towards the continent has amply demonstrated a range of very negative qualities – arrogance, greed, hypocrisy, cruelty and callousness. Edmundo will be portrayed as possessing all these qualities. Blue is often associated with coolness or coldness, and I would suggest that this is an important part of the phrase's significance. Seen in this light, the phrase becomes a highly

The Translation of Punctuation 137

compressed expression which manages to convey Edmundo's mixed emotions about his son's decision, and also a fundamental aspect of his character – his coldness, which in this instance is tempered by warmth, since for Ramón Edmundo is still *Papá* and has not yet become *el Viejo*.

Before moving on to my current translation of these sentences, I would like to note that the 1983 French translation of *Gracias por el Fuego* also amalgamates all three sentences:

Papa sourit et pose sur moi son regard bleu mais tendre.

(Benedetti 1983:40)

[Papa smiles and fixes me with his blue but tender eyes.]

(my translation)

This is not an isolated example of the altering of sentence boundaries by both merging and splitting which appears in the French version, and supports May's observation that 'translators take the liberty of changing sentence boundaries as a prerogative of their craft' (1994:129). The foregoing analysis of the importance and effect of the three separate sentences has led me to revise my initial translation, which now reads:

ST: Papá sonríe. Me mira. Esos ojos azules y sin embargo cálidos.
TT2: Papá smiles. Gazes at me. Those eyes blue and yet still warm.

This version retains key ST features – sentence structure, word count (13 as opposed to 12), syntactic structure (in sentences [1] and [3]) and word balance in sentence [3] (two phrases of three words balanced around the conjunction 'and'). The tendency to amalgamate sentences and include the subject of the verb *gazes* has been resisted, producing a starker, but more camera-like sequence of sentences as images. Spanish is a 'pro-drop' language (Pešková 2013:117), where the subject is often included in the verb form, but English is not, and it is unusual for this to occur. The word order has undergone an inevitable structural change in sentence [2] because English can hardly ever start a sentence with an object pronoun followed by a verb. What emerges from the translation of this sequence of three sentences, and the previous pair of sentences, is that for the creation of an English Benedetti, English has on occasion to be placed under strain in the service of stylistic effect.

5.3 Long Sentences: ST Style and TL Conventions

The quantitative analysis of sentence length revealed not only the dominance of short sentences, but also highlighted the existence of 30 much longer sentences of between 101 and 713 words. These constitute a mere 0.5% of the total of 6,475 in the novel, but they stand in very marked contrast to the dominant short sentences, and prompted closer examination. Figure 5.3 shows the sentence length distribution within this group of 30.

This shows the dominance of sentences between 101 and 150 words (66%) and the existence of six very long sentences of over 300 words. Quantitative analysis also revealed the location of these sentences, and I analysed the contexts in which they occurred, to see if they contained any common themes, and had particular narrative significance. This involved undertaking a qualitative analysis, a summary of whose key features is shown in *Tables 5.3* and *5.4*.

All three of these chapters have particular narrative significance and constitute the three longest chapters in the novel. In Chapter 9 Ramón reflects on death – that of Sr. Ríos whom he admires for being able to meet certain death from cancer with equanimity; his own near-death experience on the railway as a young man, brought about by a combination of bad luck and carelessness; and the realisation that the only way out of his own existential crisis is to bring about Edmundo's death. In Chapter 10, Ramón reviews his life and has conversations with a wider range of characters than at any other point. He also continues to ruminate on death at length, both the putative death of his father and that of Señor Ríos. Chapter 13 describes his last day alive and his suicide, and represents the peak of sustained emotional intensity in the novel. In many ways it acts as a summary of the novel, its themes and message.

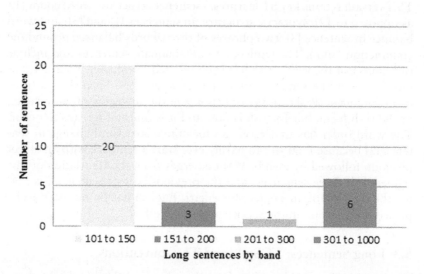

Figure 5.3 Distribution of the sentences of 101 words or more in *Gracias por el Fuego*.

Table 5.3 Occurrences of the 30 sentences of 101 words or more in *Gracias por el Fuego* shown in narrative and chapter context

Chapter number	No. per chapter	Length, in order of occurrence	Narrative Format and Context
4	1	148	**Interior monologue (IM):** Ramón is admiring the courage of the trade union leader who has stood up to his father, something he cannot do.
7	5	101, 115, 105, 101, 101	**Free indirect speech (FID):** Gloria is reflecting on her life as Edmundo's mistress, her possibly misplaced faithfulness to him, and what life might have been like had she married and had children like her sister, Berta.
9	6	103, 119, 713, 146, 132, 131	The first three **(IM)** relate to Ramón's reflections on death, including an account of a near-death experience. Numbers 4 and 5 (Dialogue) form part of his father's lecture to him when he goes to warn him that a journalist has damaging information about his (Edmundo's) dirty dealings. Number 6 shows Ramón reflecting on his appreciation of creature comforts.
10	7	314, 133, 125, 128, 161, 103, 140	**IM:** The first six are reflections by Ramón. The first four are about his time as a young man in Buenos Aires, and describe emotionally intense experiences of joy, humiliation, sexual attraction, humour and friendship. The other two are about, respectively, Montevidean middle-class pretentiousness; and how gambling can ruin someone's life. The final one is a love poem, written by a childhood friend, which Ramón has memorised and now uses to think of Dolores.
11	2	468, 512	**IM:** The first relates how Dolly informs Ramón that she has decided to sleep with him, just once; the second is after this has happened, and Ramón is reflecting on sex and death while she lies asleep beside him.
13	7	103, 141, 400, 113, 182, 297, 152	**IM:** The first four sentences come very close together, and form a sequence of reflections on the past and future by Ramón on the day he has chosen for the killing of his father.
14	1	129	**IM:** This comes near the end of Dolly's interior monologue chapter, in which she reflects on if and how she will be able to carry on with her life after Ramón's suicide.
15	1	113	**FID:** This comes on the penultimate page of the novel, and is Gloria's realisation that she needs a loving man, not one who treats her like a piece of furniture.

number: the five longest sentences.
Of the 30 sentences, 20 occur in only three chapters: 9, 10 and 13.

140   *The Translation of Punctuation*

Table 5.4 Summary of long sentences in Chapters 9, 10 and 13 of *Gracias por el Fuego*

Chapter	Sentences of 101 words or more	Sentences in chapter	Words in chapter	Av. sentence length
9	6	824	11,094	13.5
10	7	994	11,697	11.8
13	7	707	9,808	13.8

The 30 sentences all relate to three characters, Ramón accounting for 20 of them. Twenty-two occur as part of interior monologues: 21 of Ramón's and 1 of Dolly's; 2 occur in dialogue, spoken by Edmundo to Ramón; and 6 occur as free indirect speech and relate to Gloria. They are therefore predominantly embedded in an interior monologue and deal with a range of negative emotions, including fear, anger, disillusionment, loneliness and resignation. They also contain extended reflections on morality, immorality and sex. But the most recurrent theme is that of death. In contrast to Ramón's often disjointed thoughts, frequently represented by short sentences, the focus on death seems to release a flow of ideas and images, rambling but connected, which require the space of long sentences for their expression.

In assessing the stylistic function and significance of long sentences in the novel it is important to note that they are marked in the original Spanish. In Irizarry's corpus, for example, the longest sentence contains 245 words (1990:272).[9] *Gracias por el Fuego* features 6 sentences containing over 300 words, the longest totalling 713. Given how different these are from a Spanish sentence norm, it seems reasonable to conclude that Benedetti employed unusual punctuation for a reason. In this section I draw on the work of Rachel May (1994, 1997) to arrive at an interpretation of Benedetti's use of long sentences, which informs my translation approach to them.

My starting point is her simple observation that 'long sentences can produce a very different effect than short ones' (1994:122). Long sentences typically retain a wider, 'global' feel of uniting a series of disparate ideas or a sequence of actions or events; whereas short ones, as we saw earlier, often foreground a succession of discrete ideas or steps in a process and are held together by the larger grammatical unit of the paragraph. In both cases, May argues, 'one thing a sentence does is break up the narrative into manageable pieces, both for the reader and the translator' (1994:133). She goes on to suggest that

> there is no conclusive proof that readers always pay attention to sentence boundaries in making sense of a piece of writing... There is, however, experimental evidence for the sentence as the "unit of decoding", with the reader processing entire sentences at once. Thus

The Translation of Punctuation 141

longer sentences are more difficult to process, since the reader must keep the early parts of the sentence in mind... until all the information, the "message as a whole", is received.

(ibid: 133–134)

The overall effect of long sentences on the reader is often to speed up the pace of reading, because the gaps between full stops are much greater, but as noted above this longer gap may require more retentive mental effort on the reader's part. *Gracias por el Fuego* is a psychological novel, whose dominant narrative format is the interior monologue. Long sentences are largely used to represent the flow of thoughts, emotions and sensations, sometimes in a clear and focused way and sometimes in a disorganised fashion. These differences are reflected in different kinds of sentence structure, and in particular in the ways in which clauses are linked and punctuation is used, as the following examples will demonstrate.

In Chapter 11 Benedetti produces a list as part of a two-page sentence, in this case of the types and occupations of women who have gone to a rented flat to have sex with one of three men who use it for this purpose:

Donde se han tendido y abierto de piernas tantas secretarias, actrices, modelos, cajeras, pitucas, viuditas, manicuras, locutoras, bachilleras, azafatas, nínfulas, turistas, maestras de primer grado, feligresas, nadadoras, poetisas, escribanas, taquígrafas, bailarinas, profesoras de corte y confección, morfinómanas, ex suicidas, ascensoristas, dueñas de *boutiques*, presidentas de comités, esposas de diputados, vendedoras de calzoncillos, lectoras de Henry Miller, postulantes a Miss Uruguay, *teenagers* del Crandon, *jeunes filles* de la Alliance

(pp. 237–238)

[Here where so many so many secretaries, actresses, models, cashiers, snobs, widows, manicurists, presenters, bluestockings, air hostesses, nymphettes, tourists, first grade teachers, parishioners, swimmers, poetesses, notaries, typists, ballerinas, dressmaking teachers, morphine addicts, ex-suicides, lift attendants, owners of *boutiques*, chairs of committees, wives of MPs, sellers of underpants, readers of Henry Miller, Miss Uruguay contestants, *teenagers* from Crandon, *jeunes filles* from the Alliance have lain down and opened their legs]

(my translation)

The hyperbolic nature of this long, comma-separated list creates its humour and also highlights another of Benedetti's stylistic traits, namely the heavy use of commas. This is particularly noticeable in the way they

142   *The Translation of Punctuation*

Table 5.5 Raw, normalised and average frequency analysis of commas in
Gracias por el Fuego and four major Boom novels

Title	Word total	Commas: raw frequency	Normalised frequency (per 1,000 words)	Average frequency
Gracias por el Fuego	76,442	6,968	91.15	1 per 11.0 words
La Muerte de Artemio Cruz	95,569	7,768	81.28	1 per 12.3 words
Rayuela	172,818	13,552	78.40	1 per 12.7 words
La Ciudad y los Perros	128,936	9,848	76.37	1 per 13.1 words
Cien Años de Soledad	137,918	8,851	64.17	1 per 15.6 words

are used to segment long sentences (in conjunction with semicolons) and
also to structure lists. The use of lists occurs throughout the novel, the
overall effect being to ram home the point being made and often to add
humour. The results from a comparison of Benedetti's use of commas in
Gracias por el Fuego with the same four Boom novels already used for
stylistic reference, set out in *Table 5.5*, suggest that Benedetti's use of
commas is distinctive, and that consequently this feature of punctuation
needs to be treated with care in translation.

The second example is taken from Ramón's final interior monologue
in Chapter 13, in which he realises that since he cannot go through with
Edmundo's murder, suicide would be an alternative solution to all his
problems.

> caer por ejemplo entre el plátano robusto y el otro raquítico a medio
> metro de los policías que vigilan la entrada del diario para que los
> inexistentes conspiradores no se arrimen en medio de todo sería una
> solución lo extraño es que no se me haya ocurrido antes o quizá
> estuvo siempre en el fondo de mis falsos proyectos
> eh eh y si me estrellara eh la idea empieza a tentarme y esto a lo
> mejor es peligroso porque evidentemente sería una solución no ver
> nunca más la cara del Viejo borrar la imagen de mi retina mediante
> el procedimiento de convertir en nada mi retina no ver más mi pro-
> pia cara en el espejo no recordar mi cadena de derrotas mediante el
> procedimiento de convertir en nada mi memoria no reprocharme la
> aceptación de la plata del Viejo no ser consciente de que Larralde tuvo
> el coraje que a mí me falta no sentir nunca más nostalgia de Dolores
> mediante el procedimiento de convertir en nada mi nostalgia no tem-
> blar de pánico si algo empieza a triturar suavemente mi riñón no
> retener el vómito cada vez que veo a los andrajosos votar por los mil-
> lonarios no inmovilizarme en el insomnio fulminado por la repentina

The Translation of Punctuation   143

conciencia de que mis decisiones están para siempre enajenadas no estar obligado a sonreír a los candidatos a turistas y a su alma de picnic no acostarme junto a Susana y sentirla increíblemente remota ajena indiferente no pensar en la muerte de Mamá con sus uñas clavadas en mi mejilla no escuchar que el Viejo me diga torpe más que torpe no volver a proyectar nunca más ni para mí ni para nadie aquella película de terror y de asco con la voz de Mamá diciendo no pueeedo no llorar en la noche ni sentirme un imbécil no no no cada vez más no tal vez sería una solución o por lo menos un modo de negar esta pobre mugre que soy este sofocante fracaso en que he venido a parar.

(pp. 288–289)

[to fall for instance between the strong plane tree and the other stunted one half a metre from the policemen who guard the entrance to the newspaper so that the non-existent conspirators don't get in would be one solution the strange thing is that it hasn't occurred to me before or maybe it was always lurking behind my false projects

eh eh and what if I smashed myself to pieces eh the idea begins to tempt me and this is probably dangerous because clearly it would be a solution never to see The Old Man's face again erase his image from my retina through the act of obliterating my retina not to see my own face in the mirror not to remember my series of defeats through the act of obliterating my memory not to reproach myself for accepting The Old Man's money not to be aware that Larralde had the courage that I lack never again to feel nostalgia for Dolores through the act of obliterating my nostalgia not to tremble in panic if something starts to tighten my kidney gently not to stop myself being sick every time I see the tatterdemalions vote for millionaires not to paralyse myself in insomnia struck down by the sudden awareness that my decisions are forever alienated not to be forced to smile at the would-be tourists and their picnic souls not to sleep next to Susana and feel her incredibly remote estranged indifferent not to think about the death of Mamá with her fingernails sunk into my cheeks not to listen to The Old Man call me stupid more than stupid not to show ever again for myself nor for anyone else that disgusting horror movie with the voice of Mamá saying I caaan't not to cry during the night nor feel silly no no no ever more no perhaps it would be a solution or at least a way of disowning this poor wretch that I am this suffocating failure that I've become]

(my translation)

This Joycean passage is almost punctuation-free. However, paragraph separation has been retained through the use of white space. In a stream-of-consciousness passage paragraphs are unusual, and here it is clear that each paragraph contains thoughts linked to a particular theme.

144   *The Translation of Punctuation*

The first spells out the idea of jumping to the pavement below as a solution; the second lists all the things from which suicide would free him forever. The fact that paragraph markers are the only form of punctuation used here lends some support to the suggestion, put forward by Mark Algee-Hewitt, Ryan Heuser and Franco Moretti in their study of the function of the paragraph in narrative, that 'paragraphs are probably the best starting point [for a search for themes]: by concentrating thematic material within their limited space, they act as *the textual habitat of themes*' (2015:8, emphasis in original).

These examples demonstrate the creative use of punctuation in long sentences to help shape reader response. It is worth remembering, as Charles Lock reminds us, that white spaces between words only emerged in the West in the ninth century, 'opening up gaps between words to ease their reading in silence', as opposed to being used as an aid to reading a text aloud, and that 'punctuation holds words apart, and it holds the page together' (Lock 2016:170). However, punctuation use is in many cases a culture-specific phenomenon, and so deep-rooted and unconscious that when it comes to translation the tendency to normalise in accordance with TL conventions is marked. In the case of the translation of long sentences into English, this manifests itself as the tendency to break them up.

The Translation Challenges of Long Sentences

The fact that punctuation is deeply internalised and often language-specific, and that the translator is working with two languages, implies, as May suggests, 'a dichotomy between the translator-as-reader (who is extracting essential information from a sentence) and the translator-as-writer (who is exercising a perceived liberty with regard to punctuation)' (1994:121). Mona Baker argues that:

> English generally prefers to present information in relatively small chunks and to signal the relationship between these chunks in unambiguous ways, using a wide variety of conjunctions to mark semantic relations between clauses, sentences and paragraphs... English also relies on a highly developed punctuation system to signal breaks and relations between chunks of information.
>
> (2011:202)

This suggests a possible explanation for the fact that English translators often break up long sentences into what they see, consciously or otherwise, as manageable chunks. Referring to Russian translators of Faulkner and Woolf, May comments that

> the changes that the translators impose on punctuation have a regular, even predictable quality that suggests an overall "editorial"

The Translation of Punctuation   145

rather than interpretive or creative approach to this aspect of language. They seem to share a desire to totalize, to reduce language not just to manageable segments... but to something complete and static rather than fluid and open-ended.

(1997:10)

In this connection it is interesting to note that Anthea Bell felt the pressure to do this when translating a nine-page sentence in W. G. Sebald's *Austerlitz*, but resisted it:

In my very first draft I put a full stop about two pages into this passage, and then immediately took it out again; I knew without being told that it must remain one long, continuous sentence in English, tumbling clause after tumbling clause, to convey the mindless, busy haste of the régime in the camp as it is prepared to put on a show of being a happy holiday camp for Jews in order to impress a visiting Red Cross delegation.

(2011:213)

An example from Chapter 10 illustrates the effect of breaking up a long, unpunctuated portion of a sentence. Ramón is recalling a stay in Buenos Aires as a young man, which may well be partly autobiographical, as Benedetti spent two years there, aged 18–20, working as secretary to Raumsol, the leader of the *Escuela Logosófica* (Paoletti 1995:42–50). Here he describes an experience of people-watching, which is recounted with irony and humour. Set out below are the ST, the French translation and my translation, which adopt contrasting strategies.

ST (p. 222)	Benedetti (1983:181)	Thanks for the Light (unpublished)
Sí, era lindo ver desde la plaza San Martín, junto a la sombra filosa del Cavanagh, aquellos mateos con parejitas provincianas, y en el banco de al lado, el cochecito con vagidos junto a la niñera coruñesa, y el policía de cara aindiada junto a la niñera, sonriéndose ambos con la preciosa, irrecuperable timidez de los seres	Oui, c'etait beau de voir les fiacres avec les couples, place San Martín, et **je me souviens que** sur le banc d'à côté il y avait une nourrice espagnole tenant un enfant qui babillait, un policier aux traits indiens était resté près d'elle et **lui souriait** avec cette merveilleuse et inestimable **naïveté** des primitifs qui, pour parvenir à l'amour, n'ont pas besoin	True, it was lovely to see, from the plaza San Martín, <u>next to the pointed shadow of the Cavanagh building,</u> those cabs with provincial couples, and on the next bench along, <u>the little pram</u> with crying coming from it beside the nanny from <u>Coruña</u>, and the policeman with indian features next to the nanny, both smiling with

(Continued)

146 *The Translation of Punctuation*

ST (p. 222)	Benedetti (1983:181)	*Thanks for the Light (unpublished)*
primitivos, que para llegar al sexo no precisan dar, como nosotros, clase media frustrada y pretenciosa, tantos rodeos previos por zonas en que moran la religión y Jean-Paul Sartre y la carestía de la vida y el teatro independiente y vio el último asalto y su cara me resulta conocida y dónde pasará Carnaval y Turismo y los partidos tradicionales están caducos y hace años que no había un verano tan caluroso y esto del dólar siempre a once es una situación artificial e insostenible y viaja usted siempre en este trole y me daría su teléfono y me siento tan cómodo hablando contigo.	comme nous, classe moyenne frustrée et prétentieuse, de tant de détours préalables par la religion, Jean-Paul Sartre, le coût de la vie, le théâtre d'avant-garde, vous avez vu le dernier hold-up, votre visage ne m'est pas inconnu, où partez-vous à **Pâques, et à Noël**, les partis traditionnels sont périmés, cela fait des années que nous n'avons pas eu été si chaud, la cote du dollar est maintenue artificiellement, vous prenez toujours cette ligne, pourrais-je avoir votre numéro de téléphone, je me sens si bien en parlant avec toi.	the precious, irrecoverable shyness of primitive beings, who to get sex don't need, like us pretentious and frustrated members of the middle class, to go all round the houses <u>by way of the places</u> where religion and Jean-Paul Sartre <u>dwell</u> and the lack of life and the avant-garde theatre and did you see the most recent assault and I know your face from somewhere and where will you spend the Carnival season and <u>Easter</u> and the traditional parties are outdated and it's been years since we've had such a hot summer and this business of the dollar always being worth eleven is an artificial <u>and unsustainable</u> situation and do you always travel on this trolley and would you give me your 'phone number and I feel so relaxed talking to you'.

<u>text</u>: words in the ST which have been omitted in the French translation.
text: words which have been inserted in the French translation which are not in the ST.
text: the section of the ST which is unpunctuated.
,: commas which have been inserted in the French translation which are not in the ST.

This sentence of 161 words begins as a comma-separated description of a scene, but soon develops into a social commentary which takes up the whole of the second half of the sentence (88 words) and is devoid of punctuation. Here the elaborate circumlocutions of the middle-class sexual meeting ritual are parodied in a single unsegmented passage, where a catalogue of clichéd conversational gambits is stitched together with 11 instances of the connective *y*. The comic

The Translation of Punctuation 147

effect is heightened by the hyperbolic use of examples and the lack of any pause between them until the end of the sentence is reached. It also echoes a technique used by Virginia Woolf and William Faulkner, whereby a short sentence is followed by a long, often sparsely punctuated one:

> Both Faulkner and Woolf favour contrasts between a very short sentence, usually a simple statement of fact or comment from a character, followed by an extremely long, complex sentence... When Faulkner produces a long sentence, it is less a matter of interplay among different voices than a single character's ruminations on a complex theme, with sub-thoughts started but not always finished, pros and cons and ancillary considerations all strung together... The effect of Faulkner's English syntax... is to make the reader suspend logic and enter into the passions or obsessions of the character whose viewpoint the sentence reflects. The period mark comes like a deep breath after a long outpouring of feelings, and it gives the reader the welcome opportunity to assemble and make sense of all that came before.
>
> (May 1997:5–7)

This pattern is used on several occasions in the novel. What is striking here is the difference in approach between the English and French versions. While the English translation attempts to stick closely to the style and content of the ST, preserving the punctuation intact, the French version is much freer in a number of ways. For reasons which are not immediately obvious it omits a number of words and phrases altogether (underlined in the English version). The meaning of some words is altered, for example the Spanish *timidez* becomes *naïveté*. Some phrases which are not in the ST are inserted, such as *je me souviens que* (I remember that). Lastly, in the unpunctuated second half of the sentence, the French version inserts no less than 13 commas, the effect of which (on me at least) is to break up the long list of clichéd questions and comments, and thus rob them of a good deal of their comic force.

Even at the level of a single long sentence visualisation can help us to see the differences between the three versions. Without various forms of highlighting these differences would be much harder to pick out. In the screenshot the occurrences of the words *y*, *et* and *and* are shown, highlighting the fact that in the French version there are only 5 instances of this connective, whereas in the Spanish there are 16 and in the English there are 17. In the French version commas have replaced all the connectives in the second half of the sentence, as shown in Figure 5.4.

148 *The Translation of Punctuation*

Si, era lindo ver desde la plaza San Martín, junto a la sombra filosa del Cavanagh, aquellos mateos con parejitas provincianas, █ en el banco de al lado, el cochecito con vagidos junto a la niñera coruñesa, █ el policía de cara aindiada junto a la niñera, sonriéndose ambos con la preciosa, irrecuperable timidez de los seres primitivos, que para llegar al sexo no precisan dar, como nosotros, clase media frustrada █ pretenciosa, tantos rodeos previos por zonas en que moran la religión █ Jean-Paul Sartre █ la carestía de la vida █ el teatro independiente █ vio el último asalto █ su cara me resulta conocida █ dónde pasará Carnaval █ Turismo █ los partidos tradicionales están caducos █ hace años que no había un verano tan caluroso █ esto el dólar siempre a once es una situación artificial █ insostenible █ viaja usted siempre en este trole █ me daría su teléfono y me siento tan cómodo hablando contigo.	Oui, c'était beau de voir les fiacres avec les couples, place San Martín, █ je me souviens que sur le banc d'à côté il y avait une nourrice espagnole tenant un enfant qui babillait, un policier aux traits indiens était resté près d'elle █ lui souriait avec cette merveilleuse █ inestimable naïveté des primitifs qui, pour parvenir à l'amour, n'ont pas besoin comme nous, classe moyenne frustrée █ prétentieuse, de tant de détours préalables par la religion, Jean-Paul Sartre, le coût de la vie, le théâtre d'avant-garde, vous avez vu le dernier hold-up, votre visage ne m'est pas inconnu, où partez-vous à Pâques, █ à Noël, les partis traditionnels sont périmés, cela fait des années que nous n'avons pas eu été si chaud, la cote du dollar est maintenue artificiellement, vous prenez toujours cette ligne, pourrais-je avoir votre numéro de téléphone, je me sens si bien en parlant avec toi.	True, it was lovely to see, from the plaza San Martín, next to the pointed shadow of the Cavanagh building, those cabs with provincial couples, █ on the next bench along, the little pram with crying coming from it beside the nanny from Coruña, █ the policeman with indian features next to the nanny, both smiling with the precious, irrecoverable shyness of primitive beings, who to get sex don't need, like us pretentious and frustrated members of the middle class, to go all round the houses by way of the places where religion █ Jean-Paul Sartre dwell █ the lack of life █ the avant-garde theatre █ did you see the most recent assault █ I know your face from somewhere █ where will you spend the Carnival season █ Tourism █ the traditional parties are outdated █ it's been years since we've had such a hot summer █ this business of the dollar always being worth eleven is an artificial and unsustainable situation █ do you always travel on this trolley █ would you give me your 'phone number █ I feel so relaxed talking to you.

Figure 5.4 Graphic representation of the distribution of *y*, *et* and *and* in Microsoft Word 2010.

This visualisation was created in Microsoft Word and then reduced in scale to give a clear visual contrast between the three versions. It shows not only what is there in the text, but in the case of the French version, what is *not* there. The free, web-based set of visualisation and text-analytic tools, Voyant Tools,[10] can display the frequency and distribution of occurrence of selected words in a text in chart form. The frequency and distribution of *y*, *et* and *and* are shown in turn in Figure 5.5.

The same tools could be used to display the frequency and distribution of words and phrases across individual chapters and the novel as a whole, and this can be very useful when comparing ST and draft translation, as the next chapter shows.

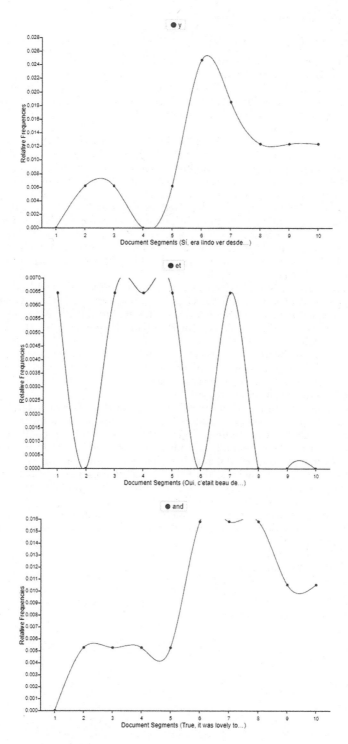

Figure 5.5 Voyant Tools representation of the frequency and distribution of *y*, *et* and *and*.

150 *The Translation of Punctuation*

Notes

1 Quoted in the revised third edition of *The New Fowler's Modern English Usage* (Burchill 1998:701).

2 Halliday, M. (1971) 'Linguistic Function and Literary Style: An Inquiry into the Language of William Golding's *The Inheritors*', in Seymour Chatman, ed., *Literary Style: A Symposium*, London & New York: Oxford University Press, pp. 330–365.

3 reg="(?<=[.?!])\s*(([^ \t\n\x0B\f\r?!.]+\s+){0,15}[^ \t\n\x0B\f\r?!.]+)[.?!]". This looks for a .,? or ! followed by 0 to 15 tokens followed by a .,? or !. The match is on the sentences excluding the starting., ? or ! This assumes that sentences end with a full stop, an exclamation mark or a question mark, and that these types do not occur within a sentence, which, while generally true, is a simplification. I also deducted the very small number of ellipses and abbreviations which use a 'full stop', such as Dr. and etc., in the novel.

4 Source: www.corpusdelespanol.org/x.asp [accessed 1 July 2015]. The search methodology involved running searches for full stops (296,174), question marks (22,943) and exclamation marks (12,067), totalling them (331,184) and then deducting ellipses (0).

5 Ayala, Azorín, Barea, Baroja, Cela, Chacel, Cunquiero, Delibes, Dieste, Espina, Galvarriato, Gironella, Gz.de la Serna, Serna, Gz. Ojea, Goytisolo, Granell, Laforet, Marsé, Martín Gaite, Matute, Miró, Pz. de Ayala, Quiroga, Sz. Ferlosio, Sender, Solana, Torrente-Ball, Unamuno, Valle-Inclán and Zunzunegui.

6 The query is: [word="tan"][tag="A.*"], which looks for the word 'tan' immediately followed by any adjective (Sketch Engine automatically tags uploaded corpora for parts of speech by language and provides a full list of the appropriate tags for all of these).

7 This is not an entirely subjective assessment of the effect of style. A recent study of reader physical responses (pupillary dilation) to suspense in literature concludes 'our findings suggest that changes of the pupil diameter provide a reliable physiological indicator of suspense, which drives recipients' attention and modulates their emotional engagement' (Riese et al. 2014:228). In other words, the field of cognitive narratology is beginning to develop ways of measuring reader response to literature via neuroscience, rather than relying entirely on self-reporting.

8 According to his biographers (Paoletti 1995) (Campanella 2009) lead soldiers were Benedetti's favourite, and practically only, toy when he was very young.

9 José Gutierrez Solana.

10 https://voyant-tools.org/

6 Applying the Methodology (Part 3)

Comparing Source Text and Draft Translation

The central argument of this chapter is that the same close and distant reading (CDR) methodology which was used to analyse the source text can also be used to compare source text (ST) and draft translation, and in so doing can help the translator to assess the extent to which they have achieved the translation goals they established for themselves and/ or which were set by the publisher or other relevant party. In the case of *Gracias por el Fuego* my translation approach was a broadly foreignising one, as set out in Chapter 3, and the goal I set myself was to stick very closely to Benedetti's style in an attempt to achieve an equivalence of stylistic effect in the translation as far as possible. Specifically, this involved an attempt to preserve sentence length and structure where this was stylistically important. CDR analysis revealed that this principally involved short sentences of 4–10 words – which posed particular translation challenges due to their syntactically compressed nature – and long sentences of over 100 words, where the heavy use of commas and the reader effort required to digest very long sequences of clauses made it tempting to break the sentences up into smaller chunks.

The four sections of the chapter deal with different ways of comparing ST and draft TT (target text). Between them they illustrate how the CDR approach allows, and indeed encourages, a translator to make the unit of translation being considered anything from a single word to the text as a whole, and to change this unit frequently in the course of a translation. Section 6.1 looks at the use of 'standard' CDR analyses, as detailed in Chapter 2, and comprises a comparison of word and sentence count, average sentence length, hapax words and lemmas, and two measures of lexical diversity. It also deals with the process of aligning the ST and TT and converting them into a searchable parallel corpus. Section 6.2 compares sentence length and structure, mirroring the analysis in Chapter 5. Where one chapter was found to have a greater observed-than-expected word count and average sentence length, it is investigated in detail and a suggested explanation put forward, involving two factors – involuntary explicitation and the contrastive linguistics of Spanish and English. Section 6.3 considers the way that repetitions were dealt with, focusing on examples of both frequent and infrequent repetition, showing how thematically important but widely distributed repetitions can easily be missed without

152   Comparing ST and Draft Translation

the aid of distant reading. Finally, Section 6.4 looks at the often-overlooked use of high-frequency function words such as *and*, showing how their patterns of usage can be stylistically important and how changing them in translation can affect the text's impact on the reader.

6.1 Comparison Using Standard CDR Analyses

In Section 6.2 of Chapter 2, I outlined five sets of potentially standard CDR analyses that could be routinely used to analyse a ST prior to translation. These were corpus summaries, word lists, keyword lists, n-grams and lexical richness. By performing the same analyses on the draft translation, it is in principle possible to assess within limits, since no two languages map onto each other directly, the extent to which certain structural elements of style have been recreated. *Table 6.1* shows a comparison of *Gracias por el Fuego* and my draft translation (2014–2015) using a number of different statistical measures drawn from corpus summaries and word lists.

Using two separate MS Word documents – the ST and the TT – it took less than 15 minutes to produce these results in Sketch Engine, including uploading the documents. The comparison of these structural linguistic features of style prompts two conclusions. First, that broadly speaking word count, sentence count and average sentence length have all been preserved in the translation. This is in line with the findings of Blum-Kulka (1986), Baker (1993) and Frankenberg-Garcia (2009) that translations tend to be more explicit than their STs, and as a consequence they are often, but not always, longer. Some research suggests that this is common (Aranda 2007:3) and in a detailed study of a corpus of Portuguese-English and English-Portuguese literary translations, Frankenberg-Garcia found that 'the translations contained on average 5% more words than the source texts' (2009:12). I have therefore used 5% as an approximate

Table 6.1 Standard CDR statistical comparisons of ST and draft TT

Measure	ST	Draft TT	% difference	Greater observed-than-expected difference?
Word count	76,442	80,600	+ 5.4	No
Sentence count	6,475	6,439	– 0.5	No
Average sentence length	11.8	12.5	+ 5.9	No
Type-token ratio*	14.7%	10.4%	– 29.2	Yes
Hapax legomena	6,436	4,602	– 28.5	Yes
Hapax legomena ÷ word count	8.4%	5.3%	– 36.9	Yes
Hapax lemmas	3,277	3,151	– 3.8	No
Hapax lemmas ÷ total lemmas	48.0%	47.7%	– 0.6	No

* (Number of types ÷ number of tokens) × 100.

figure for 'expected' increase in length, and on this basis the increased length of my translation does not seem greater than expected. Reasons advanced for this phenomenon include obligatory and what Frankenberg-Garcia (2009) calls 'voluntary' or translator-determined, explicitation, in other words making something explicit in the TT which is only implicit in the ST, where neither grammatical nor syntactical considerations demand it. In the case of Spanish to English translation there is also the fact that Spanish is a pro-drop language (see Section 6.2 for further details of both factors), whereas English only infrequently allows for the subject of a verb to be included in it. The value of this kind of simple statistical analysis is that as the translator I now *know*, rather than just think or hope, that I have broadly achieved the goal of maintaining sentence length in translation (for a more detailed analysis of this see Section 6.2).

The second conclusion is that the translation appears to exhibit a lower degree of lexical diversity than the original, as measured by the type-token ratio (TTR) and the number of hapax legomena expressed as a percentage of total word count. When hapax lemmas are divided by total lemmas, however, there is virtually no difference between the ST and TT. Using lemmas rather than words as a basis of comparison, as explained in Chapter 2, is more representative of real lexical variety, since it takes account of the inflected nature of Spanish which would otherwise artificially inflate the number of different words.

The apparent discrepancy between ST and TT indicated by two statistical measures should not, however, be ignored. Some possible explanations for this include the already mentioned inflected nature of Spanish, and English polysemy in relation to Spanish (Prior, MacWhinney and Kroll 2007). For example, the English verb *to know* can be expressed in Spanish as either *saber* or *conocer*, and the verb *to be* can be either *ser* or *estar*, depending on context. There is also, however, the question of translator choice, and one implication of the comparison is that care should be taken when revising the draft to try to use words and phrases that match the degree of lexical diversity present in the original. It would, for example, be easy to see whether a word that was unique in the ST had been translated by a word that was unique in the TT, and if not, whether there was a case for reconsidering the translation. In this regard, close reading is significantly enhanced by the use of one CDR technique in particular, the creation of a searchable parallel corpus of the ST and TT in Sketch Engine.

Creating and Using a Parallel Corpus

The free, open-source software LF Aligner[1] will create an aligned corpus from an ST and draft TT saved in a variety of file formats, allowing the user to segment at the sentence or paragraph level. While the automated segmentation process often produces good results, the resulting alignment still needs to be checked visually and manually adjusted where necessary by splitting or merging segments, or shifting them up or down. The LF Aligner workspace screen is shown in Figure 6.1.

154 *Comparing ST and Draft Translation*

7½ LF Alignment Editor 1.5 - aligned_Gracias por el Fuego - complete ST-GpF - Complete TT, 2014-2015 (first draft).txt

File Edit Help

5558	Sólo quisiera desprenderme del odio, en el instante en que apriete el gatillo, no antes.	It's just that I would like to rid myself of the hate, at the moment of squeezing the trigger, not before.
5559	Quisiera que mi crimen se convirtiera en un acto de amor.	I would like my crime to become an act of love.
5560	Matar al Viejo para que resurja Papá, el que me compró en lo de Oddone diez cajas de soldados, el que entendió que yo había visto la muerte de Víctor, el que acudía todas las noches a liberarme de la oscuridad.	To kill The Old Man in order to resurrect Papá, the one who bought me the ten boxes of soldiers at Oddone's, the one who understood that I had witnessed Victor's death, the one who came every night to free me from the darkness.
5561	Ahora el Viejo es tan abyecto que no me deja pensar en Papá, tapa con su presencia odiosa la presencia querida de Papá, desaloja con su espesa prepotencia la sensación de seguridad que Papá me otorgaba.	Now The Old Man is so despicable as to make it impossible to think about Papá, he smothers with his odious presence the beloved presence of Papá, he dislodges with his deep arrogance the sense of security that Papá gave me.

Merge (F1)   Split (F2)   Shift up (F3)   Shift down (F4)

Figure 6.1 The LF Aligner 4.1 workspace.

While this takes some time – the 300 pages of *Gracias por el Fuego* required nearly six hours to check – the procedure only needs to be used once per translation, and within the overall timescale needed to translate a complete novel arguably represents a relatively modest investment of time in exchange for considerable benefits. In addition to ensuring search accuracy in the eventual bilingual corpus, it highlights missing and untranslated sentences: in my case I had omitted to translate ten short sentences. It also shows very clearly where sentences have been split or merged in the translation, affording the translator the opportunity to edit it since text can be edited as well as segments. Furthermore, since the process involves rereading and comparing the texts, albeit fairly quickly, it provides an opportunity to identify any aspects of the translation which might benefit from more in-depth searching and checking.

In Figure 6.1, for example, the verb *otorgaba* appears at the end of the bottom ST segment, where it has been translated as *gave*. *Otorgar* has a range of meanings, which while including the common verb *to give*, often signify a more formal act such as *to confer, to award* or *to bestow*. Given that the lexical diversity comparison already referred to highlighted the potential use of simpler language in the TT, there was a case for revising the translation here and substituting the less common *bestowed* for *gave*, which also fitted the context.

Once the two texts are satisfactorily aligned, they can be saved and exported as a single Translation Memory eXchange(TMX) file to a CAT tool or a TMX viewer such as TMX Editor,[2] or to Sketch Engine where it can quickly be converted into a fully searchable parallel corpus. This means that the actual translation(s) of any word, phrase or group of words can quickly and easily be checked against the original for accuracy, consistency – where appropriate – and various linguistic and stylistic features. Revisions to the translation cannot be made in Sketch Engine, but the results of searches can be saved, downloaded and used to inform changes.

In Section 2.2 of Chapter 2, I referred to my initial translation of the phrase *el Viejo* – used by Ramón to refer to Edmundo – as *Father*, and my subsequent decision to alter this to *The Old Man*. A parallel corpus search revealed that of the 129 occurrences of *el Viejo* in the ST, I had translated 105 as *The Old Man* and 24 as *Father*, due to the fact that the decision to alter the translation of the phrase was made during rather than before the first draft. Figure 6.2 shows how parallel corpus search results are displayed.

The value of the parallel corpus is that it allowed me to find these 24 instances very easily and decide which needed to be revised. In the passages of dialogue where Ramón addresses Edmundo and calls him *Viejo*, the phrase *Old Man* does not work as its connotations are either affectionate or ageist, neither of which fit the context. In those instances, I·have used *Father* or *Sir* in an attempt to convey both distance and lack of affection. Converting a ST and draft TT into a searchable parallel corpus provides the translator with a powerful tool for translation revision and for helping to assess whether specific translation goals have been achieved. It also allows and encourages the translator to move between the micro- and macro-levels of a text since it enables her/him to treat the word, the phrase, the sentence, the paragraph, the chapter or the work as a whole as the relevant unit of translation comparison.

6.2 Comparing Sentence Length

In Chapter 5, I argued that punctuation overall, and sentence length and structure in particular, can be important features of literary style. In relation to *Gracias por el Fuego* I suggested that the dominance of sentences of ten words or less is a distinctive feature and has identifiable effects on the translator-as-reader, which dovetail with the interior monologue narrative format, and which provide a framework for the communication of the novel's message. Similarly, that the small number of sentences containing 101 words or more also make an important stylistic contribution to the novel. My conclusion, therefore, was that sentence length and structure should be generally preserved in the TT because they constitute structural features of style. The CDR approach identified and then analysed the extent, location and effects of both short and long sentences in the ST, and can also be used to analyse the TT to see whether the broad aim of preservation has been achieved.

Comparison acts as an investigative tool, capable of identifying areas of marked difference between ST and TT, and then exploring them at

Figure 6.2 Parallel corpus search results in Sketch Engine.

Comparing ST and Draft Translation 157

different levels of detail from the novel as a whole down to sentences of a particular length in an individual chapter. The aim is to identify and explain any greater observed-than-expected differences, and where appropriate, to revise the translation in line with established translation goals. At the time of writing the only text-analytic software I have been able to find which is available for general use which can display features such as average sentence length as a visualisation is TextDNA.[3] There are, however, some interesting examples of specific research projects which have done this.

In their 2007 article 'Literature Fingerprinting: A New Method of Visual Literary Analysis', for example, Daniel Keim and Daniela Oelke used the *LiteratureVis* software programme to create a display of some key features of a document in the form of a visualisation in which each text block is represented by a coloured square with colour indicating a feature value. Features visualised included frequency of occurrence of function words and parts of speech, average word and sentence length, vocabulary richness as measured by Simpson's Index[4] and hapax legomena. The results for a comparison of average sentence length in corpora of work by Jack London and Mark Twain were displayed as shown in Figure 6.3.

Although their research was monolingual, the authors refer to how their approach could be used when comparing languages: 'Sentence length is an indicator of style that can be used to estimate how good [sic] the rhythm of a text is preserved in a translation of the text' (Ibidem); and how analysis of parts of speech is seen as relevant because 'By this, the degree of formality of a text can be measured or the style of a text can be compared to its translation in another language' (Ibidem). Using visualisation for comparing published translations and their STs, and as a tool for practising translators to use when analysing STs and revising their translations, is a field ripe for development.

Using Computer-Aided Textual Markup and Analysis (CATMA), I analysed the draft translation in exactly the same way as I had analysed the ST. *Table 6.2* shows a comparison of short and long sentences in ST and TT for the novel as a whole. This suggests that while the proportions of sentences of 1–10 words and of 101 words or more have been broadly maintained, there has been a reduction in the number of sentences of 1–6 words.

Table 6.3 shows the average sentence length in ST and draft TT by chapter and the novel as a whole,[5] with the results ranked according to the increase in TT sentence length, with the highest at the top.

As explained in the previous section, my view was that the results suggested that the translation had broadly retained average sentence length. However, the fact that the highest increase in word count (which is shown in *Table 6.4*) and average sentence length both occurred in Chapter 14, suggested the need for further examination of that chapter.

This chapter consists entirely of an interior monologue by Dolly, much of which she addresses to the dead Ramón.

I focused on the very short sentences (six words or less), on the basis that it seemed more likely that I would find explicitation and/or an increase in

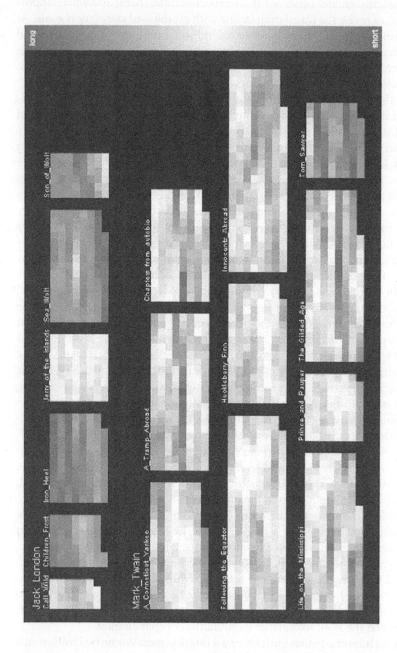

Figure 6.3 Visualisation of the average sentence length of two corpora of books written by Jack London and Mark Twain, using the LiteratureVis programme. (Keim and Oelke 2007:4).

Comparing ST and Draft Translation 159

Table 6.2 Percentages of short and long sentences: ST and draft TT

Sentence length	ST%	Draft TT%
1–6 words	45.3	40.1
1–10 words	65.6	62.3
101 words plus	0.5% (30)*	0.5% (34)

*Note: actual number of sentences.

Table 6.3 Average sentence lengths: ST and draft TT

Chapter	Av. ST sentence length	Av. TT sentence length	TT av. sentence length increase in words
14	**14.7**	**16.3**	**1.6**
11	20.2	21.4	1.2
6	9.3	10.4	1.1
12	12.4	13.5	1.1
5	9.9	11.0	1.1
7	17.9	19.0	1.1
13	13.8	14.8	1.0
4	10.7	11.5	0.8
2	11.3	12.0	0.7
9	13.5	14.0	0.7
15	10.2	10.9	0.7
10	11.8	12.4	0.6
3	6.2	6.8	0.6
8	17.0	17.4	0.4
1	9.1	9.4	0.3
Novel	**11.8**	**12.5**	**0.7**

Top row in **bold:** the chapter with the highest increase in average sentence length.
The overall rise in average sentence length of 0.7 words represents a 5.9% increase.

Table 6.4 Word count: ST and draft TT

Chapter	ST word count	TT word count	Word count increase	% increase (descending)
14	**1,856**	**2,059**	**203**	**10.9**
6	1,396	1,517	121	8.7
3	2,288	2,476	188	8.2
4	8,469	9,080	611	7.2
12	2,315	2,481	166	7.2
5	1,551	1,656	105	6.8
15	2,999	3,202	203	6.8
13	9,808	10,425	617	6.3
2	4,766	5,063	297	6.2
10	11,697	12,356	659	5.6
11	2,750	2,892	142	5.2
7	5,204	5,452	248	4.8
9	11,094	11,580	486	4.4
8	1,842	1,897	55	3.0
1	8,407	8,464	57	0.7
Novel	**76,442**	**80,600**	**4,158**	**5.4**

Top row in **bold:** the chapter with the highest increase in word count.

160 *Comparing ST and Draft Translation*

word count in them, which might have implications for the translation. In the ST there are 50 such sentences, whereas in the draft TT there are only 43, a reduction of 7. I wanted to find out whether I had merged any short sentences or had merely produced longer English sentences in these cases. A comparison of sentence totals in the ST (126) and TT (125) showed a difference of one. On further investigation, I realised that this was due to my simply omitting to translate a single two-word sentence, by mistake, 'Oh, seguir' [Oh, to continue.] (p.285). This meant that sentence totals were actually identical, thus eliminating sentence merging as a possible explanation.

I decided to look at all 50 ST sentences to see how they had been translated. In CATMA I was able to run a search query which extracted all these sentences in the ST and displayed them in order of occurrence in the chapter, together with their left and right contexts, as shown in Figure 6.4.

Using this display as a guide, I highlighted the 50 sentences in my paragraph-aligned translation of Chapter 14 in MS Word,[6] to see how the individual translations matched for length. The results showed that of the 50 sentences, 39 were of 6 words or less in the TT, and 10 slightly longer.[7] I looked at these ten sentences, which are set out in *Table 6.5*, with a comment on the explanation for the increase in length in each case.

In eight out of the ten sentences, the contrastive linguistics of Spanish and English provide an explanation for the small increase in word count. The phenomenon of 'subject-drop', already referred to, occurs in five sentences. The Spanish single-word infinitives and the common *había* accounted for two more sentence increases. I would like to stress here that as a translator I am not aiming at rigid parity of word count, nor judging the 'success' of the translation on this basis. Indeed, in seven out of the ten sentences analysed above, I saw no need to alter the translations, despite their being longer than

Left Context	Keyword	Right Context	Start Poi ▲	End Point
suicidi sonó omicidi timidi.	Cesare Pavese Tonto, tontísimo.	Me hubieras convencido, claro	30	73
Pavese Tonto, tontísimo.	Me hubieras convencido, claro.	Sólo una vez dije Ramón	73	104
debajo de tu lengua.	Ahogada, feliz.	Tonto. Pobrecito. Ahí	169	185
. Ahogada, feliz.	Tonto.	Pobrecito. Ahí, en	185	192
, feliz. Tonto.	Pobrecito.	Ahí, en ti,	192	203
seguida ibas a abrirlos.	Después no.	Alguien los habrá cerrado.	405	417
abrirlos. Después no.	Alguien los habrá cerrado.	Yo no te vi.	417	444
Alguien los habrá cerrado.	Yo no te vi.	Es decir, no vi	444	457
que decían eras tú.	Los ojos, Tus Ojos.	Es todo el recuerdo,	499	519
, o casi todo.	Me mirabas ansioso.	Fue así que empezaste a	553	573
. Me mirabas ansioso.	Fue así que empezaste a convencerme.	Ramón tonto. Viejito.	573	610
que empezaste a convencerm	Ramón tonto.	Viejito. Seguramente soy culpable	610	623
convencerme. Ramón tonto.	Viejito.	Seguramente soy culpable. ¿	623	632
Ramón tonto. Viejito.	Seguramente soy culpable.	¿Quién no lo es	632	658

Figure 6.4 The results of a CATMA search for ST sentences of six words or less in Chapter 14.

Comparing ST and Draft Translation 161

Table 6.5 Short sentences which are longer in the TT than in the ST

No.	ST	TT	Comment/explanation
1	Me hubieras convencido, claro.	You would have persuaded me, you know that.	Need to translate *claro*, as *sure* or *of course.*
2	Fue así que empezaste a convencerme.	That's how you began to persuade me.	Spanish subject-drop requires *you* in English.
3	No hubo manera de contarte nada.	There was no way to tell you anything.	Spanish does *tell you* in one word.
4	Nada de eso pude contarte.	I couldn't tell you any of that.	Spanish subject-drop requires *I* in English, and Spanish does *tell you* in one word.
5	Éramos dos seres débiles y heridos.	We were two weak and wounded beings.	Spanish subject-drop requires *we* in English.
6	Pero, además, ¿de qué sirven?	But, what would be the point of that?	Need to change to: *But, really, what use are they?*
7	Había dos lunares, abultados como cicatrices.	There were two moles, thickened like scars.	Contrastive linguistics: *había = there were.*
8	Sería tan cómodo, pero no puedo.	It would be so comforting, but I can't.	Spanish subject-drop requires *it* and *I* in English.
9	Nunca podré enloquecer.	I'll never be able to go mad.	A combination of Spanish subject-drop, and the need to translate the future tense emphatically, rather than *I can never.*
10	Guardar el espanto, pero con urgencia.	To keep the ghost in check, but urgently.	Contrastive linguistics: Spanish infinitives use one word, where English uses two. Consider changing *ghost* to *fear.*

text = suggested translation revisions.

in the ST. My goal was to retain the effects created by short sentences, with a similar proportion of the total, and, where relevant, a compressed feel.

To that end I have indicated proposed translation revisions to sentences [1], [6] and [10]. In the first two cases the aim of the revision is to compress the sentence in line with the ST and also to tighten the linguistic equivalence. In the first sentence the tone of Dolores' words is one of affectionate, and sometimes uncomprehending, reproach. Here my interpretation is that she is effectively saying to Ramón: 'You knew I would have given in to your pressure on me to leave Hugo and be with you, so why did you kill yourself?' But this is only my interpretation and so must count as voluntary explicitation, in other words

162 *Comparing ST and Draft Translation*

Table 6.6 Short sentences which are longer in the ST than in the TT

No.	ST (over six words)	TT (six words or less)	Comment
1	Es todo el recuerdo, o casi todo.	It's the whole memory, or nearly.	Contrastive linguistics: English allows *the whole* to be understood after *nearly*. Spanish needs *todo* to be spelt out.
2	Claro que la mía no fue una buena pregunta.	Mine really wasn't a good question.	Contrastive linguistics: *Claro que* becomes *really*; *la mía* becomes *mine*; *no fue* becomes *wasn't* in English.
3	Tampoco la tuya fue una buena respuesta.	Nor was yours a good reply.	Contrastive linguistics: Spanish uses two words for *yours*: *la tuya*.
4	¿Por qué será la piel tan importante?	Why is the skin so important?	Contrastive linguistics: Spanish *Por qué* becomes *Why*?

making something explicit in the TT which is only implicit in the ST, where neither grammatical nor syntactical considerations demand it.

It would be a mistake, however, to assume that Spanish can always be more easily compressed into short sentences than English. Whilst tracking the translation I found that there were four sentences in the one- to six-word band where the TT was actually shorter than the ST, due to contrastive linguistics, and these are listed in *Table 6.6*.

Overall, this investigation revealed that 39 TT sentences, corresponding to 39 short ST sentences, were within the 6-word band, and that a further 4 sentences, corresponding to longer ST sentences, were also within this band, making a total of 43. It has illustrated how Spanish and English work at a compressed level, and has thrown up instances of where the translation has benefitted from revision in the light of applying the CDR methodology.

6.3 Comparing Repetitions

While researching the occurrences of the word *fuego* in relation to the translation of the title, I came across two related instances of the verb *estallar* (to explode, erupt, burst) in Chapter 8. I remembered that this verb had also been used in other chapters, but could not recall exactly where or how often. So I decided to see whether its use across the novel formed a significant pattern, and if so, whether this pattern suggested the need for consistency of translation. A CATMA search revealed ten occurrences, shown in Figure 6.5, nine being parts of the verb and one being a noun, spread across seven chapters from 2 to 14.[8]

Contextual analysis reveals that eight of the ten occurrences relate to individuals – Ramón, Edmundo, Dolly and Sr. Ríos' granddaughter – and the likelihood of their pent-up emotions leading to an explosion or eruption. The other two occurrences, contained in the same sentence in Chapter 8, relate to an explosion or eruption on a societal scale, in other words rebellion or revolution. Locational analysis further revealed that all the occurrences come either at or close to the beginnings and ends of chapters. Thus, the word appears to be used either to help set the scene for an unfolding chapter or to help bring a chapter to an emotional climax. Further confirmation of the importance of the choice of this word was provided by running CATMA searches for two other very common words related to fire and explosion: *incendio* [a fire] and *llamas* [flames]. There were no instances of *incendio*, and only one of *llamas* (or the singular *llama*), which was found in the same sentence as both *estallar* and *fuego* in Chapter 8. This suggests that Benedetti used *estallar* to elaborate one of the central themes of the novel, that of the buildup of emotional and psychological pressure to the point where an explosion or eruption is inevitable.

A combination of the results of these searches and their analysis suggests that the use of this particular word forms a pattern, and also that consistency of translation is needed to try to create equivalence of stylistic effect. It is important to acknowledge that this approach does not always mean that a word or phrase needs to be translated the same way. The example of the two different translations of *fuego* illustrates this well. In the case of *estallar*, however, a CDR examination of the draft translation of the ten occurrences in *Table 6.7* shows that I had actually translated it in six different ways: *explode, rise up, 'have done so', snap, outburst* and *burst*.

This exercise demonstrates a tension between two principles. On the one hand, in my original version I felt free to choose the word which I initially felt best fitted the specific instance – such as *explode* or *burst* – without considering the wider context of the novel and its themes. On the other, my CDR analysis showed that the idea of eruption was central

Left Context	Keyword	Right Context	Start Poir ▲	End Point
sé que nada va a	estallar	. ¿Qué puedo decirme	51,258	51,266
siempre que algo va a	estallar	. Dolly, tu radar	140,641	140,649
adquiere por decreto. Si	estallamos	, no por propia convicción	200,035	200,045
sino pura y exclusivamente porque	estallan	nuestros vecinos y el fuego	200,107	200,115
manos extendidas, entonces algo	estalla	dentro de mí, y	277,196	277,203
gran desaliento, y nada	estalla	en mí, sino que	277,478	277,485
yo vi que vivía,	estallé	en una carcajada eléctrica y	336,548	336,555
rabietas, rencores, pobres	estallidos	. Tengo que matarlo para	348,248	348,258
me parece que voy a	estallar	. ¿Usted cree que	364,071	364,079
que no podré soportarlo y	estallaré	, o me echaré a	431,844	431,853

Figure 6.5 CATMA search for instances of the lemma *estallar*.

Table 6.7 Occurrences of *estallar* and its draft translations

	Speaker/narrator	Location	ST	Draft TT and date
1	Ramón (interior monologue) (IM)	Ch. 2 (very near the start), p. 45	El aire está tenso, pero ya sé que nada va a estallar.	The air is tense, yet I know that nothing is going to explode. (Sept 2014) (**erupt**)
2	Dolly (dialogue with Ramón)	Ch. 4 (very near the end), p. 104	¿A mi padre? Sí, Ramón, cuando los veo juntos me parece siempre que algo va a estallar.	About my father? Yes, Ramón, when I see you together it always seems to me that something's going to explode. (March 2015) (**erupt**)
3 & 4	Ramón (dialogue with Gustavo)	Ch. 8 (very near the end), p. 144	Si estallamos, no por propia convicción, sino pura y exclusivamente porque estallan nuestros vecinos y el fuego se propaga, lo más probable es que las llamas recibidas no nos sirvan de nada, como no sea para destruirnos.	If we rise up, not through our own convictions, but purely and simply because our neighbours have done so and the fire spreads, the most likely outcome is that the flames that reach us will only serve to destroy us. (Aug 2014) (**erupt** and **erupt**)
5	Ramón (dialogue with Dolly)	Ch. 10 (a few pages in from the start), p. 195	Si un extranjero llega y nos mira con desprecio, ese mismo sonriente desprecio con que los yanquis deben mirar nuestras manos extendidas, entonces algo estalla dentro de mí, y siento rabia, eso es lo que siento.	If a foreigner comes here and regards us with contempt, that same smiling contempt with which the Yanks must look at our outstretched hands, then something snaps inside me, and I feel rage, that's what I feel. (March 2015) (**erupts**)
6	Ramón (dialogue with Dolly)	Ch. 10 (a few pages in from the start), p. 195	Pero si es uno de nosotros, el Viejo por ejemplo, quien mira lo nuestro con desprecio y todos sus actos se convierten en sórdidos pormenores de una misma burla, entonces ya no siento rabia, sino un gran desaliento, y nada estalla en mí, sino que algo se desmorona.	But if it's one of us, The Old Man for instance, who looks at us with contempt and all his actions become the sordid details of the same mockery, then I no longer feel rage, but a great dismay, and nothing snaps inside me, but something crumbles. (March 2015) (**erupts**)

7	Ramón (IM)	Ch. 11 (near the start), p. 233	Cuando, a los pocos minutos, Víctor abrió primero un ojo, después el otro, y dijo quejoso: Ay, cómo me duele, ¿quién fue?; cuando yo vi que vivía, estallé en una carcajada eléctrica y empecé a decirle a tía Olga: Viste, tía, yo no lo maté, él se había escondido, yo tiré la herradura para atrás sin mirar, como vos me enseñaste, pero a Víctor no le trajo suerte.	When, after a few minutes, Victor opened first one eye, then the other, and said complainingly: Ay, how it hurts, who was it?; when I saw that he was alive, I exploded into nervous laughter and began to say to tía Olga: You see, tía, I didn't kill him, he'd been hiding, I threw the horseshoe backwards without looking, as you taught me, but it didn't bring Victor luck. (April 2015) (**erupted**)
8	Ramón (IM/ talking to a sleeping Dolly)	Ch. 11 (near the end), pp. 240–241	Me siento libre de una hostilidad frívola, armada con rabietas, rencores, pobres estallidos. Tengo que matarlo para recuperarme a mí mismo, para hacer de una vez por todas algo generoso, algo desprovisto de falso orgullo, de cálculo mezquino.	I feel liberated from a petty hostility, fuelled by tantrums, resentments, weak outbursts. I have to kill him to recover myself, to finally do something generous, something shorn of false pride, of mean calculation. (April 2015) (**eruptions**)
9	Sr. Ríos' granddaughter (dialogue with Ramón)	Ch. 12 (last sentence), p. 252	Perdóneme, en este viaje aprendí a ser fuerte y siempre me contengo, pero cuando me acuerdo de ese solo episodio, tengo que llorar porque si no me parece que voy a estallar.	Forgive me, I learned how to be strong on that trip and I usually manage to control myself, but when I remember that one episode, I have to cry because I think if I don't I'll burst. (April 2015) (**erupt**)
10	Dolly (IM)	Ch. 14 (last sentence), p. 297	Porque al llegar a La Goleta es casi seguro que no podré soportarlo y estallaré, o me echaré a llorar tan convulsivamente como ahora, o perderé el sentido y mi cabeza caerá sobre el volante, y la bocina empezará a sonar, y acaso suene un rato largo, como una pobre alarma en el desierto.	Because I'm sure that when I get to La Goleta I won't be able to bear it and I'll explode, or I'll sob uncontrollably like I am now, or I'll pass out and my head will hit the steering wheel, and the horn will start to blare, and maybe blare for a long time, like a weak alarm in the desert. (May 2015) (**erupt**)

estall – occurrences of the verb or noun based on the root.
text – different translations of *estallar*.
erupt – suggested change to the draft TT in the light of the analysis.
IM – interior monologue.

166 *Comparing ST and Draft Translation*

to the novel's narrative, and that there was a good case for consistency of translation. In other words, I had to make a judgement about the relative 'stylistic value' of both approaches and decide on a 'hierarchy of values'.

The temptation for a translator is to focus on the immediate context and to use that as a criterion for translation choices. The iterative linking of close reading and quantitative analysis can provide a broader perspective, and reveal deeper narrative and linguistic layers, which can inform the translation in a more holistic way. As Umberto Eco notes, 'translating is not only connected with linguistic competence, but with intertextual, psychological, and narrative competence' (2001:13). My conclusion, based on close reading, was that the overall narrative theme was the more important in this case, and that I needed to change the translations by using the same word in each case if possible. The question then became: which word? The two obvious candidates were *explode* and *erupt*. While often used as synonyms, there are subtle differences of semantic field between the two, and this is where 'translatorliness' or 'writerliness' comes into play, deciding how to use the enormously rich resource of the English language in the light of sometimes conflicting considerations.

The Oxford English Dictionary (OED) states that an explosion in relation to a person involves giving 'sudden, violent, or free expression to an emotion or reaction' and to explode also means 'to be unable to contain one's emotions, impatience, etc.'[9] While this certainly applies to all ten occurrences, there is an additional element to the semantic field of *erupt*, which I would suggest is not always associated with *explode*. This is the idea that the sudden bursting forth is normally the result of a buildup of pressure or tension, often over an extended period of time, as with volcanoes, the context in which the term is probably most frequently used. In *Gracias por el Fuego* this is a central idea, which would be emphasised by the use of *erupt*, and so I opted for this word.

6.4 Comparing the Use of 'small' Words

This section is based on the premise that literary style is comprised of various elements, some of which are almost invisible, not because they occur rarely, but because they occur very frequently and are seldom noticed, 'hidden in plain sight' in fact. David Holmes explains how this relates to the style of an author:

> Essentially, computational stylistics assumes that a writer has a finite number of words at his/her disposal and, at any given moment, each writer will have certain subconscious habits of using those words, depending on such things as context and literary genre and subject to the constraints of syntax. An analyst searches for features particular to a given writer, features of which the writer is probably unaware and which can be measured quantitatively in order to have a basis for comparison with other writers.
>
> (1985:329)

Comparing ST and Draft Translation   167

This approach underlies the discipline of stylometry, which is largely concerned with authorship attribution. In his survey of modern authorship attribution methods Efstathios Stamatatos argues that 'the most common words [found in texts] (articles, prepositions, pronouns etc.) are found to be among the best features to discriminate between authors' (2009:5). In other words, the way an author, or a translator-as-author, uses high-frequency function words such as *by, that, and,* etc., has often been found to be distinctive. Forming part of the fabric of a text, yet rarely foregrounded, such elements constitute part of its underlying stylistic structure and are therefore relevant to translation. Furthermore, as Stamatatos also argues, 'function words are used in a largely unconscious manner by the authors and they are topic-independent' (ibidem). One of their distinguishing characteristics is that they are only detectable by the use of quantitative, usually computer-assisted, analysis.

So far the use of the CDR approach has followed a particular pattern: close reading has identified the potential stylistic importance of a range of features such as culture-specific items (CSIs), forms of interpersonal address and sentence length. These have then been subjected to quantitative analysis and the results assessed and investigated using close reading. But as Saldanha has noted, 'Quantitative and qualitative methods can be combined in a number of ways' (2009:5). The CDR approach to translation is flexible in that the starting point for a given analysis can be either close or distant reading. In Chapters 4 and 5 my analyses of cultural features and punctuation in *Gracias por el Fuego* originated with questions and hypotheses generated by close reading and the initial translation of the text, to which quantitative analytical techniques were then applied for investigation. In this section I start with a more open-ended quantitative analysis of language use, using word frequency distribution as a basis, to investigate some 'hidden' features of Benedetti's style. This approach is data-driven rather than data-based, and allows the analyst to respond without any preconceptions to findings which prompt further investigation. In other words, the data is used to generate research questions rather than to test existing hypotheses. I apply this approach to Benedetti's use of high-frequency function words.

Corpus-linguistic tools can be used to help us see features of a text which are hidden in that they are rarely quantified, or even registered at all, by the conscious mind in the course of normal, and even close, reading. Such features include the use of high-frequency function words and the low-frequency repetition of words and phrases. This involves 'x-raying' a text to see the patterns hidden below the surface. As Munday observes, 'the figures produced by statistical analysis can reveal elements of a writer's style which would otherwise remain undiscovered' (1997:202). Saldanha and O'Brien also note that 'the use of corpus linguistic tools can help us to find patterns faster' (2013:92), and these patterns often have a relationship to authorial style. In this section my starting point is a frequency distribution analysis of words in the ST. Corpus linguistics have demonstrated

168 *Comparing ST and Draft Translation*

that the most frequently occurring words are usually 'closed-class' function words, and the way an author uses them can often be distinctive. I therefore investigated the most frequently occurring words in *Gracias por el Fuego* to see what they might tell me about Benedetti's literary style.

In CATMA the Wordlist tool produces a list of all the words in a text, which can be displayed alphabetically or by frequency (high to low, or low to high). I ran the Wordlist query for each chapter and for the novel as a whole, and the ten most frequently occurring words across the novel were, in descending order, *de, que, la, y, a, el, en, no, me* and *un* (all in lower case). These words collectively account for 23.8% of the text, and for between 18.6% and 26.7% of each chapter. Two aspects of the results drew my attention to the word *y* [and]: its overall position in the list, which seemed high; and its contrasting positions in two chapters, being the highest frequency word in Chapter 14 and the second lowest frequency word in Chapter 15.

As a co-ordinating conjunction *y* can be stylistically significant through its presence, its absence or its sentence position, particularly when it is sentence-initial. Benedetti's style in *Gracias por el Fuego* involves the use of *y* in all three ways. I had become aware of some of these uses while undertaking the initial translation, for example, in the long, comma-separated list sentences referred to in Chapter 5, which are devoid of conjunctions, but had no clear sense of their frequency or of how they might relate to other aspects of style. *Y* therefore seemed worthy of further investigation. For a more accurate indication of frequency of use I needed to include the capitalised occurrences of all ten words, since they can all be used to start a sentence. The results of this revised analysis are shown in Appendix A, Table A3. In relation to *Y/y* two findings drew my attention. Its overall frequency rating in the novel rose from fourth to third, featuring in the top five words in every chapter; and it was the highest frequency word in Chapters 3 and 14.

To see whether the frequency rating for *Y/y* was distinctive, I compared it to two Spanish corpora, the *Frequency Dictionary of Spanish* (FDS) (Davies 2006)[10] and the 5.7-million word twentieth-century fiction section of the *Corpus del Español* (CdE) (Davies 2016), and the four major Latin American Boom novels which were used as sentence length control comparators in Chapter 5. I did this in two ways. I compared normalised frequency ratings to see whether the number of occurrences per 1,000 words in these comparators was higher or lower than in *Gracias por el Fuego*. The results of this analysis are shown in *Table 6.8*.

This shows that Benedetti actually uses *Y/y* less often per 1,000 words than all the comparators, so is distinctive in that respect. However, when the use of *Y/y* is compared in relative terms, i.e. how often it is used in relation to other function words within a text, the picture is different. To produce the figures in *Table 6.9* I used the FDS rankings as given, searched the CdE using its built-in search engine and ran the same CATMA Wordlist queries on the four novels as I used in *Gracias por el Fuego*.

Comparing ST and Draft Translation 169

Table 6.8 Raw and normalised frequency analyses of *Y/y* in *Gracias por el Fuego*, the *Corpus del Español*, the *Frequency Dictionary of Spanish* and four major Boom novels

Title	Word total	Raw frequency of occurrence	Normalised frequency (per 1,000 words of text)
La Ciudad y los Perros	128,936	4,268	33.1
La Muerte de Artemio Cruz	95,569	3,142	32.8
Frequency Dictionary of Spanish	5,700,000	148,657	31.2
Cien Años de Soledad	137,918	4,126	29.9
Corpus del Español: twentieth-century fiction	5,144,073	148,657	28.8
Rayuela	172,818	4,908	28.4
Gracias por el Fuego	76,442	2,121	27.7

Table 6.9 Relative word frequency in *Gracias por el Fuego*, the *Frequency Dictionary of Spanish*, the *Corpus del Español* and four major Boom novels

Order	Gracias por el Fuego	Frequency Dictionary of Spanish	Corpus del Español	Cien Años de Soledad	La Ciudad y los Perros	La Muerte de Artemio Cruz	Rayuela
1	de	el/la[11]	de	de	y	de	de
2	que	de	la	la	la	la	la
3	y	que	que	que	de	y	que
4	el	y	el	y	el	el	y
5	la	a	y	el	a	que	a
6	no	en	en	en	que	a	el
7	a	un	a	a	se	los	en
8	en	ser (all forms)	se	los	los	no	un
9	un	se	no	se	en	en	se
10	es	no	un	con	un	las	no

y: frequency rankings highlighted for quick reference.

These show that relative to other function words Benedetti uses *Y/y* in *Gracias por el Fuego* more often than in the FDS, CdE, *Cien Años de Soledad* and *Rayuela*; as often as in *La Muerte de Artemio Cruz*; and less often than in *La Ciudad y los Perros*. These results, and the fact that *Y/y* was the most frequently used word in two chapters of the novel, suggested that what might be stylistically interesting was the way Benedetti uses the conjunction, rather than just its frequency of

170 *Comparing ST and Draft Translation*

occurrence, and that this was likely to be of relevance to translation. On this basis I decided to investigate it further.

The Investigation of Y/y

Of the two chapters where *Y/y* is the most frequently used word, Chapter 14 seemed more noteworthy as both the raw frequency total (105 instances[12] as compared to 60) and the percentage of chapter word count (5.6 as compared to 2.6) were higher than in Chapter 3. Chapter 14 consists of a single interior monologue by Dolly and contains both flash-backs and flash-forwards, where she envisages herself going through the motions of daily life while inwardly feeling only sadness and despair. The narrative context provides a clue to the extensive use of *Y/y*, as a means of stringing together lists of past events and sequences of projected future actions. This also ties in with the longer than average sentence length highlighted in Section 5.4 of Chapter 5, since these lists are contained in relatively long sentences. As Chapter 14 is quite short (1,856 words), I decided to experiment with a more visual way of mapping the occurrences of *Y/y*, by highlighting them in MS Word, as shown in Figure 6.6 and as illustrated in Chapter 5 in relation to the use of commas.

This shows a concentration on page 1, the bottom of page 2 and page 3. Of the 105 occurrences, 19 are of sentence-initial *Y* and 86 are of *y*. Of these 86, 33 (38%) are contained in 7 sentences, all of which start with *Y*. The first four of these, on p. 292, successively recount childhood memories. The remaining 3, also successive, which are amongst the longest sentences in the chapter, contain 28 instances which link a series of imagined routine daily actions which Dolly will perform. Outwardly normal, these actions will not reflect her inner turmoil, as illustrated in the second of this group of three sentences (shown as the first sentence on page 3 of Figure 6.6):

> Y le preguntaré si puedo llevar el coche, y él dirá que sí, y la muchacha sonreirá de lejos y correrá a abrirme el garaje, y yo daré vuelta a la llave y escucharé el ronquido familiar del motor, y pondré primera, y apretaré suavemente el acelerador, y saldré a la luz, que será una luz extraña y metálica, con las verjas estriadas como en un aguafuerte, y los árboles quietos, con sus copas en triángulo, secos.
>
> (p. 296)

> [And I'll ask him if I can take the car, and he'll say yes, and the maid will smile from a distance and rush to open the garage for me, and I'll turn the key and hear the familiar rumble of the engine, and I'll put it in first gear, and slowly depress the accelerator, and come out into the light, that will be a weird, metallic light, with the railings striated like an etching, and the trees calm, with their triangular crowns, and dry.]
>
> (my translation)

Figure 6.6 The 105 instances of Y and y in Chapter 14 of *Gracias por el Fuego*.

172 Comparing ST and Draft Translation

The stylistic effect on me of the repeated use of *y* is to separate and emphasise each act in the sequence, and encourage the reader to visualise it. Of the 126 sentences in the chapter, 19 (15%) begin with *Y*, showing that not only are clauses within sentences linked by the conjunction, but that it is used to link sentences to form longer lists. The overall effect is one of relentless regret and pessimism, tinged with dishonesty, since Dolly is unable to show her true feelings.

Comparison of ST and TT

As in Chapter 5, my methodology here is to apply the same CDR approach to the TT as I did to the ST, and to investigate greater observed-than-expected differences. I analysed the ten most frequently used words in the TT, then added the frequencies of their capitalised forms to the totals. The overall results for the two texts are shown in *Table 6.10*, and the full results are shown in Appendix A, Table A4.

While most of the words in the TT top ten mirror words in the ST top ten – with the exception of *I*, *you* and *it* – the frequency order is very different, due to the contrastive linguistics of Spanish and English. For example, *que* and *that* only partially map onto each other, as do *a* and *to* and *de* and *of*. However, if *el* and *la* are aggregated, they become the highest frequency word set, equating largely to *the*, and then *y* and *and* become the fourth highest frequency words in their respective lists.

I decided to analyse the comparative occurrences of *Y/y* and *And/and* for two reasons. Having identified the stylistic relevance of *Y/y* in the ST, I wanted to see how I had translated it. Second, I had the impression that the two words mapped onto each other fairly closely, as indicated by Spanish grammar reference books: '**Y**. "and"; used much like its English equivalent' (Butt and Benjamin 2000:445, bold in original). John Butt and Carmen Benjamin mention two differences in use. The translation of *y* as 'after' in phrases such as 'Transcurrieron días y días' [Day

Table 6.10 The ten most frequently used words in *Gracias por el Fuego* and the draft translation

Frequency order	ST	Draft TT
1	de	the
2	que	I
3	y	to
4	la	and
5	no	that
6	el	a
7	a	of
8	en	you
9	me	it
10	un	in

y/and: frequency rankings highlighted for quick reference.

Comparing ST and Draft Translation 173

after day passed] (ibid.:445), and as 'what about? in phrases such as '¿Y el perro?' [What about the dog?], and '¿Y qué?' [So what?] (ibid.:446). There is also the morphological change from *y* to *e* before a word beginning with an *i* or *y* sound, such as *hijo* or *hierro* (ibid.:445). Lastly, given the strong similarity in linguistic function and use, and the fact that the total number of occurrences was very similar: 2,239 in the ST and 2,193 in the TT, I hypothesised that there would not be a major disparity of occurrences at chapter level. A frequency comparison of *Y/y* and *And/and* is shown in *Table 6.11*, in descending order of numerical disparity.

Broadly speaking the results bore out my hypothesis, but there was a notable exception, Chapter 9 (highlighted in bold), which had by far the largest discrepancy. My investigation therefore centred on two chapters: Chapter 14 because it was investigated earlier in this section in relation to the ST, and Chapter 9 because it displayed the greatest difference in occurrences. In Chapter 14, *Y/y* and *And/and* were the most frequently occurring words:

ST occurrences	*TT occurrences*
Y : 19	And : 18
y : 86	and : 85
Total : 105	Total : 103

Investigation revealed that in the case of *And* one sentence beginning with Y in the ST had simply been left out of the translation by mistake, thus accounting for the difference of one. In the case of *y*, the discrepancy of one was not due simply to a single non-translation of *y* as *and*, as I had assumed, but was a more complex phenomenon. There were in fact a total of six non-translations of *y* as *and*, and five cases where an extra *and* had been used in the TT, making a total difference of one.

Table 6.11 Comparison of occurrences of *Y/y* in the ST and *And/and* in the draft TT

Chapter	ST	Draft TT	Difference
9	**317**	**288**	**−39**
4	238	221	−17
1	221	210	−11
13	299	288	−11
3	60	58	−2
12	62	60	−2
14	105	103	−2
5	46	45	−1
11	96	95	−1
6	40	40	0
15	67	67	0
2	117	118	+1
10	369	374	+5
7	167	174	+7
8	42	52	+10

174   *Comparing ST and Draft Translation*

The 'missing' *and*s highlighted two further differences in usage between Spanish and English. The first relates to the way that Spanish usually links two adjectives which qualify the same noun with *y*, whereas English often performs the same function with a comma. For example:

ST: 'una luz extraña y metálica'

(p. 296)

TT: 'a strange, metallic light'

The second shows how *y* can be translated as 'but':

ST: 'Ahora sí puedo y para qué sirve.'

(p.291)

TT: 'Now I can, <u>but</u> what's the point.'

The additional *and*s also highlighted two linguistic phenomena. There are instances of *y* changing to *e* before a word beginning with an *i* or *y* sound. There is also a case of TL influence, which relates to the insertion of 'and' before the last item in a list:

ST: '...mis orejas, a mi boca, a mi nariz, a mis cejas.'

(p. 295)

TT: '...my ears, my mouth, my nose <u>and</u> my eyebrows.'

The investigation of Chapter 14 led to four translation changes, including the removal of *and* in the example just quoted, in all cases resulting in a closer recreation of ST usage and syntax.

The Investigation of Chapter 9

A variation of 29 instances between ST and draft TT was revealed:

ST occurrences	TT occurrences
Y : 44	And : 42
y : 273	and : 246
Total : 317	Total : 288

As in Chapter 14, the variation is not simply due to 29 instances of non-translation of *Y/y* as *And/and* but is comprised of 68 such non-translations and 39 instances of additional *And/and*s. The findings of both chapters reveal a more complex and nuanced relationship between the Spanish and English co-ordinating conjunctions than I had been aware of, and also highlight the strength of TL influence, which I suspect operates at least partially at a subconscious level. I manually checked all the ST and TT occurrences of the conjunctions, retaining

Comparing ST and Draft Translation 175

many of the instances of non-correspondence and revising others. Thirty-one *non-and* translations and 21 additional *and*s were retained.

Grammatical and typographical conventions relating to clock time and year citation, for example, were respected:

ST: 'dos <u>y</u> veinte'
TT: 'twenty past two'

ST: 'mil novecientos treinta <u>y</u> ocho'
TT: '1938'

The English preference for comma separation of adjectives also features frequently and was mostly retained. A number of idiomatic expressions required the non-translation of *Y/y* as *And/and* or insertion of the latter, as in the following examples:

ST: 'hacia un lado <u>y</u> hacia otro'
TT: 'from side <u>to</u> side'

ST: '<u>Y</u> bien'
TT: 'Well'

ST: 'váyase a festejar su cumpleaños'
TT: 'go <u>and</u> celebrate your birthday'

More broadly, this detailed CDR examination of the actual linguistic usage of an apparently closely mapped pair of conjunctions illustrates the range of possible translation variations. Depending on context, *Y/y* can be rendered as *and, but, after, when, where, moreover, furthermore, to* and *what about?*, as well as being removed completely.

As a result of the investigation I made a total of 41 translation changes in Chapter 9, involving both the removal and insertion of *And/and*. The insertions were made, almost without exception, with a view to restoring the perceived stylistic effect of the ST, which in my judgement had been altered or lost in the draft translation. For example, in Chapter 9 in an interior monologue Ramón is trying to imagine what it would be like to be absolutely certain that he was going to die, as his client Sr. Ríos is:

ST	*TT1 (August 2014)*	*TT2 (November 2016)*
Quizá se tenga la sensación de que el tiempo comienza a transcurrir a una velocidad vertiginosa, de que uno cierra los ojos por un instante y cuando los abre ya ha pasado medio día. (p. 156)	Maybe it brings on the feeling that time is starting to pass incredibly quickly, that <u>if you close your eyes for a moment, half a day will have gone by when you open them again.</u>	Maybe you have the feeling that time is starting to pass by at breakneck speed, <u>that you close your eyes for an instant and when you open them half a day's gone by.</u>

176   *Comparing ST and Draft Translation*

I would suggest that the reinstatement of *and*, the removal of *if*, the re-tention of the past tense in 'half a day's gone by' as opposed to the use of the future perfect 'will have gone by', and the repositioning of the phrase 'half a day's gone by' at the end help to recreate the ST effect of a sentence speeding to a climax with a minimum number of words.

Another example of the reinstatement of *and* comes in the novel's longest sentence, which relives Ramón's near-death experience on a railway track:

ST	TT1 *(August 2014)*	TT2 *(November 2016)*
...lo que me importa es la absoluta seguridad de que dentro de cuatro minutos, cinco a más tardar, pasará el tren de la una y siete, y no podré escaparme porque este cepo de hierro me ha tomado casi a la altura del tobillo, y el pie queda allá abajo y sin escapatoria (p. 157)	...what worries me is the absolute certainty that in the next four minutes – five at the outside – the 1:07 will come through, and I won't be able to escape because this steel trap has caught me at nearly ankle height, with my foot below it with no means of escape,	...what worries me is the absolute certainty that within four minutes, five at the most, the 1:07 will come through, and I won't be able to escape because this iron trap has caught me almost at ankle height, and my foot is stuck there below and with no means of escape,

The context is a stream-of-consciousness sentence of 713 words, containing 43 instances of *y*, all strongly suggesting 'and' as a translation. My initial rendering of the last two instances of *y* as *with* suggests TL influence in the form of a common subordinate clause structure. It is perfectly idiomatic and the meaning is the same, but the stylistic effect is to break a clear and insistent pattern of thoughts, feelings and sensations simultaneously linked and separated by *and*, collectively creating the re-experiencing of rising panic in a living nightmare. The reinstatement of the two *and*s, I would suggest, helps to restore this effect.

A final example illustrates how two quantitative analyses can interact to produce a translation revision. The phrase *después de todo* occurs twice in Chapter 9, on p. 151 and p. 169. The first time it is used by Sr. Ríos to preface his revelation to Ramón that he has cancer, and the second by Edmundo when lecturing Ramón, telling him that *después de todo* Ramon is his son and for that reason alone he will not rebel against his father. I initially translated both instances with the phrase 'when all's said and done', thus inserting two additional *and*s. However, the phrase in the ST seems to be important at the macro-level of the novel. It occurs 23 times, and in 19 instances relates to the repetition of the fact that Ramón is Edmundo's son. It is variously imbued with frankness, sarcasm, irony, condescension, bitterness and resignation and used by four characters: Sr. Ríos, Ramón, Edmundo and Gloria. It represents another example of Benedetti's use of repetition of key words and phrases across the novel. I felt that there was an argument in this case for consistency of translation, and since I have translated the phrase as *after all* in a way which seems to fit these and all the other instances, I have revised the Chapter 9 instances to match.

What the analysis of high-frequency function words in both ST and draft TT has shown is that starting with an open-ended quantitative linguistic analysis rather than with questions and hypotheses generated by close reading can also lead, with the help of close reading, to a deeper understanding of how stylistic effects are created and sustained in a literary text, and thus lead to better informed translation choices. Distant reading can reveal the existence of linguistic patterns based on the usage of very common function words, which are hard to detect through close reading. It can also help a translator to appreciate how they themselves both write and translate, as the next chapter illustrates.

Notes

1 http://sourceforge.net/projects/aligner
2 https://sourceforge.net/projects/tmxeditor/
3 http://graphics.cs.wisc.edu/Vis/SequenceSurveyor/TextDNA.html Although free, this programme requires advanced computer knowledge to use.
4 A measure of diversity originally developed in the field of biology, but later applied to linguistics.
5 The full analysis is displayed in **Appendix A, Table A2**.
6 This was before I started using Sketch Engine, and I would now use the sentence-aligned parallel corpus.
7 The missing untranslated sentence counts as one short sentence less in the TT.
8 I would now use Sketch Engine and a sentence-aligned parallel corpus for this kind of search.
9 OED online, www.oed.com/view/Entry/66640?redirectedFrom=explode#eid [accessed 26 July 2016].
10 This lists the 5,000 most frequently used words in Spanish by frequency and alphabetically.
11 The combination of these two word forms (which are not disaggregated in the FDS), and that of all forms of the verb *ser*, skew the results for the *Frequency Dictionary of Spanish*. As a further control I therefore searched for the frequencies of the 10 words from the FDS in the 22.8 million word twentieth-century section of the CdE (from which the FDS is largely taken), excluding *ser*, and listed them here.
12 There were also two instances of 'e', which is the form taken by 'y' when the next word begins with an 'i' or 'y' sound.

7 Applying the Methodology (Part 4)

The Auto-analysis of Translator Style

So far, I have used the close and distant reading (CDR) approach to analyse source text (ST) style, to solve problems during initial translation and to compare ST and TT (target text) against clearly specified translation goals and criteria. In this chapter I illustrate a fourth use of the approach, namely enabling a translator to investigate and analyse their own style in terms of aspects of habitual patterns of linguistic usage, and in particular those habits which are widely held to be wholly or partially unconscious. The methodology employed for this investigation involved conducting an auto-stylistic analysis of two of my translations from Spanish to English, relating them both to their respective source texts, and in one case to a second translation of the same text by another translator, thus providing triangulation. This was then followed up by a second investigation, using subsequent translations, designed to test for the presence of the linguistic habits identified in the first investigation, and their impact on my translations.

The purpose of such an exercise was to begin to answer some of the following questions. What are my unconscious translation habits? How do they relate to the idea of 'translation universals' such as simplification, normalisation and explicitation put forward by Baker, Laviosa-Braithwaite, Saldanha and others? Do I actually translate in the way I think I do? Do my habits militate against the achievement of my translation goals and philosophy, e.g. do I domesticate more than I intend to? How, and to what extent, do my habits distinguish me from other translators working in my chosen genre(s) and language pair(s)? How far does my translation style differ from 'normal' English usage, as compared to reference corpora such as the British National Corpus and the British English 2006 corpus?

While a serious attempt to answer all these questions is well beyond the scope of this book, the overall motivation behind them is a desire for an increased awareness of aspects of my own style, so that in principle, at least, I render them open to the possibility of control and change. In Section 7.1, the findings of the investigation show that the translations chosen, when subjected to initial open-ended corpus linguistic analysis followed up by close reading and qualitative analysis, do indeed reveal six unconscious translation tendencies, some of which are common to both translations. In Section 7.2, searches are conducted for these six tendencies in a set of subsequent translations from both Spanish and Greek using part-of-speech (POS) tags. Evidence was found which suggests that three of these tendencies – a tendency to switch between present participles or gerunds and infinitives, to substitute pairs of dashes for pairs of commas and to add emphasis by increasing the strength of modifiers – might well be part of my translation style, and their potential impact on translation is also assessed.

7.1 Analysing One's Own Translation Style

Identifying Translator Style

Style in translation has broadly been investigated from two perspectives, the translation of style generally and individual style of translation. Scholars have investigated the 'presence' of a translator in a translated text, manifested in their attitude towards what they translate, and illustrated in a range of ways including cultural representation and the use of paratextual elements such as a translator's preface (Hermans 1996, 2014; Schiavi 1996; Munday 1998, 2007a and b, 2008a, 2011; Alvstad 2014). The idea of translators having their own individual style, as opposed to simply being vehicles for the reproduction of ST authorial style, and this in principle being identifiable across a range of translations of different authors, was first brought to prominence by Mona Baker in her article 'Towards a Methodology for Investigating the Style of a Literary Translator' (2000). In it she makes three basic claims. The first is that

> it is as impossible to produce a stretch of language in a totally impersonal way as it is to handle an object without leaving one's fingerprints on it... I understand style as a kind of thumb-print that is expressed in a range of linguistic — as well as non-linguistic — features.
>
> (2000:244–245)

The second is that

> a study of a translator's style must focus on the manner of expression that is typical of a translator, rather than simply instances of open intervention. It must attempt to capture the translator's characteristic use of language, his or her individual profile of linguistic habits, compared to other translators. Which means that style, as applied in this study, is a matter of patterning: it involves describing preferred or recurring patterns of linguistic behaviour, rather than individual or one-off instances of intervention.
>
> (245)

The third is that it is necessary to attempt to disentangle individual translator style from linguistic usage that could be the result of the influence of the source language (SL), ST, author or genre.

180   *The Auto-analysis of Translator Style*

More recent work in the field includes a range of studies focusing largely on the optional use by translators of various micro-level linguistic devices such as modal particles (Winters 2009), the connective *that* with reporting verbs (Olohan 2001; Saldanha 2005, 2011b), segmentation (Pekkanen 2010) and structural calque (Marco 2004). Summarising the work done so far, two principal elements emerge as dominant. There are investigations of quantifiable linguistic habits which are argued to be largely, but not entirely subconscious, text- and author-independent, and to be cumulatively capable of producing stylistic and narrative shifts at the macro-level of a text, and of identifying the style of individual translators. By contrast, there are a smaller number of studies which look at style as also encompassing broader, conscious attitudes to the role of the translator as cultural mediator, as evidenced not only by translations but also by what translators say about their own attitudes in this regard and how it relates to their translation practice (Munday 2007a and b, 2008a; Saldanha 2011a).

To my knowledge, the only research which has been done to date on stylistic auto-analysis by translators is a study by Jan Rybicki. This was designed to test the extent to which the authorship attribution method used in stylometry known as most-frequent-words analysis was capable of recognising 'the stylistic (or merely lexical?) traces of translators' (Rybicki 2013:195). Rybicki compared his translations into Polish of a number of English texts by John le Carré and Douglas Coupland with texts by native Polish writers, and concluded that 'the translator's lexical traces can indeed be found' (2013:202). But the focus of this research was on the possibility of identifying the translator as opposed to the author of a literary text primarily on the basis of their use of function words, rather than on trying to identify a range of possible linguistic translatorial habits with a view to greater self-knowledge as a translator.

A distinction is often made between conscious and unconscious elements of translator style. As a way of beginning to think about this, I have set out below a tentative list of some factors which can influence translator style, along a possible continuum.

Unconscious ⟵			*Conscious*

• TL influence
• SL influence
• education/idiolect/
  lexical priming
• use of high-frequency
  function words
	• segmentation
	• simplification
	• explicitation
	• normalisation
		• attitude to the
		  author and/or
		  text
		• attitude to role
		  as cultural
		  mediator
			• choice of
			  genre/
			  author/text
			• influence or
			  pressure
			  from author
			  or publisher

I do not contend that a clear dividing line can be drawn between conscious and unconscious elements. Decisions about aspects such as sentence length, explicitation, segmentation and simplification may well be partly conscious and partly unconscious, and vary from text to text and also within a text. Different aspects of style may be located at different points along the continuum, and these points themselves may vary from translator to translator and also change over time. However, on the basis that I am free to change aspects of my translatorial style which are the result of conscious choice, my focus is on those elements which for me appear to be wholly or largely unconscious, but which can in principle be detected and therefore brought into the realm of conscious awareness. This focus governed my choice of research design and methodology for a 'mini-investigation' of my own translatorial habits and style.

Investigating My Own Translatorial Style

Building on Baker's foundational work, Saldanha puts forward a refined definition of translator style as a 'way of translating' which

- is felt to be recognizable across a range of translations by the same translator
- distinguishes the translator's work from that of others
- constitutes a coherent pattern of choice
- is 'motivated' in the sense that it has a discernible function or functions, and
- cannot be explained purely with reference to the author or source-text style, or as the result of linguistic constraints.

(2011b:31)

I have used this as a set of guiding principles, with the addition to the third bullet point of the phrase 'whether conscious or unconscious'. The central idea underlying both Baker's and Saldanha's arguments is clear: in order to identify a translator's individual style it must be possible to convincingly separate it out from a variety of other possible explanations for particular patterns of linguistic behaviour, the most important of which will normally be ST, SL and TL influence.

In line with a suggestion by Marion Winters, I have used

> a comparative research design that enables most variables in the translation process (the author of the source text, the source and target languages, the time of publication of the original and the translation, etc.) to be held constant, so that the remaining variable, the *translator*, and his or her style, becomes the source of explanations for divergences between two translations.

(2009:75, emphasis in original)

To that end I have triangulated the investigation of aspects of my own style by using two sets of comparisons: ST and TT in two translations

182 *The Auto-analysis of Translator Style*

of different authors, and two different translations of the same ST, mine and another, carried out in the same month. In both cases I used a combination of quantitative and qualitative analysis.

The first part of the investigation involved comparing my translation of a section of *El Discurso Vacío* (1996), a novel by Mario Levrero (1940–2004), with a section of the same length from my draft translation of Chapter 13 of *Gracias por el Fuego*, carried out between 2014 and 2015. The translation of Mario Levrero was undertaken in August 2014, so is close in time to that of *Gracias por el Fuego*, and like that translation precedes the use of corpus tools which came to be central to my translation methodology from mid-2015 onwards. It came about by chance, as the text was provided by Stefan Tobler, the founder of the And Other Stories publishing house, who organised a mini-competition amongst the students of the Spanish class at the London *Translate in the City* summer school, which I attended in June 2014. This short translation was the only other translation which could form part of my investigation, since it was the only other literary translation I had done at the time. The second translation of the Mario Levrero text was the one which won the competition, and whose author kindly sent me a copy when I requested it in December 2016.

Mario Levrero was Uruguayan, and *El Discurso Vacío* is, like Benedetti's *La Tregua*, written as a diary. There are elements of similarity and difference from both *La Tregua* and *Gracias por el Fuego*. The story centres around the constant struggle of the narrator to complete simple calligraphic exercises, whose only aim is to shape letters correctly and pleasingly, while each time he sits down to practise, he finds himself composing stories and musing philosophically, and his handwriting goes to pot. Levrero has been described as belonging to a surrealist school of writers, dubbed *los raros* by the critic Ángel Rama (1966), which included the well-known author Felisberto Hernández. In contrast to *Gracias por el Fuego*, *El Discurso Vacío* contains no clear political message or coherent social critique. The extract chosen by And Other Stories comprises the consecutive diary entries for 13th, 15th and 20th November, which are on pages 42–46 of the 196-page novel. In these entries the narrator talks about his inability to maintain a routine with his calligraphic exercises, his frustration at giving in to the temptation to put them aside to do some writing to earn money and how his planned day of peaceful practice turned into one of resentful childcare when his son returned home from school, having complained of feeling ill. The extract contains 689 words. Both source text extracts and my two translations are reproduced in full in **Appendix B** for reference.

The extract chosen from *Gracias por el Fuego*, containing 660 words, comes from Chapter 13, and was selected according to the following criteria. It needed to be of very similar length, to be representative of the novel as a whole in broad stylistic and thematic terms, but also to provide some stylistic contrasts with the extract from *El Discurso Vacío*. The purpose of this contrast was to see if there were consistent features

The Auto-analysis of Translator Style   183

of translator style which could be identified as being independent of author style. Both texts are interior monologues, but the extract from *Gracias por el Fuego* contains some long sentences and is very different in tone and content. While the *El Discurso Vacío* extract is light, tongue-in-cheek, self-deprecatory, deeply philosophical and inward-looking by turn, that from *Gracias por el Fuego* is negative, self-critical, fatalistic and severely critical of society and its dominant elite.

Before presenting the investigation and its results, it must be acknowledged that it was based on very short samples, which necessarily limits the possibility of drawing robust conclusions. However, research in stylometry suggests that when analysing the use of high-frequency function words, 'a few hundred words' can often be 'sufficient to perform authorship attribution' (Stamatatos 2009:5). In other words, at least some unconscious aspects of translator style in principle can be revealed by the analysis of relatively small samples. The investigation was undertaken in a series of six steps, each of which is summarised below, together with its rationale.

Step 1: The Chapter 13 extract from *Gracias por el Fuego* and its translation were chosen to compare to those of *El Discurso Vacío*. As with the keyword analysis in Section 6.4 of Chapter 6, I had no preconceived hypothesis about my own style as a translator and allowed the investigation to be data-driven. While aware of how I was aiming to translate a specific novel, I did not know if I had a specific and text-independent style as a translator, and if so, of what it might consist. In line with this approach, I deliberately did not read C.C.'s translation until after I had completed its quantitative analysis, so that I would not be influenced by subjective impressions of similarities and differences from my translation. To maintain consistency of comparison, I used the same set of units of analysis in all six steps, as listed below.

Unit of analysis	Reason for use
Number of tokens (words)	A basic statistic which is used in all the ratios and percentages
Number of lemmatised types of words[1]	A more accurate representation of lexical variety than the raw count of word types
Type-token ratio (TTR)	A standard measure of lexical variety, which is, however, heavily text length-dependent
Average sentence length	A measure of syntactic and narrative style
Hapax legomena (words occurring only once)	A measure of lexical variety
Hapax legomena as % of text	A measure of lexical variety
Ten most frequently occurring words as % of text	A linguistic measure that allows for comparison with reference corpora of standard language use
Top ten most frequently occurring words, in descending order	Almost always function words, their usage patterns can often provide a distinctive linguistic 'thumb-print'

184   *The Auto-analysis of Translator Style*

The aim was to perform an 'x-ray' of basic linguistic features which close reading of even a short passage would be unlikely to reveal and see where the results led. I used the freely available AntConc text analysis programme[2] to produce the lemmatised word lists,[3] TTRs and lists of hapax legomena; and CATMA to produce sentence length statistics.

Step 2: Studies of translator style are often exclusively TT-oriented, but as Winters argues, 'reference to the source text allows for more reliable results and should provide deeper insight into the individual styles of the translations' (2009:79), and makes it easier to rule out aspects of translation which can be put down to ST and SL influence. I therefore compared my translations with their respective source texts (and not at this stage with each other) to see which features appeared to be the result of translator choice. In relation to my *Gracias por el Fuego* translation I found two examples of such features: a change from active to passive voice:

ST: ...porque las buenas cosas <u>que anunció</u> mi infancia...
TT: ...the good things <u>foreshadowed</u> in my childhood...

and an instance of added emphasis:

ST: Es bueno tomar una <u>decisión grave</u> en un día así...
TT: It's good to take a <u>decision as important as this</u> on a day like this...

While these represent examples of translator choice, they also partly support the hypothesis that translations have a tendency towards simplification, standardisation and explicitation (Blum and Levenston 1978; Blum-Kulka 1986; Laviosa-Braithwaite 2005; Toury 2012), and are not of themselves features which would identify my style vis-à-vis that of other translators.

In relation to the *El Discurso Vacío* translation I found two instances of simplification, one of which involves a flattening of a self-mocking, pretentious literary register:

ST: ...la posibilidad de un trabajo (temporario) que me permitiría re-unirme con cierta suma de dinero...
TT: ...the possibility of a job (albeit temporary) that would reunite me with sufficient money...

These are indicative of possible translation habits, which I had not been aware of, but which contribute to translation style, without on their own being distinctive.

Step 3: A comparison was made between C.C.'s translation of the *El Discurso Vacío* extract and the ST, to begin to identify features of her translation that might prompt quantitative comparison with my version of the same text.

The Auto-analysis of Translator Style   185

Step 4: I was now ready to compare both translations of *El Discurso Vacío,* and the standardised comparison I had been using threw up two interesting features, as shown in *Table 7.1*. My translation is 3.5% longer, and my average sentence length is 8.1% longer than C.C.'s. The fact that C.C.'s translation contained one more sentence than mine provided a partial explanation for her lower average sentence length, but despite the small difference, I wanted to proceed to an investigation of banded sentence length.

Step 5: The results, shown in *Table 7.2*, highlighted differences in three sentence length bands, 11–19 words, 20–35 words and 36–60 words.[4]

Given that the ST and TTs are relatively short, I decided to place all three side by side in MS Word to visually compare the sentences which fell within these three bands. What is particularly interesting about this approach is that it brought to my attention some features of my translation practice which a simple comparison of my TT with the ST had not foregrounded. It may well be that seeing your own translation through the lens of another translator's version of a text reveals features which would not otherwise be so apparent, or even revealed at all. Four tendencies were highlighted as a result of comparing my translation with that of C.C. and the ST of which I was unaware. The first is a tendency to alter present tense forms, from a present participle to an infinitive,

Table 7.1 Comparison of the two translations of the extract from *El Discurso Vacío*

Feature	*My TT*	*C.C.'s TT*
Tokens/words	730	705
Types (lemmatised)	312	309
Type-token ratio (TTR)	42.7%	43.8%
Average sentence length	29.2	27.0 words
Hapax legomena	208	209
Hapax legomena as % of text	28.5	29.6
Ten most frequently occurring words as % of text	27.1	28.8
Top ten words (frequency)		
1	the (38)	the (35)
2	to (28)	to (30)
3	I (25)	I (26)
4	and (18)	and (23)
5	that (18)	that (18)
6	of (17)	a (16)
7	with (17)	of (15)
8	a (13)	my (14)
9	my (13)	with (14)
10	for (11)	for (12)

186   *The Auto-analysis of Translator Style*

Table 7.2 Sentence length bands in my TT and C.C.'s TT

Sentence length bands	My TT	C.C.'s TT
0–6	4	6
0–10	7	8
11–19	3	1
20–35	8	12
36–60	7	4
60–100	0	1
Sentence total	25	26
Average length	29.2	27.0

and from the present indicative to the present continuous and vice versa. There were four instances of these changes, which are not dictated by TL or SL conventions, illustrated by the following examples (figures in brackets are word totals):

EDV extract	My TT	C.C.'s TT
Debo seguir pensando en esto. (5)	I must continue to think about this. (7)	I must keep thinking about this. (6)
...la chispa divina que recorre infatigablemente el Universo y lo anima, lo sostiene, le presta realidad bajo su aspecto de cáscara vacía. (39)	...the divine spark which tirelessly roams the Universe, breathing life into it, sustaining it and giving it substance behind the façade of an empty shell. (41)	...the divine spark that tirelessly works its way through the Universe and brings it to life, sustains it, lends substance to its empty-shell appearance. (41)

The second also relates to verb usage and involves a change from active to passive voice:

EDV extract	My TT	C.C.'s TT
Quiero escribir y publicar. (5)	I want to write and to be published. (7)	I want to write and publish. (6)

This choice is also optional, but may have been influenced by the broad TL tendency for authors to talk about wanting *to be published* as an ambition, rather than *to publish.*[5]

The third tendency, three instances of changing commas into dashes[6] on either side of parenthetical clauses, seems to qualify as stylistically distinctive in that there is no obvious TL or SL/ST influence involved, coupled with the fact that I noticed this tendency when I was revising

The Auto-analysis of Translator Style   187

my initial draft of *Gracias por el Fuego*. Benedetti does not use dashes in the novel at all, and I converted my dashes back into commas during the revision.

EDV *extract*	*My TT*	*C.C.'s TT*
Tengo necesidad de ver mi nombre, mi verdadero nombre y no el que me pusieron, en letras de molde. (19)	I have a need to see my name – my real name, not the one they gave me – in print. (19)	I have a need to see my name, my real name and not the one that was given to me, in print. (22)

I would suggest that the stylistic effect of dashes is to add emphasis to the separation of the clause and thus foreground its content. This is similar to the reader attention-capturing effect of mini-paragraphs noted by Emmott, Sanford and Dawydiak in their research on cognitive stylistics (2007:212,215).

The final tendency is that of simplification, as shown by this example:

EDV *extract*	*My TT*	*C.C.'s TT*
En cierto momento, y no hace mucho tiempo, el ejercicio caligráfico diario estuvo a punto de volverse un ejercicio literario. (20)	At one point, not long ago, the daily calligraphy exercise nearly turned into a literary one. (16)	At one point, and not that long ago, my daily penmanship exercise was on the verge of becoming a literary one. (21)

Here I have omitted the conjunction *y* and the modifier *mucho*, and also somewhat flattened out the phrase *estuvo a punto de*, rendering it simply as *nearly turned into*. In this instance, it was the comparison with C.C.'s translation which highlighted for me what I had done, since she has retained the ST phrasing more closely.

Step 6: The final step was to compare my translations of the two extracts to see if there were common features which suggested stylistic distinctiveness, and three emerged. The first was the change from active to passive voice, of which there was one example in each TT. The second was the addition of emphasis, which took different forms in the two translations. In the *Gracias por el Fuego* TT the added emphasis was linguistic, while in the *El Discurso Vacío* TT it was typographical, involving the use of dashes. The third feature was that of simplification, which took the form of the removal of repetition in *Gracias por el Fuego* and the linguistic simplification of a more complex phrase in *El Discurso Vacío*.

188   *The Auto-analysis of Translator Style*

Analysis of the Results of the Investigation

In terms of methodology, the results of the investigation support the idea that comparison with STs adds a useful triangulatory dimension to the auto-analysis of translator style, and of translator style in general, which an exclusive focus on different TTs cannot provide. The open-ended, data-driven approach which does not start from a predetermined hypothesis has also been shown to be productive, allowing the analyst to follow up interesting results with no preconceived idea about what these are likely to reveal. The results also highlight the value of being able to compare different translations of the same text. However, it must be acknowledged, as Saldanha notes, that 'a method based on retranslations is of limited usefulness, since it can be applied only to a relatively limited number of works' (2011b:33). But overall, the idea that a CDR approach to the auto-analysis of translator style can yield valuable results and insights into aspects of translation practice which are wholly or largely unconscious is supported by this investigation.

I acknowledged earlier that this investigation was based on very short text samples, and therefore the results must be regarded as tentative. That said, it is instructive to note that when making decisions about whether to publish a translation, publishers generally ask for samples of no more than 1,000 words,[7] which suggests that they can make important judgements about quality, style and content on the basis of this amount of text. While a larger number of translations would clearly lend greater weight to any common features found, the key would seem to be not necessarily the length, but the representativeness of the sample(s) chosen for analysis. In this regard, I must also acknowledge that there was no form of independent check on the sample from *Gracias por el Fuego* which I chose to use, other than the criteria which I outlined, and that my much greater familiarity with that novel than with *El Discurso Vacío*[8] may also have influenced the investigation in various ways.

The results of the analysis in terms of tendencies found can be divided into two groups. On the one hand, there are those features, such as added emphasis and simplification, which provide support for the idea of translation universals already referred to, and which by definition can be found in the work of many, if not most, translators. On the other, there are habits such as the conversion of parenthetical commas into dashes and present participles into infinitives, and the changing of present tense verb forms from indicative to continuous (and vice versa), which would appear to be independent of text, author and SL or TL conventions. These might be considered potential identifiers of an individual translatorial style.

What all these features have in common, however, is that I was not aware of them prior to undertaking this auto-stylistic investigation. Its

The Auto-analysis of Translator Style   189

value for me, therefore, lies not so much in being able to claim that I have discovered unique identifiers of my style, as in bringing into the realm of consciousness translation habits which are cumulatively capable of influencing the style of my translations and their relationships to their source texts. The methodology does not end, however, with the discovery of possible patterns of linguistic usage hitherto unknown to the translator. Two more important questions need to be addressed: which of these possible linguistic habits are probable or definite habits? And do they have a significant impact on the way the translator translates?

7.2 Assessing the Impact of Stylistic Auto-analysis on How One Translates

The exercise in auto-analysis of translator style described in the previous section identified six possible unconscious linguistic habits. These were the altering of present tense verb forms; the conversion of present participles or gerunds into infinitives; the changing of active to passive verb constructions; the substitution of dashes for parenthetical commas; an increase in the degree of emphasis used relative to the original, which may also relate to the dashes for commas tendency, since I think that dashes tend to emphasise the separation of the clause contained by them from the rest of the sentence; and simplification. In this section I show how CDR analyses can be used to help assess whether these six tendencies were evidenced by two translations completed in 2018, after the translation of *Gracias por el Fuego*.

I translated four short stories from a collection by the contemporary Bolivian author Edmundo Paz Soldán entitled *Desencuentros* [Dis-appointments] (2018),[9] and a chapter from a contemporary Greek autobiographical novel entitled *Ο πόνος της επιστροφής* [Bittersweet nostalgia] (2015:85–91) by Άγγελος Μανουσόπουλος [Angelos Manousopoulos]. The chapter is entitled 'Άγγελοι πάνω από το Βερολίνο' [Angels over Berlin].[10] The Spanish and Greek texts are very different in content and style from each other, and both are different from *Gracias por el Fuego*. The 104 stories in the 'Dis-appointments' collection are all very short, ranging from a single sentence to six pages. They are characterised by dark humour and a form of Kafkaesque urban magical realism which has been dubbed 'McOndo' to distinguish it from the rural magical realism of García Márquez' Macondo (O'Bryen 2011).

The Greek novel consists of a series of chapters which are very similar to self-contained short stories, each dealing with a particular experience or theme forming part of the author's adolescence and early adulthood. Written in the first person they are humorous and often nostalgic accounts which nevertheless portray a series of relationships – family, peer group and neighbourhood – in perceptive and often uncompromising terms. I consider the stories and chapter chosen to be representative of

190 *The Auto-analysis of Translator Style*

the style of each author. The advantage of using translations from different languages and genres for analysis is that it helps to isolate linguistic usage features that are specific to the translator. If some or all of the six tendencies can be shown to be present in both translations this provides evidence that they are less likely to be the result of SL, genre or author influence.

Methodology

The four short stories were compiled into separate ST and TT corpora by merging individual files in MS Word, and the book chapter was saved as two separate files, ST and TT. Parallel corpora were then constructed in each case, by using LF Aligner 4.1 and uploading the resulting Translation Memory eXchange(TMX) file to Sketch Engine. The four individual corpora are comparable in size: the Spanish ST is 1,594 words and its English TT is 1,600 words; the Greek ST is 1,368 words and its English TT is 1,532 words. Two different approaches were taken to the testing for the presence of the six translation tendencies: the 'manual' comparison of the sentence-aligned STs and TTs using the free, open-source TMX Editor, which displays and allows for the editing of TMX files created in LF Aligner; and the use of corpus query language (CQL) queries for specific words, parts of speech and linguistic phenomena such as hapax legomena.

Sketch Engine automatically tokenises,[11] counts and parses the text so that a POS tag can be assigned to each word. The tests I used to look for evidence of the five tendencies are set out in *Table 7.3*, which includes the specific CQL queries used. It is important to remember that the tagsets – the lists of letters and symbols used to construct the individual tags – vary from language to language, both as regards the specific letters and symbols used and the range of parts of speech which are tagged. In terms of verbs, for example, neither the English nor Spanish tagsets allow searches for the active and passive voices, whereas the Greek one does. By contrast, only the English tagset allows searches for different forms of the verbs 'to be' and 'to have'.

Sketch Engine automatically chooses the appropriate tagset for each language, and a complete list of available tags can be accessed by clicking on the Tags button in either the Concordance or Parallel Concordance Advanced tab search screens, when CQL is selected as the search method. On a more cautious note, it should be remembered that tagging errors do occur and that CQL search results need to be carefully reviewed if accuracy of evidence and robustness of conclusions are to be maintained.

In all cases the methodology involved analysing both the ST and TT, but the starting point varied according to the linguistic phenomenon being searched for. In the case of the tendency to change the present indicative tense to the present continuous, I ran queries on the STs and then looked to see how the translation corresponded. In the case of

The Auto-analysis of Translator Style   191

Table 7.3 CQL queries used to identify possible specific translation habits

Possible translation habit	CQL query/queries	Search purpose
Changing present indicative to present continuous and vice versa	Spanish: [tag="VMIP.*"] Greek: [tag="VbMnIdPr.*"]	To find all main verbs in the present indicative tense.
	English: [tag="VVG.*"]	To find all present participles.
Changing present participles or gerunds to infinitives	Spanish: [tag="VMG.*"] Greek: [tag="VbMnPp.*"]	To find all gerunds/ participles.
	English: [tag="TO.*"]	To find all infinitives.
Changing active to passive voice	English: [tag="VVN.*"]	To find all past participles.
Changing parenthetical commas to dashes	English: [word ="--"]	To find all dashes.
Adding emphasis	English: [tag="JJS.*"]	To find all superlative adjectives.
	English: [word="very"] [tag="J.*"]	To find all instances of *very* followed by an adjective.
Simplification	English: [tag="V.*"|tag="N.*"|tag="J.*"|tag= "RB.?"] Spanish: [tag="V.*"|tag="N.*"|tag="A.*"|tag="R.*"] Greek: [tag="Vb.*"|tag="No.*"|tag="Aj.*"|tag="Ad.*"]	To find all verbs, nouns, adjectives and adverbs ('content' words).

the tendency to substitute the passive for the active voice, I ran a query on the TTs for past participles which are needed to form the passive in English – for example 'was shown' and 'had been taken' – and then looked to see if these formed part of a passive construction, and if so, if this corresponded to a passive or active voice construction in the ST.

Results and Analysis

Before summarising the results of each set of analyses it is worth noting that the process of analysing linguistic usage in three languages

192 *The Auto-analysis of Translator Style*

highlighted some important differences between them, and showed some of the different ways in which English 'responds' to contrasting grammars. This is particularly true of verbs, aspects of whose usage formed the focus of the first three translation tendencies investigated.

1. Changing from the present indicative tense to the present continuous: The Spanish present indicative frequently needs to be translated as the present continuous in English, as, for example, in *Ya voy* [*I'm coming*, rather than *I come*], and is generally used for action which is actually in progress (Butt and Benjamin 2000:230). Greek does not have a present continuous tense, so its present indicative can be translated by either the present indicative or the present continuous in English, according to context. My methodology involved looking for all the instances of verbs in the present indicative in the Spanish and Greek corpora to see how they had been translated. Of the 41 hits in Spanish and the 105 in Greek, the vast majority of the translations were grammatically determined, as in the Spanish example above. Where there was a non-grammatically determined choice as to which tense to use, I could find no instance of a change from indicative to continuous. However, in the course of reviewing the results of the searches, I did notice that I had changed not only present participles into infinitives, but also vice versa.

2. Changing participles or gerunds to infinitives, and vice versa: All three languages possess participles, and infinitives, and Spanish and English possess gerunds,[12] but I would hazard the suggestion that present participles are used more frequently in English. Given this, it was possible to search in both directions for tendencies to change verb forms: from STs to TTs and vice versa. In terms of changes from participles or gerunds to infinitives, I found two instances of non-grammatically determined changes in the Spanish corpus and one in the Greek corpus, as illustrated below.

ST: ...los grafitis continuaron <u>apareciendo</u>

(Paz Soldán 2018:215, emphasis added)

TT: ...the graffiti continued <u>to appear</u>

(emphasis added)

ST: πόσο δύσκολη υπόθεση είναι η <u>παρακολούθηση</u> μιας τέτοιας ταινίας κάτω από τέτοιες συνθήκες...

(Μανουσόπουλος 2015:88, emphasis added)

TT: ...what a difficult business it is <u>to watch</u> films like this under such circumstances...

(emphasis added)

The Auto-analysis of Translator Style   193

In the Greek example the word παρακολούθηση is used as a noun-participle meaning *following* or *observation*. On reflection I decided to revise the translation to read 'what a difficult business it is <u>following</u> films like this under such circumstances', in other words to preserve the participle on the basis of improved fluency, and to change the translation of the verb for greater accuracy of meaning, since *following* is a more attention-rich activity than merely *watching*.

In terms of changing infinitives into participles or gerunds, I found two instances of non-grammatically determined change in the Spanish corpus and two in the Greek corpus, as illustrated below.

ST: El presidente de la compañía ha anunciado la imposibilidad de <u>rescatar</u>los

(Paz Soldán 2018:46, emphasis added)

TT: The Company president has declared the impossibility of <u>rescuing</u> them

(emphasis added)

which could have been translated as '...declared it impossible <u>to rescue</u> them'.

ST: Και μάλιστα στις πιο καθημερινές και τετριμμένες εκφάνσεις της: <u>να</u> <u>γυρνάς</u> κουρασμένος από τη δουλειά, <u>να μουτζουρώνεις</u> τα δάχτυλά σου από την εφημερίδα...

(Μανουσόπουλος 2015:88, emphasis added)

TT: And certainly its most common, everyday occurrences: <u>coming</u> home from work tired, <u>smudging</u> your fingers on the newspaper...

(emphasis added)

which could have been translated as '<u>to come</u> home from work tired, <u>to smudge</u> your fingers on the newspaper...' as in the ST. The four instances, involving changes in both directions, provide some evidence that this might be a translation tendency, but there is much less evidence that the changes have a significant impact on the translation.

3. Changing verbs from the active to the passive voice: Sketch Engine provides tags for the active and passive voice in Greek, but not in Spanish or English. So, the main search query I used was for past participles in English, needed to form the passive tenses, designed to help identify instances of the passive voice and see how these related to the STs. No examples of a change of voice were found.

194　*The Auto-analysis of Translator Style*

4. Changing parenthetical commas to dashes: Although often considered interchangeable, Houston suggests that 'the dash's modern use [is] to surround parenthetical clauses, which when spoken, warrant a pause on either side' (2014:150). The University of North Carolina's Writing Center goes further, suggesting that 'Where parentheses indicate that the reader should put less emphasis on the enclosed material, dashes indicate that the reader should pay <u>more</u> attention to the material between the dashes'[13] (emphasis added). This accords with my view that dashes add emphasis relative to commas as well as brackets. Searching for the presence of dashes in the TTs, and seeing if they corresponded to dashes in the STs, was straightforward and revealed one instance in the Spanish corpus and two in the Greek corpus where I had substituted dashes for commas, as illustrated below:

ST: … todas las frases que eran borradas un día retornaban insidiosas, a la vez ambiguas y precisas, reveladoras e impenetrables, al día siguiente.

(Paz Soldán 2018:217)

TT: … all the phrases that were rubbed out one day returned insidiously – being at once ambiguous and exact, revealing and impenetrable – the next.

I would suggest that the dashes in this case are slightly more emphatic than the commas they replace but are primarily aids to reading, making it easier to sort out the main and subordinate clauses. A tendency to use pairs of dashes to separate subclauses is one of which I had been semi-aware before conducting these investigations, and evidence revealed by the latter serves as a reminder to use this stylistic device with care.

5. Adding emphasis: In addition to looking for paired dashes as a possible form of added emphasis, I searched for instances in the TTs of *very* followed by an adjective to see if these corresponded to weaker modifiers in the STs, as this is what had been found in the initial auto-stylistic investigation. I only found one example, in the Greek corpus, but it was telling. The context is a scene where the author and his friend, both teenagers at the time, are watching a film and the main characters have the ability to read people's minds. The friend comments that he would especially love to be able to read girls' minds, and the author replies:

ST: Ειδικά οι γκόμενες καλύτερα να μη μάθεις ποτέ τι σκέφτονται για σένα, είπα από μέσα μου και <u>χάρηκα</u> που ο φίλος μου δεν μπορούσε να διαβάσει τη σκέψη μου.

(Μανουσόπουλος 2015:87, emphasis added)

TT: It would be better if you never knew what the babes in particular think of you, I thought to myself, and was <u>very pleased</u> that my friend couldn't read my mind.

(emphasis added)

The Auto-analysis of Translator Style 195

The Greek verb χάρηκα simply means *I was glad* rather than *I was very pleased*, and this suggests that where a contrast is involved – in this case between the author's opinion and that of his friend – I may be prone to overemphasising the contrast. This particular example is relatively mild in its effect on the translation (and having spotted it, I revised the translation accordingly), but if regularly practised this kind of linguistic alteration could have a significant cumulative stylistic and narrative impact on translation.

6. Simplification: As Ekaterina Lapshinova-Koltunski observes, 'If core patterns of lexical use are observed [...] we can identify simplification comparing the proportion of content (or lexical) words vs. grammatical words' (2015:96). This proportion is a measure of lexical density or richness (see Chapter 2, Section 2.2), and the higher the proportion of content words, the lexically richer the text. As previously mentioned, there are different ways of defining 'content' words, but a commonly used measure comprises all verbs, nouns, adjectives and adverbs. These can easily be searched for in all three languages, using a single CQL query for each language, and the results show an increase of 9% in the content word proportion in the Spanish corpus TT (from 52.0% to 56.8%) and a decrease of 2.8% in that of the Greek corpus TT (from 56.2% to 54.6%). Neither result provides any clear evidence of simplification. There are other kinds of simplification, particularly syntactical and semantic, but testing for these is a more complex process and is more easily done if specific linguistic phenomena to search for have been identified beforehand.

Conclusions and Possible Methodologies for Future Stylistic Auto-analysis

As with the translation samples investigated in the first section of this chapter, it is necessary to acknowledge the limitations of the analysis. The corpora used are short, 1,594 words of Spanish and 1,368 of Greek, and conclusions based on them are necessarily tentative. Furthermore, translator style and the various linguistic habits which comprise it are not set in stone, but may change over time, particularly in response to experience, and may also vary to some extent according to author, genre, period and SL. Nevertheless, the purpose of the exercise was simple. Having identified six possible translation habits of which I had hitherto been unaware, I wanted to see if evidence could be found of their presence in subsequent translations, and if so, what their impact on how I translate might be.

The picture which emerges from the results is a mixed one. There was no evidence of a tendency to change the present indicative to the present continuous, to change the active voice to the passive, or of simplification as measured by lexical richness. There was some evidence of a tendency

196   *The Auto-analysis of Translator Style*

to switch between present participles or gerunds and infinitives, to substitute pairs of dashes for pairs of commas and to add emphasis by increasing the strength of modifiers. These latter three tendencies raise some interesting questions. The first two do not appear to alter meaning, only style, while the last one has a potentially more significant impact on content as well.

After reviewing the instances in which a non-grammatically determined choice was made to switch between participles or gerunds and infinitives, it seems that the unconscious motivation was to retain linguistic rhythm and flow. Using a sequence of participles or gerunds can feel smoother and more fluent than a series of infinitives. For example, 'I like walking, sailing and playing the guitar' has a more fluent feel than 'I like to walk, to sail and to play the guitar', which involves more of a stop-start rhythm that emphasises each activity separately. The appropriateness of changing the verb forms in translation will, of course, depend on how well they reflect the style of the ST and, indeed, whether equivalence of stylistic effect is a translation goal.

The same applies to the use of dashes instead of commas. Depending on the context, the lengthened mental pauses that I have argued are created by dashes may result in real added emphasis, or may simply help to prevent a clause being 'buried' in a long and syntactically complex sentence which might be normal for a SL reader, but not a TL reader. The possible tendency to add emphasis through augmenting the strength of modifiers is of greater concern. A brief analysis of the contexts in which this occurs suggests that it is where two attributes or actions or situations are contrasted. I appear to want to emphasise this contrast more strongly than the ST does, and this could result in both stylistic and narrative distortions. As with the other two tendencies, an awareness of its existence should now make it easier to control.

The aim of this application of the CDR approach is to develop simple but reliable methods for identifying one's own unconscious or semiconscious linguistic habits and propensities, capable of affecting translation, which can be used by literary translators without the need for specialist computing or statistical knowledge. As Pekkanen notes, this would also be very useful for students:

> making student translators aware of their own and others' personal [linguistic] propensities will allow students to develop as translators who can make conscious choices with an awareness of the macrolevel effects of their decisions.

(2010:168)

In principle, a literary translator interested in analysing their own style could use the same kind of methodologies as those used by translation

The Auto-analysis of Translator Style   197

scholars to identify translator style. These centre on various forms of linguistic patterning including usage of the reporting verbs *say* and *tell*, and the optional use of *that* with these verbs (Baker 2000; Saldanha 2011b); the use of emphatic italics (Saldanha 2011c); the use of alliteration and syntactic amplification (Munday 2008a); a variety of formal shifts such as expansion, contraction, addition and deletion of linguistic elements; and shifts in the order of those elements (Pekkanen 2010).

However, in addition to the analytical complexity of some of these studies, they often include both conscious and unconscious choices on the part of the translator. On the assumption that translators are aware of their conscious choices and can therefore in principle control them, my focus is on ways of discovering habits and choices which are likely to be unconscious, but which can be identified as occurring regularly across a range of translations of different authors, genres and ideally from different languages. There are essentially three ways of doing this, which are not mutually exclusive. All three ways do, however, rely on there being a body of source texts and their translations which are available in digital format and which can be compiled into searchable corpora in a programme such as Sketch Engine or CATMA. The first is to use analyses which look for the presence of specific linguistic phenomena in a translator's work, particularly those which have been shown to be used by other translators. The second is to start with more open-ended analyses, such as those used in the investigation of my own translation habits earlier in this section, and see where the results lead. The last is to compare different translations of the same text in the same language, where available.

Some examples of each approach will illustrate how I envisage the methodology being applied. To see whether they had a propensity for linguistic expansion or contraction, a translator could run simple queries for total word count and average sentence length for several ST-TT pairs. If there was evidence of a consistent pattern either way it could be further investigated if desired, for example, by means of a more fine-grained analysis of sentence length. Similarly, analyses of standardised TTRs and proportions of content words could be used to see if there was a tendency to use simpler or more complex language relative to the original. It should be noted that these particular analytical measures are all quick and easy to use, and could be used on STs and TTs separately, without the need to create a parallel corpus.

A more open-ended, but by definition less frequently available, approach would involve a translator using retranslations to compare their version with that of another translator. In the case of my own self-investigation this proved to be the most revealing method of all. Similar queries could be run on the ST and both TTs, and if the results suggested further investigation, the creation of a sentence-aligned, triple parallel

198   *The Auto-analysis of Translator Style*

text – ST, TT1 and TT2 – could be created, as in the case of Rothwell's retranslation of Zola's *Joie de vivre*, cited in Chapter 1. The investigations have also highlighted for me some subtle distinctions between different forms of linguistic expression, such as between gerunds and infinitives, and how languages differ in their possession and use of such distinctions. As Andrew Rothwell says, 'it is only when a text is viewed through the lens of another language that its hidden linguistic riches and lacunae become visible' (2009:270).

Notes

1 The lemma of a word is its base root, and a lemmatised list of word types would count the inflections of that lemma as a single type: for example, the lemma *say* would represent instances of *say, says, saying* and *said*. The purpose of lemmatisation is to help provide a more accurate representation of lexical variety. In Spanish, for instance, inflections are far more numerous than in English, but this does not mean that its higher raw type count indicates greater lexical variety.

2 www.laurenceanthony.net/software/antconc/ [accessed 17 March 2017].

3 I had difficulty finding Spanish lemma lists that could be successfully imported into AntConc, to act as a reference corpus against which to process the Spanish text loaded into the programme. However, the programme's developer, Laurence Anthony, kindly built me a Spanish lemma list after I contacted him about this problem, and this is now available on his website for anyone else who wishes to lemmatise Spanish texts. I would now use Sketch Engine, which has built-in lemma lists for a wide range of languages.

4 For consistency I decided to use the same sentence length bands as in the Chapter 5 analyses.

5 C.C. is Canadian, and it is possible that some subtle differences between North American and British English may be significant.

6 These are technically known as 'em dashes', so-called because their length is held to equate to the width of the lower case letter *m* (Houston 2014:145).

7 Comment by panel members at the Publishers' Armchair session at International Translation Day, British Library, 30 September 2016.

8 I read the entire novel before translating the extract, but have not reread it since 2014.

9 The stories are as follows: Kathia [Kathia], p. 78; Anaheim, California [Anaheim, California], pp. 46–47; Cuento con dictador y tarjetas [The dictator and the greetings cards], pp. 202–203; and Fábula de la Ciudad Blanca y los grafitis [The tale of Ciudad Blanca and the graffiti], pp. 214–217.

10 These translations have not been published, and the Greek novel appears to be self-published online. Available at: https://free-ebooks.gr/βιβλίο/3a4V/o-πόνος-της-επιστροφής

11 'Tokens' include punctuation marks as well as words.

12 Gerunds and participles have the same form in English, namely the addition of the ending–*ing* to the root (e.g. *walk* becomes *walking*), but their usage differs. A gerund is a verb form used as a noun, e.g. *I like walking*; whereas a participle is a verb form used as an adjective, e.g. *the walking wounded,* or with an auxiliary verb, e.g. *I was walking* (Burchill 1998:328–329).

13 https://writingcenter.unc.edu/tips-and-tools/semi-colons-colons-and-dashes/

8 Conclusions

Assessing the Potential of the Methodology

This book began with a question: why do literary translators, and their trainers, often give the impression that they are at best ambivalent about the use of technology in literary translation, and at worst simply antagonistic? The answer seems to be that 'technology' in this context is generally assumed to mean machine translation (MT), computer-aided translation (CAT) tools or a combination of both, which are seen as either inappropriate or a threat to the skills and livelihoods of literary translators. While not ruling out the idea that these two technologies may become more relevant to literary translation in the future, the approach advocated in this book is one that broadens the field of what is coming to be called 'computer-assisted literary translation' (CALT).[1] The central argument has been that a combination of close and distant, or computer-assisted, reading can bring corpus-linguistic (CL) and text-visualisation tools and techniques to bear creatively and productively on the process of literary translation. Specifically, it is claimed that the use of this methodology can produce better informed translations than those which rely on close reading alone, and does not deskill or attempt to replace human translation, but actually enhances it.

This argument has been supported by the case study of a book-length translation from Spanish to English, initially drafted using traditional methods and then subjected to the close and distant reading (CDR) approach, which resulted in significant revisions. In addition, it has been argued that the CDR methodology offers translators a possible way of identifying and analysing their own translatorial style, and some evidence for this was provided by analyses of the case study translation and six other shorter translations by the author. The first section of this final chapter attempts to assess the strengths and limitations of the methodology, while the second looks at the potential for its future development and its relevance to translation studies (TS) scholars, postgraduate translation students and professional literary translators.

200 *Assessing the Potential of the Methodology*

8.1 Assessing the Strengths and Limitations of the Methodology

In Chapter 1 it was argued that this methodology can be used in three specific ways as part of the literary translation process, and in one more general way:

1. In analysing the source text (ST) during and after initial reading, and in helping the translator to formulate specific translation goals.
2. In undertaking the first draft of the translation.
3. In comparing the ST and draft translation, with a view to seeing if certain translation goals have been achieved, and what has actually happened in the translation process.
4. In the auto-analysis of translator style.

Each of these is discussed below in more detail.

1 ST analysis

In Section 2.2 of Chapter 2 five types of potentially standard CDR analyses were listed that could be used on a literary text in order to help build a computer-aided stylistic profile of some of its key structural and linguistic aspects. These were corpus summaries, word lists, keyword lists, n-grams and simple measures of lexical richness. The criteria used to select these as standard tests were speed and ease of use, the production of results which were likely to be able to inform translation decisions and goal-setting, and the capacity to provide potential benchmarks against which to compare the draft translation. For each type of analysis an explanation of the kind of data it can provide and the potential relevance of that data to translation was given, supported by an example of information extracted that could not have been obtained by close reading alone.

A summary was also given of the potential benefits to a literary translator of using this set of computer-aided analytical tools, which can identify

*   the frequency, distribution and context of occurrence of words and phrases, including words which only occur once (word lists and n-grams)
*   themes and potentially hidden aspects of authorial style (word lists, keyword lists and n-grams)
*   structural features of style such as sentence length and the range and register of vocabulary used (corpus summaries, lexical richness measures).

In addition to these standard analyses, two detailed examples were given of how the CDR approach was applied to the case study translation: characterisation (in Chapter 2) and sentence length (in Chapter 5). These analyses are summarised below.

An investigation of characterisation in the novel was carried out through frequency and distribution analysis of named character references; analysis of a single character – Edmundo – by concordance and discourse analysis of his direct speech; and by a network analysis visualisation which produced a map of the 87 interacting characters in the novel, showing certain key aspects of their relationships. These analyses were collectively able to inform the translation by producing a deeper and more rounded appreciation of character portrayal, showing how they can help the translator to find an appropriate voice for each character and also to make decisions about the translation of register, dialect and idiolect.

In Chapter 5, I analysed the stylistic and narrative importance of punctuation, in particular sentence length and structure. My impression that short sentences were often used and that they had particular effects on me as reader-then-translator – tending to draw me into the narrative – was confirmed by initial quantitative, and subsequent qualitative, analysis. A detailed analysis of banded sentence length by chapter and for the novel as a whole was undertaken, and the average sentence length of *Gracias por el Fuego* was also compared to reference corpora of Spanish and Latin American twentieth-century fiction, showing that it was significantly shorter. When seen in the light of a translation approach, detailed in Chapter 3, which aimed to preserve both the form and content of the ST as closely as possible, this led to a decision to attempt to broadly preserve both sentence length and boundaries in the target text (TT). Triangulation for this decision was provided in the form of comparisons with the French translation of the novel, in which sentences are frequently split or merged, which demonstrated how such alterations can lead to narrative and stylistic shifts. For example, the amalgamation of short sentences in interior monologues can lead to a reduction in the overall intensity of the narrative and in the significance of individual acts, thoughts and descriptions.

As a final example, in Chapter 6 I investigated Benedetti's use of the high-frequency function word *y* [and], which emerged from an open-ended word frequency analysis as being potentially stylistically relevant. The way an author uses such words is considered within the field of stylometry often to be beyond her/his conscious control, and in part for that reason to be capable of acting as a unique identifier or linguistic 'fingerprint' of an author's style (Mosteller and Wallace 1964; Burrows 1997; Holmes 1998; Stamatatos 2009; Jockers 2013). The use of such words is, however, something which as human readers we are not programmed to register or keep track of, unless it deviates substantially from the normal range of usage. The fact that both the repeated presence and also the repeated absence of *y* in long sentences could be stylistically relevant, each producing different effects, was brought out and helped to provide more information about the nature of Benedetti's authorial style.

202 *Assessing the Potential of the Methodology*

2 As an aid to translation

In Chapter 2 the analysis of the title of the novel, *Gracias por el Fuego,* centred on whether the word *fuego* should be translated as *fire* or *light.* Three kinds of CDR analysis were used: a frequency, distribution and contextual analysis of occurrences of the word *fuego* in the text; a comparison of the titles of six other translations of the ST into different languages; and an analysis of the book cover illustrations of 25 different ST editions and the 6 published translations already mentioned. The consensus of the results of these analyses suggested that the word should be translated as *light.*

Corpora offer powerful aids to solving specific translation challenges. This is important given that translators spend a good deal of their time looking for information, and yet there is strong evidence that very few professional translators actually use corpora at all in their work. There are two main kinds of corpora that a translator could use to look up problematic words and phrases:

- monolingual source language (SL) corpora such as the *Corpus del Español*[2] and the TenTen Corpus Family[3] which is built into Sketch Engine
- parallel bilingual corpora, where texts in one language are sentence-aligned with their translations in another.

An example was given in Section 1.3 of Chapter 1 of an uncommon phrase which neither dictionaries nor online searches were able to resolve satisfactorily: *soga y cabrito.* Using two features of Sketch Engine – Word Sketch and a monolingual Spanish reference corpus – its meaning [everything] became clear. In Section 2.4 of Chapter 2 another example was given of an uncommon verb, *arrebolarse,* used by Edmundo. Character analysis helped to contextualise the use of this word, and monolingual corpora helped to identify the degree of its unusualness, leading to thesaurus searches for a correspondingly rare word in English and a decision to use the word *rubifying,* rather than the more common *reddening.*

3 Comparison of the ST and the draft translation

In Chapter 6 it was argued that the same CDR methodology used to analyse the ST can also be used to compare ST and draft translation, thus assisting the revision process and helping the translator to assess the extent to which they have achieved certain translation goals. These goals include overall strategies such as aiming for equivalence of stylistic effect and specific subsidiary goals such as the preservation of average sentence length. It was argued that this comparison could be undertaken in different ways, including applying the same standard CDR analyses to the TT as were used for the ST. Three examples from the case study translation

Assessing the Potential of the Methodology 203

were given to illustrate the comparison process in detail: sentence length, frequent and infrequent repetition, and the use of the high-frequency function word *and*.

A total of eight standard CDR analyses, drawn from those available via corpus summaries and word lists in Sketch Engine, were used: word and sentence count; average sentence length; TTR; and hapax in terms of total count, total divided by overall word count, as total lemmas and as a proportion of total lemmas. The results showed that word count, sentence count and average sentence length had broadly been maintained, while measures of lexical diversity gave a more mixed picture. Measures based on simple word count, such as TTR, showed a greater difference between ST and TT than those based on lemmas, which it was argued in Chapter 2 provide a more accurate basis for cross-linguistic quantification comparisons between Spanish and English. The process of converting an ST and draft TT into a fully searchable, POS (part of speech)-tagged parallel corpus was also explained, and the benefits of using a sentence-aligned Translation Memory eXchange(TMX) file for translation revision were illustrated. These included being able to see where sentences had been left untranslated by mistake, where they had been merged or split, and identifying specific issues which might benefit from further investigation, such as repetitions or unusual words.

The sentence length data of the TT was analysed in exactly the same way as that of the ST (for full details of both, see **Appendix A, Tables A1 and A2**). The results showed that the total number of sentences, average sentence length and the proportions of sentences in the 1–10 word and 101 word plus bands had been broadly maintained, but that there was a reduction in the proportion of 1–6-word sentences. Statistics for word count and average sentence length showed that there was a greater observed-than-expected difference in Chapter 14, and this was investigated in detail. The suggested explanation for this involved a combination of voluntary explicitation and the contrastive linguistics of Spanish and English.

The ability of CL software, and sentence-aligned parallel corpora in particular, to search for repetitions of specific words and phrases and to show how they have been translated on each occasion was also illustrated in Section 6.3 of Chapter 6. The ten occurrences of the verb *estallar*, for example, were originally translated in six different ways. The word was shown to have both narrative and stylistic importance, but its occurrences were widely spread across the novel, meaning that without the use of computer analysis it was easy not to see a linguistic pattern which was relevant to translation. The result of the analysis was to opt for a single, consistent translation for all ten instances: *erupt*.

A CDR analysis of the use of the Spanish high-frequency function word *y* and its primary English counterpart *and* is a good example of a pattern of language use which can often be of stylistic significance, but

204 *Assessing the Potential of the Methodology*

which close reading alone is incapable of detecting because as readers we simply do not register this kind of information. Having identified the occurrences of the word as of interest due to their particularly high frequency in two of the novel's chapters, CDR analysis of their translations in those chapters produced two interesting findings. First, while forming an apparently closely mapped pair of co-ordinating conjunctions, *y* and *and* in fact possess a much more nuanced relationship: *y* can be translated in at least ten different ways in English according to context. Second, the word's presence or absence can create marked stylistic and narrative effects – such as increasing or reducing the reading rhythm – particularly in the context of long sentences. A reassessment of the translation in the light of this analysis resulted in a significant number of revisions designed to try to recreate perceived ST stylistic effects.

4 Stylistic auto-analysis

As with the previous example, the CDR methodology opens up possibilities for the auto-analysis of translator style that highlight the benefits of a partnership between close and distant reading. In Chapter 7 an experimental two-stage investigation of my own translatorial style was undertaken. The first stage involved comparing three translations in different ways. Two of the translations were my own – one from the case study and another of an extract from a novel by another Uruguayan author, Mario Levrero – and one was by another translator. Standard CDR analyses – corpus summaries, word lists and lexical diversity measures – were combined with close reading, and all three translations were initially compared with their respective STs, and then with each other, which provided some triangulation.

The results provided possible evidence for the existence of six linguistic habits related to translation, ranging from added emphasis and simplification to grammatical alterations to verb tense and voice, none of which I had been aware of. The second stage involved a follow-up analysis of a further five short translations from Spanish and Greek which postdated the case study and Mario Levrero translations by three years. The aim was to see if these translations provided any evidence to support the existence of the six tendencies originally identified. The Spanish and Greek originals and their translations were saved as separate corpora and then converted into sentence-aligned parallel corpora in Sketch Engine.

The analysis involved two linked processes: close reading of the sentence-aligned corpora and running a series of CQL queries on the parallel corpora based on searches for specific parts of speech. The results provided some evidence for three of the six tendencies. Two appear to be more related to style – switching between present participles or gerunds and infinitives, and substituting dashes for parenthetical commas – while one, adding emphasis, could affect meaning as well. Identifying these hitherto unconscious linguistic tendencies not only affords me a

Assessing the Potential of the Methodology   205

chance to exercise greater control over how I translate in the future, but also gives me some insight into how I *think* as a translator, since I was able to identify some possible causes for these three tendencies.

Summary

An overall assessment of the results of applying the CDR approach to the translation of *Gracias por el Fuego* and other texts suggests that it has provided evidence for the benefits of all four aspects of the CDR methodology, but to differing degrees. The first three – relating to ST analysis, assistance with the process of initial translation and comparison of the ST with a draft translation – are more strongly supported than the fourth, the auto-analysis of translatorial style. Multiple examples have been given of linguistic and stylistic information which has been produced by using the CDR methodology which close reading alone could either not have extracted at all or only at the cost of disproportionate time and effort.

These examples have also shown that this information is directly relevant to translation decision-making in relation to literary style, and can inform translation decisions at all levels of a text from the sentence upwards both during initial translation and at the revision stage. I hope to have shown that the tools and techniques used are either cheap or free, do not involve a steep learning curve in order to use successfully and can produce valid and meaningful results in most cases very quickly. Neither does the methodology result in the deskilling or replacement of human translators. On the contrary, by allowing the translator access to more information about a text and their translation than would otherwise be possible, translation as both process and product is enhanced.

While the emphasis in this book has been on the distant reading element of the CDR methodology, since this is most obviously what is new about the approach, it is important to stress that the methodology only works because it combines both types of reading in a partnership of equals. Either can be used as the starting point for an analysis, depending on context. The value of the methodology lies not in the simple addition of CL and text-visualisation tools to traditional close reading, like an extra tool in a toolbox. It resides in the fact that this is a methodology that involves a recursive dialogue between close reading and quantitative analysis, each suggesting tasks and research questions for which the other is admirably suited, and each responding to the challenges of these tasks. Close reading is empowered rather than diminished by a partnership with quantitative analysis.

The limitations of the approach, listed in Section 3 of the Introduction, must also be fully acknowledged. The need to choose stylistic features for reasons in addition to quantifiability is crucial since not everything which can be counted is of stylistic or translational relevance. There are

206 *Assessing the Potential of the Methodology*

also many important stylistic features, such as humour, irony and metaphor, which at present are undetectable by readily available computer software, if at all. The inevitable decontextualisation which accompanies computer-assisted literary analysis must always be borne in mind, and an important aspect of the methodology is both the need to move between the micro- and macro-levels of a text and the corresponding ability to 'zoom' in and out as required. Literary style is and will always be more than a collection of statistically measurable features, but such features can make a valuable contribution to its overall appreciation and translation. And lastly, the methodology is arguably of most relevance where the aim is to recreate ST style as closely as possible in the TT, which is not always the case.

8.2 Relevance of the Methodology for Translation Scholars, Students and Professional Literary Translators

The origin of this book was my PhD dissertation (Youdale 2017) which developed the CDR methodology and applied it to the case study translation. What made this a new approach in both theoretical and practical terms was that, to the best of my knowledge, it represented the first study in which a combination of close reading and computer-assisted quantitative analysis was applied to the process of translating a text, rather than to the product(s) of already completed translations. Since then I have extended and documented the range of analyses and software which can be used as part of the CDR approach, and applied them to more translations. Consequently, one aim of the book has been predominantly practical: to show by means of a wide range of examples and analytical techniques how CDR can be applied to the process of translating literary style.

The overall aim, as stated in the Introduction, is for this book to act as an open invitation to the community of translation scholars and literary translators to engage in a wider debate about how computer technology might be productively and creatively integrated into the practice of literary translation. This debate needs to take account of MT and CAT tools, but goes beyond these technologies and incorporates the use of CL and text-visualisation in partnership with close reading. It has been written with three groups in mind: translation scholars, students and literary translators.

Translation Scholars

The CDR approach has one foot in the Digital Humanities and one in TS, and it is a further aim of this book to help develop greater links between the two. The use of computer-assisted analysis in the broad field of literary studies is now an established part of the discipline. Apart from the work of Franco Moretti and the Stanford Literary Lab[4] there are the related fields of corpus stylistics, CL, stylometry, literary and

Assessing the Potential of the Methodology 207

linguistic computing, and computational narratology. Since 2012 an annual workshop has been organised by the Association for Computational Linguistics in North America under the title of 'Computational Linguistics for Literature' (Toral and Way 2018). Much of this research appears to be monolingual and Anglophone-centred, but nevertheless has insights to offer TS, such as Moretti's concept of 'operationalizing' and testing judgements and claims made about literary texts (Moretti 2013b), and Rybicki's recent use of stylometric authorship attribution techniques to identify translatorial as well as authorial presence in literary translations (Rybicki 2013; Rybicki and Heydel 2013).

In TS, CDR relates to three areas of study – translation technology, corpus-based translation studies (CTS) and style in and of translation. The use and effects of technology in non-literary translation have been, and continue to be, well documented (see Section 1.1 of Chapter 1). Research using eye-tracking, think-aloud protocols and analysis of the integration of MT and CAT tools into translator workflow are all well developed, and recently there has been a focus on MT post-editing in relation to quality and effort involved (see, for example, Toral, Wieling and Way 2018; Vieira and Alonso 2018). Since 1978 there has been an annual conference, now organised by the International Association for Advancement in Language Technology (ASLING),[5] entitled 'Translation and the Computer'. Since 2014 the possible uses of MT in literary translation have been, and continue to be, explored more seriously (see Section 1.2 of Chapter 1).

In relation to style in, and of, translation this book embraces both aspects but places more emphasis on the former. It is primarily concerned with more effective ways in which the perceived style of the ST can be analysed and recreated in translation. The focus on the effects of style on readers, central to this study, also links to what might be called the 'cognitive turn' in several related fields: cognitive TS, cognitive stylistics, cognitive narratology and reception theory more generally. But CDR is also concerned with style *of* translation and the identification by translators themselves of often unconscious linguistic habits. This is an area ripe for exploration and development, drawing on both stylometry and corpus stylistics.

It is in the field of CTS that CDR could perhaps make its most obvious contribution to TS. The use of corpora in research in CTS is now nearly 30 years old, and while the CDR methodology adapts a number of CTS' analytical tools and techniques to a different purpose, its contribution goes further than that. The broad trend in CTS has involved a move away from the detailed comparison of individual STs and TTs towards the analysis of multiple texts, both mono- and bilingual (Laviosa 2004; Shen 2010; Ji 2012). This has been influenced by the focus in TS since the 1980s on descriptive rather than prescriptive research (Blum-Kulka 1986; Toury 2012). My research runs counter to both trends in that it

208 *Assessing the Potential of the Methodology*

focuses on the analysis and translation of a single text, and also advocates the use of a particular methodology rather than simply describing it as a way of translating. In this way theory is related to practice very directly.

Students of Translation[6]

The CDR methodology has important implications for the training of literary translators. For translators the balance between the use of traditional translation skills, such as a high level of competence in both SL and TL and source culture knowledge and awareness, and the use of various forms of translation technology is changing rapidly. An ability to use both CAT tools, and now increasingly MT, has become a professional necessity rather than an option for non-literary translators. One implication of this technological trend for both students and practitioners is, as Pym notes, the need for translator training to involve a greater emphasis on 'skills (*knowing how*) rather than knowledge (*knowing that*)' (2013:496, emphasis in original). The methodology advocated in this book builds on the idea of technological skill development, but without downplaying the importance of traditional linguistic and cultural knowledge and expertise. It retains an emphasis on identifying possible translation solutions as well as selecting between them, both through close reading and computer-assisted pattern recognition and analysis. It preserves a balance between human intuition, experience and creativity, and the targeted application of computerised literary analysis.

According to the Postgraduate Search website, there are currently 41 universities in the UK offering a total of 129 postgraduate translation courses, 92 of which are MA programmes.[7] There are also MA or equivalent programmes in translation in a large number of other countries. Many of these cover literary translation, and given what has been said above regarding the widespread use of CAT tools and MT in the commercial translation sector, it has been suggested that 'translation software features heavily in virtually all [MA] translations studies courses' (Declerq 2015:366). A typical example is the unit on translation technology offered by the University of Bristol as part of its MA in Translation entitled 'Computer-Aided Translation (CAT)'. This kind of unit would provide a very appropriate framework within which to test and evaluate the methodology with students. Here it should also be noted that the use of the CDR approach is by no means confined to the Anglophone world. Its principles and applications are not specific to English, and key software programmes such as Sketch Engine can be used in a variety of other languages.

In addition to MA programmes in translation there is a framework which brings together a comprehensive but flexible model of competences needed by literary translators during training and also during

Assessing the Potential of the Methodology 209

their careers. This is the Framework of Reference for the Education and Training of Literary Translators, known as the PETRA-E Framework,[8] developed by the Dutch-Flemish Centre for Expertise in Literary Translation. The Framework aims to produce a foundational, but in no way exhaustive, map of the skills and competences needed by a literary translator at each of five stages: LT1 – beginner, LT2 – advanced learner (MA graduate), LT3 – early career professional, LT4 – advanced professional and LT5 – expert.

Eight competences are listed, with relevant sub-competences: transfer competence, language competence, textual competence, heuristic competence, literary-cultural competence, professional competence, evaluative competence and research competence. In the grid formed by the vertical list of eight competences and the horizontal list of the five levels, the only specific reference to the use of digital tools is in relation to the sub-competences of 'searching the internet' and 'using reference material', both of which form part of 'heuristic competence'. This minimal reference to the use of digital tools suggests that there is room for a debate to be opened up within the profession about the possibility of incorporating approaches such as CDR which draw on both the humanities and computer science. Indeed, the leaflet summarising the project explicitly states that 'The PETRA-E Framework does not aim at standardization; on the contrary, it wants to open up the discussion about the qualities of literary translators by describing their competences in an analytical model'.

Literary Translators

For literary translators to adopt the CDR methodology they first need to hear about it and then to be persuaded to try it for themselves. The first steps in this direction have already been taken. In September 2018 there was a presentation and short workshop on CDR as part of the European School for Literary Translation in Rome, organised by CEATL (the European Council of Literary Translators' Associations).[9] Swansea University organised two two-day workshops on CALT in January and May 2019, bringing together leading scholars in the field of technology and translation such as Dorothy Kenny and Andrew Way, postgraduate students and literary translators. As part of the January workshop I presented a summary of the CDR approach and also ran two hands-on training sessions for the 40 participants with Professor Andrew Rothwell. The reception was very positive, and it is to be hoped that both the Rome and Swansea workshops will help to create the basis for a network of people interested in pursuing the area of CALT in the future. It is also hoped that the proceedings of these workshops will be published. Lastly, the publication of this book will hopefully generate both discussion and interest in this area. I would argue that literary translators have nothing

210 *Assessing the Potential of the Methodology*

to lose and much to gain by experimenting with the approach advocated in it.

The case has been made that the software required is either cheap or free, has a shallow learning curve and in many cases is capable of yielding meaningful results in seconds. Its use represents no more than a simple extension of a range of computer skills that most literary translators already possess. Above all, the CDR approach does not represent a threat to their skills or livelihood, but an opportunity to enhance what they do. One important feature of the methodology as a whole has been validated: its scalability. While translation researchers may be in a position to conduct a range of in-depth analyses, students and professional translators may find it more appropriate to use a more limited repertoire of analytic tools, concentrating on those techniques which can be shown to yield quick and meaningful results. The methodology is a work-in-progress which before it can claim any broader applicability needs to be used many more times, by different translators working on different authors, genres and periods and with different language pairs. But it challenges the world of literary translation to open itself up to new approaches which embrace both the 'digital' and the 'humanities', with all the opportunities they can bring.

Notes

1 This is the title given to two workshops held at Swansea University in January and May 2019.
2 Available at: www.corpusdelespanol.org/
3 Details available at: www.sketchengine.eu/documentation/tenten-corpora/
4 https://litlab.stanford.edu/
5 www.asling.org/tc40/?page_id=85
6 I am here mainly referring to MA students.
7 www.postgraduatesearch.com/pgs/search?course=translation [accessed 26 November 2018]
8 https://petra-education.eu/framework-literary-translation/
9 www.ceatl.eu/

Appendix A: Research Data

Table A1 Sentence length and word count in *Gracias por el Fuego* by chapter and overall

Chapter	6 words or less (%)	10 words or less (%)	11–19 words (%)	20–35 words (%)	36–60 words (%)	61–100 words (%)	101–1000 words (%)	Words in chapter	Sentences in chapter	Average sentence length
1	445 (48.4%)	634 (68.9%)	212 (23.0%)	61 (6.6%)	11 (1.2%)	2 (0.2%)	0	8,407	920	9.1
2	159 (37.8%)	263 (62.6%)	92 (21.9%)	55 (13.1%)	9 (2.1%)	1 (0.2%)	0	4,766	420	11.3
3	252 (68.7%)	321 (87.5%)	33 (9.0%)	10 (2.7%)	3 (0.8%)	0	0	2,288	367	6.2
4	387 (48.9%)	530 (66.9%)	155 (19.6%)	75 (9.5%)	26 (3.3%)	5 (0.6%)	1 (0.1%)	8,469	792	10.7
5	79 (50.3%)	110 (70.0%)	27 (17.2%)	15 (9.6%)	5 (3.2%)	0	0	1,551	157	9.9
6	64 (42.7%)	105 (70.0%)	33 (22.0%)	9 (6.0%)	2 (1.3%)	1 (0.6%)	0	1,396	150	9.3
7	67 (23.0%)	130 (44.7%)	69 (23.7%)	59 (20.3%)	24 (8.2%)	4 (1.4%)	5 (1.7%)	5,204	291	17.9
8	24 (22.2%)	47 (43.5%)	30 (27.8%)	19 (17.6%)	10 (9.3%)	2 (1.8%)	0	1,842	108	17.0
9	348 (42.2%)	514 (62.4%)	169 (20.5%)	90 (10.9%)	35 (4.2%)	10 (1.2%)	6 (0.7%)	11,094	824	13.5
10	447 (45.0%)	655 (65.9%)	207 (20.8%)	83 (8.4%)	32 (3.2%)	10 (1.0%)	7 (0.7%)	11,697	994	11.8
11	58 (42.6%)	80 (58.8%)	26 (19.1%)	18 (13.2%)	9 (6.6%)	1 (0.7%)	2 (1.5%)	2,750	136	20.2
12	54 (28.9%)	95 (50.8%)	62 (33.1%)	27 (14.4%)	3 (1.6%)	0	0	2,315	187	12.4
13	346 (48.8%)	482 (68.0%)	123 (17.3%)	56 (7.9%)	27 (3.8%)	14 (2.0%)	7 (1.0%)	9,808	709	13.8
14	50 (39.7%)	80 (63.5%)	20 (15.9%)	13 (10.3%)	8 (6.3%)	4 (3.1%)	1 (0.8%)	1,856	126	14.7
15	153 (52.0%)	205 (69.7%)	60 (20.4%)	19 (6.5%)	7 (2.4%)	2 (0.7%)	1 (0.3%)	2,999	294	10.2
Novel	2,933 (45.3%)	4,251 (65.6%)	1,318 (20.3%)	609 (9.4%)	211 (3.3%)	56 (0.9%)	30 (0.5%)	76,442	6,475	11.8

1 Sentences have been counted by using full stops, question and exclamation marks as delimiters. This ignores ellipses, which distort the figures by increasing the number of very short sentences (all three of the dots are counted as sentences), but I have counted the ellipses and deducted them from the totals. They are only significant in Chapter 10, where there are 24, nearly all contained in one paragraph.
2 **Number**: chapter with the highest percentage of short sentences, and the lowest average sentence length (Chapter 3).
3 Number: chapter with the longest average sentence length (Chapter 11).

Table A2 Sentence length and word count in the 2014–15 draft translation of *Gracias por el Fuego* by chapter and overall

Chapter	6 words or less (%)	10 words or less (%)	11–19 words (%)	20–35 words (%)	36–60 words (%)	61–100 words (%)	101–1000 words (%)	Words in chapter	Sentences in chapter	Average sentence length
1	391 (43.2%)	599 (66.2%)	218 (24.1%)	76 (8.4%)	10 (1.1%)	2 (0.2%)	0	8,464	905	9.4
2	146 (34.7%)	251 (59.6%)	98 (23.3%)	58 (13.8%)	12 (2.8%)	1 (0.2%)	1 (0.2%)	5,063	421	12.0
3	**232 (63.6%)**	**309 (84.7%)**	**41 (11.2%)**	**11 (3.0%)**	**4 (1.1%)**	0	0	2,476	365	6.8
4	335 (42.4%)	498 (63.0%)	166 (21.0%)	91 (11.5%)	29 (3.7%)	5 (0.6%)	2 (0.3%)	9,080	791	11.5
5	70 (46.3%)	99 (65.6%)	30 (19.9%)	16 (10.6%)	5 (3.3%)	1 (0.7%)	0	1,656	151	11.0
6	50 (34.2%)	100 (68.5%)	33 (22.6%)	10 (6.8%)	2 (1.4%)	1 (0.7%)	0	1,517	146	10.4
7	66 (23.0%)	112 (39.0%)	75 (26.1%)	61 (21.3%)	30 (10.5%)	5 (1.7%)	4 (1.4%)	5,452	287	19.0
8	25 (23.0%)	46 (42.2%)	31 (28.4%)	18 (16.5%)	13 (12.0%)	1 (0.9%)	0	1,897	109	17.4
9	308 (37.3%)	496 (60.0%)	178 (21.5%)	94 (11.4%)	39 (4.7%)	13 (1.6%)	6 (0.7%)	11,580	826	14.0
10	393 (39.5%)	619 (62.2%)	218 (22.9%)	104 (10.5%)	38 (3.8%)	9 (0.9%)	7 (0.7%)	12,356	995	12.4
11	48 (35.6%)	73 (54.1%)	27 (20.0%)	20 (14.8%)	10 (7.4%)	2 (1.5%)	3 (2.2%)	2,892	135	21.4
12	43 (23.4%)	83 (45.1%)	66 (35.9%)	30 (16.3%)	5 (2.7%)	0	0	2,481	184	13.5
13	311 (44.1%)	457 (64.8%)	132 (18.7%)	63 (8.9%)	33 (4.7%)	11 (1.6%)	9 (1.3%)	10,425	705	14.8
14	43 (34.1%)	76 (60.3%)	21 (16.7%)	13 (10.3%)	11 (8.7%)	4 (3.2%)	1 (0.8%)	2,059	126	16.3
15	122 (41.6%)	192 (65.5%)	64 (21.8%)	27 (9.2%)	5 (1.7%)	4 (1.4%)	1 (0.3%)	3,202	293	10.9
TOTALS	2,583 (40.1%)	4,010 (62.3%)	1,398 (21.7%)	692 (10.7%)	246 (3.8%)	59 (0.9%)	34 (0.5%)	80,600	6,439	12.5

1 Sentences have been counted by using full stops, question and exclamation marks as delimiters. This ignores ellipses, which distort the figures by increasing the number of very short sentences (all three of the dots are counted as sentences), but I have counted the ellipses and deducted them from the totals. They are only significant in Chapter 10, where there are 24, nearly all contained in one paragraph.
2 **Number**: chapter with the highest percentage of short sentences, and the lowest average sentence length (Chapter 3).
3 Number: Chapter with the longest average sentence length (Chapter 11).

Table A3 Word frequency in *Gracias por el Fuego* by chapter and overall

Chapter	1st	2nd	3rd	4th	5th	6th	7th	8th	9th	10th	Word %
1	de (329)	que (260)	y (221)	el (200)	la (199)	no (187)	a (178)	en (155)	un (118)	es (131)	23.5
2	de (174)	que (157)	la (144)	el (128)	y (117)	a (100)	no (89)	me (70)	en (65)	un (64)	23.2
3	y (60)	no (54)	que (51)	de (48)	a (41)	la (40)	en (35)	me (34)/el (34)		con (27)	18.6
4	que (298)	de (283)	y (238)	no (207)	la (205)	el (186)	a (181)	en (161)	me (129)	un (87)	23.3
5	de (73)	la (50)	que (47)	y (46)	el (45)	a (27)/no (27)		los (22)/en (22)		con (17)	24.2
6	que (59)	no (42)	y (40)	de (37)	a (31)	en (27)	la (26)	me (25)	es (23)	lo (22)	23.8
7	de (217)	que (194)	la (176)	y (167)	el (148)	en (128)	a (96)	no (95)	se (67)	su (63)	26.0
8	que (86)/de (86)		la (63)	no (50)	y (42)	el (38)	en (37)	a (32)	es (30)	con (28)	26.7
9	que (422)	de (418)	y (317)	la (285)	no (273)	a (265)	el (217)	en (204)	me (183)	un (132)	24.5
10	que (484)	de (450)	y (369)	la (282)	a (267)	no (234)	el (222)	en (210)	me (168)	lo (154)	24.3
11	de (120)	que (110)	y (96)	a (62)	la (60)	no (59)	el (55)	por (38)	en (36)	me (35)	24.4
12	que (89)	de (83)	la (67)	y (62)	el (58)	en (54)	a (52)	se (41)	un (31)	lo (32)	24.6
13	que (402)	de (400)	y (299)	la (244)	no (256)	a (217)	en (216)	el (205)	me (157)	es (122)	25.7
14	y (105)	que (60)	la (51)	el (49)	de (46)	en (37)	no (35)	a (34)	una (31)	los (29)	25.7
15	de (108)	que (99)	no (94)	la (88)	y (67)	a (63)	el (62)	un (51)	se (50)	su (40)	24.1
Novel	**de (2,872)**	**que (2,821)**	**y (2,239)**	**la (1,856)**	**no (1,738)**	**el (1,671)**	**a (1,648)**	**en (1,445)**	**me (1,036)**	**un (891)**	**23.8**

1 The top ten words are listed in descending order of frequency from left to right, with the number of occurrences in brackets. The figures include both lower and upper case occurrences.[1]

2 The **Word %** column gives the percentage of chapter word count accounted for by the total of the top ten word occurrences.

3 y (...): frequency rankings highlighted for quick reference.

Table A4 Word frequency in the draft translation by chapter and overall

Chapter	1st	2nd	3rd	4th	5th	6th	7th	8th	9th	10th	Word %
1	the (367)	to (222)	you (215)	and (210)	a (200)	it (159)	of (157)	that (152)	in (112)	is (76)	22.1
2	the (292)	to (126)	and (118)	a (112)	of (107)	that (101)	it (66)	my (56)	with (55)	is (53)	21.4
3	the (81)	to (64)	a (60)	you (59)	and (58)	that (40)	of (38)	it (37)	my (36)	me (27)	20.2
4	the (396)	to (240)	and (221)	that (212)	of (197)	you (192)	a (183)	it (135)	me (116)	in (105)	22.0
5	the (105)	of (47)	and (45)	a (40)	I (37)	to (32)/that (32)		you (25)	is (20)	with (16)	24.1
6	you (55)	the (54)	to (50)	that (45)	and (40)	a (31)	it (29)	in (23)/me (23)		of (21)	24.5
7	the (293)	and (174)	that (154)	to (142)	of (133)	a (125)	her (116)	he (109)	she (89)	1 (74)	25.8
8	the (89)	you (69)	to (68)	that (56)	of (54)	and (52)	a (37)/is (37)		about (33)	in (22)	27.3
9	the (494)	I (440)	to (350)	that (291)	and (288)	a (256)	you (236)	of (232)	in (157)	me (144)	25.0
10	the (558)	I (481)	to (368)	and (374)	that (304)	you (290)	a (255)	of (231)	in (165)	it (183)	26.0
11	the (115)	and (95)	to (88)	that (63)	of (62)	me (45)	it (41)	her (40)/my (40)		a (39)	21.7
12	the (125)	to (82)	he (66)	a (60)/and (60)		I (57)	that (49)	of (44)	in (43)	it (35)	25.0
13	the (502)	I (397)	to (315)	that (277)	of (246)	and (288)	a (187)	my (139)	in (142)	it (164)	25.5
14	and (100)	the (88)	a (56)	to (55)	my (53)	that (51)	you (43)	in (30)	was (29)	of (27)	25.8
15	the (138)	to (107)	he (96)	that (86)	of (73)	and (67)	his (56)	she (53)	you (46)	her (38)	23.7
Novel	the (3,698)	I (2,703)	to (2,309)	and (2,193)	that (1,913)	a (1,705)	of (1,677)	you (1,435)	it (1,248)	in (1,030)	24.7

1 The top ten words are listed in descending order of frequency from left to right, with the number of occurrences in brackets. The figures include both lower and upper case occurrences.[2]

2 The **Word %** column gives the percentage of chapter word count accounted for by the total of the top ten word occurrences.

3 And (...): frequency rankings highlighted for quick reference.

Notes

1 The original frequency order was derived from lower case occurrences, and I then added in the upper case occurrences to produce a complete picture of word occurrences. This changed the frequency order in a number of cases.
2 The original frequency order was derived from lower case occurrences, and I then added in the upper case occurrences to produce a complete picture of word occurrences. This changed the frequency order in a number of cases.

Appendix B: Translations used for Chapter 7

Table B1 Extract from Chapter 13 of *Gracias por el Fuego* and my 2015 draft translation

ST (660 words)	TT (682 words)
Tengo la sensación de estar haciendo aquella vieja prueba de baraja basada en las palabras: Mutus, Nomen, Dedit, Cocis. Habré de pasar el día manteniendo conversaciones, realizando actos, haciendo gestos, que parecerán iguales a los cotidianos, a los opacos actos, palabras y gestos de todos los días, pero que en cambio serán un solo naipe de cada grupo. Sólo yo tengo el secreto de la prueba, sólo yo conozco dónde debo colocar el otro, es decir, sólo yo conozco el significado que esas conversaciones, esos actos, esos gestos, habrán de tener mañana, cuando yo tenga una muerte sobre mi espalda, y, a pesar de (o, mejor, a causa de) esa muerte, pueda echar mis hombros hacia atrás, en un gesto de buena respiración y libertad recuperada, y mirar sin rencores el prodigioso cielo vacío. Sí, será mejor que esperen todos hasta mañana: los deudores, los acreedores, los turistas, los intérpretes, los guías, las viejas que quieren ver la Semana Santa de Sevilla y después morir, los calaveras que quieren consejos sobre cómo correrla en Estocolmo sin hablar sueco, los exigentes que se inscriben en la excursión de noventa y dos días siempre y cuando la Agencia les brinde garantías de que la Aduana no dificultará ese espléndido y minucioso contrabando que es el motivo cultural de su viaje. Sí, mejor que vengan todos mañana, con el diario abierto en su gran titular a toda página: TRÁGICA MUERTE DE EDMUNDO BUDIÑO. Mi gran curiosidad actual es cómo se las arreglarán, blancos y colorados, para revelar que el hijo, nada menos que el hijo, de uno de sus próceres, mató nada menos que al Prócer. La inmunidad del procerato es, para blancos y colorados, tan inconmovible como el contrabando, como el matrimonio, como la venerada Ley de Lemas. En eso están de acuerdo.	I have the feeling that I'm doing the old Latin card trick based on the words: Mutus, Nomen, Dedit, Cocis. I'll have to spend the day holding conversations, performing acts, making gestures, which will seem the same as the daily routine, the dull everyday acts, words and gestures, but which in fact will be only one card from each group. I alone hold the secret of the trick, I alone know where I must place the other one, in other words, I alone know the meaning that those conversations, those acts, those gestures will have tomorrow, when I have a death hanging around my neck, and, in spite of (or, rather, because of) that death, I can push my shoulders back, in a gesture of deep breathing and freedom regained, and look without bitterness at the wonderful empty sky. Yes, it'll be better for them all to wait until tomorrow: the debtors, the creditors, the tourists, the interpreters, the guides, the old women who want to see Easter in Seville and then die, the revellers who want advice on how to live it up in Stockholm without speaking Swedish, the demanding ones who sign up for the 92-day excursion on condition that the Agency offers them guarantees that Customs will not interfere with that splendid and meticulous contraband which is the reason for their trip. Yes, better if they all come tomorrow, with the newspaper open showing its huge headline on every page: TRAGIC DEATH OF EDMUNDO BUDIÑO. I am really curious to know how they'll arrange things, the *blancos* and *colorados*, to reveal that the son, the son no less, of one of their great leaders, killed the Great Leader no less. The immunity of the great leadership is, for *blancos* and *colorados*, as unshakeable as the contraband, as marriage, as the revered double simultaneous voting system. On that they're agreed.

(Continued)

En este país en que los escasos revolucionarios vocacionales suspenderían su revolución a causa del mal tiempo, o la postergarían hasta abril para no perderse la temporada de playas, en este amorfo país de andrajosos que votan a millonarios, de peones rurales que están contra la reforma agraria, de una clase media que cada vez encuentra más dificultades para imitar los tics y los cócteles de la alta burguesía y sin embargo piensa en la palabra solidaridad como si se tratase del séptimo círculo infernal, en este país de tipos como yo mismo, desacomodado en mi apellido porque reniego de toda la inmundicia que hoy lleva implícita el nombre Budiño; desacomodado en mi clase porque mi bienestar económico me duele como una culpa, como una mala conciencia, en tanto que mis iguales disfrutan del confort como podría hacerlo una hembra regalona; desacomodado en mis creencias, sobre todo políticas, porque extraigo mis recursos de un sistema de vida totalmente opuesto al que prefiero; desacomodado en mis relaciones, porque quienes participan de mi nivel social me consideran poco menos que un bellaco, y quienes participan de mis creencias políticas me consideran poco menos que un tránsfuga; desacomodado en mis sentimientos, en mi vida sexual, porque he conocido la plenitud y desde entonces soy consciente de que lo demás es un pobre sucedáneo; desacomodado en mi profesión, porque el malón de turistas y candidatos a tales me apabulla con su grosería, con sus contrabandos, con su guaranguería esencial, con su gloriosa estafita, con su obsesión de rebaja, con su alma de picnic; desacomodado frente a mi memoria, porque las buenas cosas que anunció mi infancia, las protecciones, las esperanzas, las osadías, se han quedado todas en el camino, y el recordar se me vuelve así un mero registro de frustraciones.
Está linda la calle. Ni frío ni calor. Un sol bien amarillo, pero tibio. Una brisa que mueve apenas los banderines del caramelero y las hojas de los plátanos. Es bueno tomar una decisión grave en un día así, que no repele, más bien invita a que lo disfrutemos. Me gusta mi ciudad; siento que de algún modo formo parte de ella.

In this country in which the few career revolutionaries would put their revolution on hold because of bad weather, or postpone it until April so as not to miss the beach season, in this amorphous country of beggars who vote for millionaires, of farm labourers who are against agrarian reform, of a middle class who find it increasingly difficult to mimic the tics and cocktails of the gentry and yet think about the word solidarity as if they were talking about the seventh circle of hell, in this country of people like me, alienated from my surname because I disown all the filth that is now implicit in the Budiño name; alienated from my class because my economic well-being afflicts me like a sin, like a guilty conscience, while my peers enjoy their comfort like a spoilt bitch; alienated from my beliefs, above all my politics, because I earn my living from a way of life totally opposite to the one I would prefer; alienated from my relationships, because my social equals consider me practically a pariah, while those who share my political beliefs consider me practically a defector; alienated from my feelings, with my sex life, because I've known full satisfaction and ever since I've been conscious that everything else is a pale substitute; alienated from my profession, because the herd of tourists and would-be's overwhelm me with their coarseness, with their contraband, with their wholesale crudeness, with their glorious rackets, with their obsession about discounts, with their 'picnic' mentality; alienated by my memory, because the good things foreshadowed in my childhood, the protections, the hopes, the daring ambitions, have all fallen by the wayside, and the act of remembering them just turns me into a mere record of frustrations.

The street is beautiful. Not too cold, not too hot. A very yellow sun, but warm. A breeze which scarcely ruffles the pennants of the sweet seller and the plantain leaves. It's good to take a decision as important as this on a day like this, that doesn't diminish, but rather invites enjoyment. I like my city; I feel that in some way I form part of her.

Table B2 Extract from *El Discurso Vacío* and my translation, 2014

ST (689 words)	TT (730 words)
13 de noviembre	13th November
Usted sabrá (y escribo "Usted" porque necesitaba practicar la U mayúscula) que he comprobado la eficacia de estos ejercicios para templar la mente y disponerla para la jornada; por ello es una grave falta comenzar el día con otro tipo de tarea (como por ejemplo los aniquiladores crucigramas) y dejar este saludable ejercicio para un momento posterior, que a veces no llega, o llega demasiado tarde.	Usted will be aware (and I write "Usted" because I need to practise the capital U) that I have proved the effectiveness of these exercises for calming the mind and preparing it for the day's work; which is why it is a serious mistake to start the day with any other sort of task (such as, for example, the crosswords which banish everything else) and put aside this healthy exercise for a later time, which sometimes never comes, or else comes too late.
En cierto momento, y no hace mucho tiempo, el ejercicio caligráfico diario estuvo a punto de volverse un ejercicio literario. Tuve la fuerte tentación de transformar mi prosa caligráfica en prosa narrativa, con idea de ir fabricando una serie de textos como peldaños de una escalera que me elevara de nuevo a las añoradas alturas que había sabido frecuentar hace ya mucho tiempo. Pero el Tentador siempre mete la cola, siempre está agazapado espiando el corazón del Hombre, y eligió ese momento para tentarme con la posibilidad de un trabajo (temporario) que me permitiría reunirme con cierta suma de dinero, necesaria para ponerme al día, para no tener deudas y para tener una cierta cantidad de dinero, tranquilizadora, en el bolsillo. Así que terminé por aceptar ese trabajo, y allí se fue al diablo mi determinación de escribir y, por unos días, también estos ejercicios. Ahora, al retomarlos, me vuelve el deseo de escribir. Quiero escribir y publicar. Tengo necesidad de ver mi nombre, mi verdadero nombre y no el que me pusieron, en letras de molde. Y más que eso, mucho más que eso, quiero entrar en contacto conmigo mismo, con el maravilloso ser que me habita y que es capaz, entre muchos otros prodigios, de fabular historias o historietas interesantes. Ese es el punto. Esa es la clave. Recuperar el contacto con el ser íntimo, con el ser que participa de algún modo secreto de la chispa divina que recorre infatigablemente el Universo y lo anima, lo sostiene, le presta realidad bajo su aspecto de cáscara vacía.	At one point, not long ago, the daily calligraphy exercise nearly turned into a literary one. I was strongly tempted to transform my calligraphic prose into narrative prose, with the idea of gradually producing a series of texts, like the steps of a staircase, that would elevate me once more to the much missed heights which I had experienced a long time ago. But the Tempter is always sticking his oar in, always crouching down, spying on the heart of Man, and he chose this moment to tempt me with the possibility of a job (albeit temporary) that would reunite me with sufficient money to catch up with things, clear my debts and still be left with a reassuring sum in my pocket. So I ended up accepting the job, and that's when my resolve to write went to the devil, along with – for a few days – these exercises. Now, as I return to them, the desire to write also returns. I want to write and to be published. I have a need to see my name – my real name, not the one they gave me – in print. But more than that – much more – I want to make contact with my very self, with that wonderful being which lives within me and which is capable, amongst many other miracles, of composing interesting stories and tales. That's the point. That's the key. To re-establish contact with that intimate being, that being which partakes in some secret way of the divine spark which tirelessly roams the Universe, breathing life into it, sustaining it and giving it substance behind the façade of an empty shell.
15 de noviembre	15th November
Tratemos, mediante este ejercicio, de templar la mente para la jornada (que se presenta difícil, aunque esas presentaciones no quieren decir mucho: ayer, por ejemplo, todo se presentaba de maravillas y en eso me avisan los	Let's try, using this exercise, to calm my mind for the day's work (which appears difficult, although such appearances don't mean very much: yesterday, for instance, everything appeared to be hunky-dory, and

(Continued)

vecinos que Ignacio estaba en viaje hacia aquí, porque se había sentido mal en la escuela. Eso borró de un plumazo mi tranquilidad del resto del día de ayer y también del de hoy, que estaba destinado a mi absoluta y placentera soledad porque la escuela había planeado una excursión. De modo que ahora Ignacio —quien se siente lo más bien— está en casa, en la cama por abulia y propia decisión, llamándome de tanto en tanto para tenerme bajo su control y hacerme sentir su poder, y yo teniendo que obedecer —pues su madre está en Caracas—con la culpable solicitud debida a un enfermo).

20 de noviembre
Veamos si hoy puedo recuperar el aplomo necesario para dibujar convenientemente las letras. Hoy me desperté con una marcada sensación de disgusto conmigo mismo. Ese disgusto tiene que ver, según he podido percibir, con el hecho de llevar ya demasiado tiempo —demasiados años— viviendo fuera de mí mismo, ocupándome de cosas que suceden fuera de manera exclusiva. Y, de todos modos, cuando en algunas oportunidades he logrado llevar la mirada hacia adentro, no me he conectado con las partes más sustanciales de mí mismo, sino con los aspectos más triviales, "subconscientes". ¿Qué se ha hecho de mi alma? ¿Por dónde andará? Hace un rato le decía a Alicia que me sentía mal porque hace mucho tiempo que no me conecto con la eternidad. Esto quiere decir que percibo las cosas superficialmente, que no tengo vivencias, que estoy apartado del Ser Interior; demasiado apartado, y sin tener la menor noción de los caminos posibles para acercarme. No importa qué es lo que se está viviendo cuando uno está apartado de Sí Mismo; todo carece igualmente de peso, todo transcurre sin dejar ninguna huella memorable.
La causa de todo no está, como a menudo tiendo a creer, en los reclamos del mundo exterior, sino en mi apego, o mi compromiso, con estos reclamos. Debo seguir pensando en esto.

then the neighbours told me that Ignacio was on his way here, having felt sick at school. In one fell stroke this destroyed my tranquillity for the rest of yesterday, and for today, too, which had been earmarked for complete and agreeable solitude, because the school had planned a trip. So now Ignacio – who feels as right as rain – is at home and in bed through wilful laziness, calling me from time to time to keep me under his thumb and make me feel his power, and I have to respond – since his mother is in Caracas – with the guilty solicitude due to the sick).

20th November
Let's see if today I can recover the self-possession needed to draw the letters properly. Today I woke up with a marked feeling of self-dissatisfaction. This dissatisfaction has to do, as far as I can tell, with the fact that I have lived for far too long – far too many years – outside my self, concerning myself exclusively with things that happen externally. And, anyway, when on occasion I have managed to turn my gaze inwards, I haven't connected with the most important parts of that self, only with the most trivial, 'subconscious' ones. What's happened to my Soul? Where's it gone? I recently told Alicia that I felt bad because it had been a long time since I had connected with eternity. This means that I perceive things superficially, that I don't have experiences, that I am separated from my Inner Being; too separated, and without the least idea of the possible ways of approaching it. It doesn't matter what is being experienced when one is separated from One's Self; everything is equally flat, everything happens without leaving any memorable impression.
The cause of all this lies not, as I often tend to believe, in the attractions of the external world, but in my attachment to those attractions.
I must continue to think about this.

References

Aarts, B., Chalker, S. and Weiner, E., 2014. *The Oxford Dictionary of English Grammar*, 2nd ed., Oxford: Oxford University Press.

Agarwal, A. and Lavie, A., 2008. Meteor, m-bleu and m-ter: Evaluation metrics for high-correlation with human rankings of machine translation output. *Proceedings of the Third Workshop on Statistical Machine Translation*. Columbus: Association for Computing Linguistics, pp. 115–118.

Aixelá, J., 1996. Culture-specific ítems in translation. In R. Álvarez and C. Vidal, eds., *Translation, Power, Subversion*. Clevedon: Multilingual Matters, pp. 52–78.

Algee-Hewitt, M., Heuser, R. and Moretti, F., 2015. *On Paragraphs. Scale, Themes, and Narrative Form*. Literary Lab Pamphlet No. 10. Stanford: University of Stanford. Available at: https://litlab.stanford.edu/LiteraryLabPam phlet10.pdf

Allen, E., 2013. The will to translate: Four episodes in a local history of global cultural exchange. In E. Allen and S. Bernofsky, eds., *In Translation: Translators on Their Work and What It Means*. New York: Columbia University Press, pp. 82–104.

Alvstad, C., 2014. The translation pact. *Language and Literature*, 23(3), pp. 270–284. Available at: doi:10.1177/0963947014536505

Antón, J., 1992. *Novelas y Cuentos de Mario Benedetti*. PhD. Universidad Complutense de Madrid.

Aranda, L., 2007. *Handbook of Spanish-English Translation*. Lanham, Boulder, New York, Toronto and Plymouth (UK): University Press of America.

Baker, M., 1993. Corpus linguistics and translation studies: Implications and applications. In M. Baker, G. Francis and E. Tognini-Bonelli, eds., *Text and Technology: In Honour of John Sinclair*. Philadelphia and Amsterdam: John Benjamins, pp. 233–250.

——— 1995. Corpora in translation studies: An overview and some suggestions for future research. *Target*, 7(2), pp. 223–243.

——— 2000. Towards a methodology for investigating the style of a literary translator. *Target*, 12(2), pp. 241–266.

——— 2011. *In Other Words,* 2nd ed., London and New York: Routledge.

Bal, M., 1997. *Introduction to the Theory of Narrative,* 2nd ed., Toronto, Buffalo, London: University of Toronto Press.

Beberfall, F., 1981. Bibliografía de y sobre Mario Benedetti. *Revista Iberoamericana*, 47(114), pp. 359–411.

222 References

Bell, A., 2004. Translation as illusion. In R. Beard and B. Garvey, eds., *Oxford: Shelving Translation Conference. EnterText*, 4(3), Supplement, pp. 13–28. Available at: www.brunel.ac.uk/__data/assets/pdf_file/0005/110696/Anthea-Bell-pdf,-Translation-as-Illusion.pdf

―――― 2011. Translating W. G. Sebald – with and without the author. In J. Catling and R. Hibbitt, eds., *Saturn's Moons: W. G. Sebald – A Handbook*. Cambridge: Legenda, pp. 209–216.

Bellow, S., 2007. *Herzog*. London: Penguin Books.

Benedetti, M. 1959a. Familia Iriarte. In M. Benedetti, *Montevideanos*. Montevideo: Alfa, pp. 78–85.

―――― 1959b. Los Novios. In M. Benedetti, *Montevideanos*. Montevideo: Alfa, pp. 94–114.

―――― trans. Rothenberg, G., 1963. The Iriarte family. *Odyssey Review*, 3(2), pp. 200–207.

―――― trans. Graham, B., 1969. *The Truce*. New York: Harper & Row.

―――― 1970. *El País de la Cola de Paja*. Montevideo: Alfa.

―――― trans. Tricario, L. and Levine, S. J., 1976. The Iriartes. *Fiction*, 5(1), pp. 12–14.

―――― trans. Riva, C. and Namer, T., 1983. *L'Étincelle*. Paris: Belfond.

―――― trans. Morales, H., 2010. The Iriarte family. In H. Morales, ed., *The Rest is Jungle and Other Stories*. Austin: Host Publications, pp. 158–165.

―――― 2014. *Gracias por el Fuego*, 3rd ed., Madrid: Alianza Editorial.

―――― trans. Morales, H., 2015. *The Truce*. London: Penguin Random House.

Benedetto, U., 1977. *EDAF nuevo diccionario general inglés-español: new-comprehensive English-Spanish dictionary*. Madrid: EDAF.

Benjamin, W. trans. Zohn, H., 2004. The task of the translator. In L. Venuti, ed. *The Translation Studies Reader*. [ebook] London and New York: Routledge, pp. 15–25.

Berman, A., trans. Venuti, L., 2004. Translation and the trials of the foreign. In L. Venuti, ed., *The Translation Studies Reader*. [ebook] London and New York: Routledge, pp. 285–297.

Bermejo, E., 1973. El caso Benedetti. In J. Ruffinelli, ed., *Variaciones críticas*. Montevideo: Libros del Astillero, pp. 26–41.

Bernaerts, L., De Bleeker, L. and De Wilde, J., 2014. Narration and translation. *Language and Literature*, 23(3), pp. 203–212. Available at: doi:10.1177/0963947014536504

Besacier, L. and Schwartz, L., 2015. Automated translation of a literary work: A pilot study. In *4th Workshop on Computational Linguistics for Literature (CLfL 2015)*. Denver: Association for Computational Linguistics, pp. 114–122. Available at: www.aclweb.org/anthology/W/W15/#0700

Biber, D., 2011. Corpus linguistics and the study of literature: Back to the future? *Scientific Study of Literature*, 1(1), pp. 15–23.

Birdwood-Hedger, M., 2006. *Tension between Domestication and Foreignization In English-Language Translations of Anna Karenina*. PhD. University of Edinburgh.

Blum, S. and Levenston, E., 1978. Universals of lexical simplification. *Language Learning*, 28(2), pp. 399–415. Available at: http://search.ebscohost.com/login. aspx?direct=true&db=psyh&AN=2013-21751-011&site=ehost-live&scope=site

References 223

Blum-Kulka, S., 1986. Shifts of cohesion and coherence in translation. In J. House and S. Blum-Kulka, eds., *Interlingual and Intercultural Communication: Discourse and Cognition in Translation and Second Language Acquisition Studies*. Tubingen: Gunter Narr, pp. 17–35.

Boase-Beier, J., 2002. Style and choice: Recreating patterns in translation. *Studies in Cross-Cultural Communication*, 1, pp. 1–28.

———— 2010a. *Stylistic Approaches to Translation*, 3rd ed., London and New York: Routledge.

———— 2010b. Who Needs Theory? In A. Fawcett, K. Guadarrama García and R. Hyde Parker, eds., *Translation: Theory and Practice in Dialogue*. London and New York: Continuum, pp. 25–38.

———— 2011. Stylistics and translation. In K. Malmkjaer and K. Windle, eds., *The Oxford Handbook of Translation Studies Online*. Oxford: Oxford University Press.

———— 2014a. Translation and the representation of thought: The case of Herta Müller. *Language and Literature*, 23(3), pp. 213–226.

———— 2014b. Stylistics and translation. In M. Burke, ed., *The Routledge Handbook of Stylistics*. London and New York: Routledge Taylor & Francis Group, pp. 393–407.

Boll, T., 2013. César Vallejo in English: Stanley Burnshaw, Paul Muldoon, and Lawrence Venuti's ethics of translation. *Translation and Literature*, 22(1), pp. 74–102.

Bortolussi, M. and Dixon, P., 2003. *Psychonarratology: Foundations for the Empirical Study of Literary Response*. Cambridge: Cambridge University Press.

Bucheli, G., 2012. Organizaciones "demócratas" y radicalización anticomunista en Uruguay, 1959–1962. *Contemporánea*, 3(3), pp. 11–30. Available at: www.geipar.udelar.edu.uy/wp-content/uploads/2014/10/Contemporanea03_2012-11-23-webO-02.pdf

Burchill, R., 1998. *The New Fowler's Modern English Usage*, rev. 3rd ed., Oxford: Oxford University Press.

Burrows, J., 1997. Style. In E. Copeland and J. McMaster, eds., *The Cambridge Companion to Jane Austen*. Cambridge: Cambridge University Press, pp. 170–188.

Busa, R., 2004. Foreword: Perspectives on the digital humanities. In S. Schreibman, R. Siemens and J. Unsworth, eds., *A Companion to Digital Humanities*. Malden, MA; Oxford and Carlton (Australia): Blackwell, pp. xvi–xxii.

Bush, P., 1999. Translating Juan Carlos Onetti for Anglo-Saxon readers. In G. San Román, ed., *Onetti and Others: Comparative Essays on a Major Figure in Latin American Literature*. New York: State University of New York, pp. 177–186.

———— 2003. The act of translation: The case of Juan Goytisolo's *A Cock-Eyed Comedy*. *Quaderns. Revista de traducció*, 10, pp. 121–134. Available at: https://ddd.uab.cat/pub/quaderns/11385790n10/11385790n10p121.pdf

———— 2012. Toil, trouble and jouissance: A case study - editing Juan the landless. In R. Wilson and L. Gerber, eds., *Creative Constraints: Translation and Authorship*. Clayton: Monash University Publishing, pp. 119–131.

Butazzoni, F., 2009. Literature: Mario Benedetti, the most beloved of Uruguayan writers. *Inter Press Service*. Available at: www.ipsnews.net/2009/05/literature-mario-benedetti-the-most-beloved-of-uruguayan-writers/

224 References

Butt, J. and Benjamin, C., 2000. *A New Reference Grammar of Modern Spanish*, 3rd ed., London: Arnold.

Campanella, H., 2009. *Mario Benedetti: Un Mito Discretísimo*. Barcelona: Seix-Barral.

Carillo, G., 1976. La biopsia como técnica literaria en *Gracias por el Fuego*. In A. Fornet, ed., *Recopilación de textos sobre Mario Benedetti*. La Habana: Casa de las Américas, pp. 127–140.

Carl, M., Bangalore, S. and Schaeffer, M., 2016. Computational linguistics and translations studies: Methods and models. In Y. Gambier and L. van Doorslaer, eds., *Border Crossings: Translation Studies and Other Disciplines*. Amsterdam: John Benjamins, pp. 225–244.

Carter, R., 2012. Coda: Some rubber bullet points. *Language and Literature*, 21(1), pp. 106–114. Available at: doi:10.1177/0963947011432048

Céspedes, F., 1976. Otras opiniones. In A. Fornet, ed., *Recopilación de textos sobre Mario Benedetti*. La Habana: Casa de las Américas, pp. 257–258.

Chan, S.-W., 2015a. Computer-aided translation: Major concepts. In S.-W. Chan, ed., *The Routledge Encyclopedia of Translation Technology*. London and New York: Routledge, pp. 32–67.

——— 2015b. The development of translation technology: 1967–2013. In S.-W. Chan, ed., *The Routledge Encyclopedia of Translation Technology*. London and New York: Routledge, pp. 3–31.

Chesterman, A., ed., 1989. *Readings in Translation Theory*. Helsinki: Finn Lectura.

——— 1997. *The Memes of Translation: The Spread of Ideas in Translation Theory.*Amsterdam: John Benjamins.

Choudhury, R. and McConnell, B., 2013. *Translation Technology Landscape Report*. De Rijp: TAUS.

Cincotta, M., 1996. Naturalising linguistic aliens: The translation of code-switching. In *Conference on Interpreting and Translation*. Sydney: University of Western Sydney, pp. 2–11. Available at: http://files.eric.ed.gov/fulltext/ED404868.pdf

Cortázar, J., trans. Rabassa, G., 1998. *Hopscotch*. London: The Harvill Press.

——— 2013. *Rayuela*. Madrid: Santillana Ediciones Generales.

da Costa, O., 2007. Foregrounding and refamiliarization: Understanding readers' response to literary texts. *Language and Literature*, 16(2), pp. 105–123. Available at: doi:10.1177/0963947007075979

van Dalen-Oskam, K., 2013. Names in novels: An experiment in computational stylistics. *Literary and Linguistic Computing*, 28(2), pp. 359–370.

Davies, E., 2003. Goblin or a dirty nose? The treatment of culture-specific references in translations of the Harry Potter books. *The Translator*, 9(1), pp. 65–100.

Davies, M., 2006. *A Frequency Dictionary of Spanish: Core Vocabulary for Learners*. Abingdon and New York: Routledge.

——— 2016. Corpus del Español. *Brigham Young University*. Available at: www.corpusdelespanol.org/x.asp

Declerq, C., 2015. Translation technology in the United Kingdom. In S-W. Chan, ed., *The Routledge Encyclopedia of Translation Technology*. London and New York: Routledge, pp. 364–374.

Delabastita, D. and Grutman, R., 2005. Introduction: Fictionalising representations of multilingualism and translation. In D. Delabastita and R. Grutman,

References 225

eds., *Fictionalising Translation and Multilingualism. Special issue of Linguistica Antverpiansia, NS4.* pp. 11–34.

Dorfman, A., 1976. Otras opiniones. In A. Fornet, ed., *Recopilación de textos sobre Mario Benedetti.* Havana: Casa de las Américas, pp. 253–254.

Eagleton, T., 2014. *How to Read Literature.* New Haven, CT and London: Yale University Press.

Eco, U., 2001. *Experiences in Translation.* Toronto, Buffalo and London: University of Toronto Press.

Elson, D., Dames, N. and McKeown, K., 2010. Extracting social networks from literary fiction. In *Proceedings of the 48th Annual Meeting of the Association for Computational Linguistics.* pp. 138–147. Available at: http://dl.acm.org/citation.cfm?id=1858696%5Cnhttp://dl.acm.org/citation.cfm?id=1858681.1858696%5Cnhttp://dl.acm.org/ft_gateway.cfm?id=1858696&type=pdf%5Cnhttp://www.aclweb.org/anthology-new/P/P10/P10-1015.pdf

Emerson, C., 1983. Translating Bakhtin: Does his theory of discourse contain a theory of translation? *University of Ottawa Quarterly*, 53(1), pp. 23–33.

Emmott, C., Sanford, A. and Dawydiak, E., 2007. Stylistics meets cognitive science: Studying style and readers' attention from an interdisciplinary perspective. *Style*, 41(2), pp. 204–226.

Evison, J., 2010. What are the basics of analysing a corpus? In A. O'Keeffe and M. McCarthy, eds., *The Routledge Handbook of Corpus Linguistics.* London and New York: Routledge, pp. 122–135.

Feltrin-Morris, M., 2016. Persuasive spaces: Translators prefaces to the divine comedy. *Forum Italicum: A Journal of Italian Studies*, 50(1), pp. 38–49. Available at: doi:10.1177/0014585816636339

Fernández Retamar, R., 1976. La obra novelística de Mario Benedetti. In A. Fornet, ed., *Recopilación de textos sobre Mario Benedetti.* La Habana: Casa de las Américas, pp. 101–113.

Fludernik, M., 2009. *An Introduction to Narratology*, 2nd ed., Abingdon: Routledge.

Fornet, A., 1975. Mario Benedetti y la revolucion posible. *Revista de Crítica Literaria Latinoamericana*, 1(2), pp. 63–72.

Franco Arcia, U., 2012. Translating multilingual texts: The case of "Strictly Professional" in *Killing Me Softly. Morir Amando* by Francisco Ibáñez-Carrasco. *Mutatis Mutandis*, 5(1), pp. 65–85. Available at: https://dialnet.unirioja.es/descarga/articulo/5012619.pdf

Frankenberg-Garcia, A., 2009. Are translations longer than source texts? A corpus-based study of explicitation. In A. Beeby, P. Rodríguez-Inés and P. Sánchez-Gijón, eds., *Corpus Use and Translating: Corpus Use for Learning to Translate and Learning Corpus Use to Translate.* Amsterdam and Philadelphia: Benjamins, pp. 47–58.

——— 2015. Training translators to use corpora hands-on: Challenges and reactions by a group of thirteen students at a UK university. *Corpora*, 10(3), pp. 351–380.

Frérot, C., 2016. Corpora and corpus technology for translation purposes in professional and academic environments. Major achievements and new perspectives. *Cadernos de Traduçao*, 36(1), pp. 36–61.

226   References

Fuentes, C., 1999a. Las Amigas. In J. King, ed., *Short Stories in Spanish*. London: Penguin, pp. 106–140 (even page numbers only).

―――― 1999b. Las Amigas, trans. Mac Adam, A. In J. King, ed., *Short Stories in Spanish*. London: Penguin, pp. 105–141 (odd page numbers only).

Gallego-Hernández, D., 2015. The use of corpora as translation resources: A study based on a survey of Spanish professional translators. *Perspectives*, 23(3), pp. 375–391. Available at: doi:10.1080/0907676X.2014.964269

Garcia, I., 2015. Computer-aided translation: Systems. In S.-W. Chan, ed., *The Routledge Encyclopedia of Translation Technology*. London and New York: Routledge, pp. 68–87.

Gardner-Chloros, P. and Weston, D., 2015. Code-switching and multilingualism in literature. *Language and Literature*, 24(3), pp. 182–193. Available at: doi:10.1177/0963947015585065

Genette, G., trans. Lewin, J., 1997. *Paratexts: Thresholds of Interpretation*. Cambridge: Cambridge University Press.

Geng, Z., Cheesman, T., Laramee, R., Flanagan, K. and Thiel, S., 2015. ShakerVis: Visual analysis of segment variation of German translations of Shakespeare's Othello. *Information Visualization*, 14(4), pp. 273–288.

Gonçalves, L., 2016. A contribution of corpus linguistics to literary analysis. *Transversal*, 2(2), pp. 42–53.

Greene, E., Ave, L., Knight, K. and Rey, M., 2010. Automatic analysis of rhythmic poetry with applications to generation and translation. In H. Li and L. Màrquez, eds., *Proceedings of the 2010 Conference on Empirical Methods in Natural Language Processing (EMNLP'10)*. Cambridge, MA: Association for Computing Linguistics, pp. 524–533. Available at: www.aclweb.org/anthology/D10-1051

Grutman, R., 2005. Refraction and recognition: Literary multilingualism in translation. *Target*, 18(1), pp. 17–47.

Gutt, E.-A., 1991. *Translation and Relevance: Cognition and Context*. Oxford and Cambridge MA: Blackwell.

Guyot, J., 1976. Retrato de un caudillo en *Gracias por el Fuego*. In A. Fornet, ed., *Recopilación de textos sobre Mario Benedetti*. La Habana: Casa de las Américas, pp. 141–158.

Halliday, M., 1971. Linguistic function and literary style: An inquiry into the language of William Golding's *The Inheritors*. In S. Chatman, ed., *Literary Style: A Symposium*. London and New York: Oxford University Press, pp. 330–365.

Harker, J., 1999. Contemporary Japanese fiction & "Middlebrow" translation strategies: The case of Banana Yoshimoto's "Kitchen." *The Translator*, 5(1), pp. 27–44.

Herman, D., 2002. *Story Logic: Problems and Possibilities of Narrative*. Lincoln and London: University of Nebraska Press, pp. 27–51.

―――2013.Cognitivenarratology(revisedversion;uploaded22September2013). *The Living Handbook of Narratology*. Available at: www.lhn.uni-hamburg.de/article/cognitive-narratology-revised-version-uploaded-22-september-2013

Hermans, T., 1996. The translator's voice in translated narrative. *Target*, 8(1), pp. 23–48.

―――― 2014. Positioning translators - voices, views and values in translation. *Language & Literature*, 23(3), pp. 285–301.

References 227

Hervey, S., Higgins, I. and Haywood, L., 2004. *Thinking Spanish Translation*. London, New York: Routledge.

Hockey, S., 2004. The history of humanities computing. In S. Schreibman, R. Siemens and J. Unsworth, eds., *A Companion to Digital Humanities*. Malden, MA; Oxford; Carlton (Australia): Blackwell, pp. 3–19.

Holmes, D., 1985. The analysis of literary style – a review. *Journal of the Royal Statistical Society. Series A (General)*, 148(4), pp. 328–341.

—— 1998. The evolution of stylometry in humanities scholarship. *Literary and Linguistic Computing*, 13(3), pp. 111–117.

Hoover, D., 2004. Quantitative analysis and literary studies. In S. Schreibman, R. Siemens, and J. Unsworth, eds., *A Companion to Digital Humanities*. Oxford: Blackwell. Available at: http://digitalhumanities.org/companion/view?docId=blackwell/9781405148641/9781405148641.xml&chunk.id=ss1-6-9&toc.id=0&brand=9781405148641_brand

Houston, K., 2014. *Shady Characters: The Secret Life of Punctuation, Symbols and Other Typographical Marks*. New York and London: W. W. Norton & Company.

Hunston, S., 2010. How can a corpus be used to explore patterns? In A. O'Keeffe and M. McCarthy, eds., *The Routledge Handbook of Corpus Linguistics*. London and New York: Routledge, pp. 152–166.

Hutchins, J., 2010. Machine translation: A concise history. *Journal of Translation Studies*, 13(1 & 2), pp. 29–70. Available at: www.hutchinsweb.me.uk/CUHK-2006.pdf

Hyde-Parker, R., 2008. Corpora and corpus stylistics in literary translation pedagogy. *Norwich Papers*, 16. Norwich: University of East Anglia, pp. 21–40.

Irizarry, E., 1990. Stylistic analysis of a corpus of twentieth-century Spanish narrative. *Computers and the Humanities*, 24(4), pp. 265–274. Available at: https://link.springer.com/article/10.1007/BF00123413

Iser, W., 1972. *The Implied Reader*. Baltimore, MD: Johns Hopkins University Press, pp. 279–299. Available at: www.jstor.org/stable/10.2307/468316

Jääskeläinen, R., 1999. *Tapping the Process: An Explorative Study of the Cognitive and Affective Factors Involved in Translating*. Joensuu: University of Joensuu.

Jänicke, S., Franzini, G., Cheema, M. and Scheuermann, G., 2015. On close and distant reading in digital humanities: A survey and future challenges. In R. Borgo, F. Ganovelli, and I. Viola, eds., *Eurographics Conference on Visualization (EuroVis) (2015)*, pp. 1–21. Available at: www.researchgate.net/publication/282156818_On_Close_and_Distant_Reading_in_Digital_Humanities_A_Survey_and_Future_Challenges_A_State-of-the-Art_STAR_Report

Ji, M., 2012. Hypothesis testing in corpus-based literary translation studies. In M. Oakes and M. Ji, eds., *Quantitative Methods in Corpus-Based Translation Studies*. Amsterdam and Philadelphia: Benjamins, pp. 53–72.

Jockers, M., 2013. *Macroanalysis: Digital Methods and Literary History*. Urbana, Chicago and Springfield: University of Illinois Press.

Johansson, V., 2008. Lexical diversity and lexical density in speech and writing: A developmental perspective. *Working Papers in Linguistics*, 53. Lind: Lind University, pp. 61–79.

Johnson, J., 2008. *Corpus Stylistics and Translation*. Quaderni del CeSLiC. Centro di Studi Linguistico-Culturali. Bologna: Università di Bologna. Available at: www.academia.edu/25479479/Corpus_stylistics_and_translation

228 References

Jones, R. and Irvine, A., 2013. The (un)faithful machine translator. In *Proceedings of the 7th Workshop on Language Technology for Cultural Heritage, Social Sciences, and Humanities*. Sofia: Association for Computational Linguistics, pp. 96–101.

Joyce, J., 2010. *Ulysses*. Ware: Wordsworth Editions.

Keim, D. and Oelke, D., 2007. Literature fingerprinting: A new method for visual literary analysis. In *IEEE Symposium on Visual Analytics Science and Technology*. Sacramento: IEEE, pp. 115–122.

Kenny, A., 1992. *Computers and the Humanities*. London: British Library.

Kenny, D., 2016. The translator and the machine. *The Linguist* (online). Available at: www.ciol.org.uk/translator-and-machine-dorothy-kenny

——— ed. 2017. *Human Issues in Translation Technology*. Abingdon and New York: Routledge.

King, J., 2005. The boom of the Latin American novel. In E. Kristal, ed., *The Cambridge Companion to the Latin American Novel*. Cambridge: Cambridge University Press, pp. 59–80.

Klarer, M., 2004. *An Introduction to Literary Studies*, 2nd ed., London and New York: Routledge Taylor & Francis Group.

Koller, W., 1989. Equivalence in translation theory. In A. Chesterman, ed., *Readings in Translation Theory*. Helsinki: Finn Lectura, pp. 99–104.

Kornai, A., 2008. *Mathematical Linguistics*. New York: Springer.

Kübler, N. and Aston, G., 2010. Using corpora in translation. In A. O'Keeffe and M. McCarthy, eds., *The Routledge Handbook of Corpus Linguistics*. London and New York: Routledge, pp. 501–515.

Kucher, K. and Kerren, A., 2014. Text visualization browser: A visual survey of text visualization techniques. *InfoVis*, (November 2014), pp. 1–3.

——— 2015. Text visualization techniques: Taxonomy, visual survey, and community insights. *2015 IEEE Pacific Visualization Symposium (PacificVis) (PACIFICVIS)*, Hangzhou, China, pp. 117–121. Available at: www.computer. org/csdl/proceedings/pacificvis/2015/6879/00/07156366-abs.html

Lagos, J., 2013. *Una "Zona Intermedia" entre el Benedetti Moral y el Benedetti Político*. Montevideo: Universidad de la República. Available at: www.geipar. udelar.edu.uy/jose-gabriel-lagos-benedetti-entre-la-moral-y-la-politica-a-principios-de-los-60/

Lan, L., 2015. Corpus. In S.-W. Chan, ed., *The Routledge Encyclopedia of Translation Technology*. London and New York: Routledge, pp. 465–479.

Lapshinova-Koltunski, E., 2015. Variation in translation: Evidence from corpora. In C. F. and F. Zanettin, eds., *New Directions in Corpus-Based Translation Studies (Translation and Multilingual Natural Language Processing 1)*. Berlin: Language Science Press, pp. 93–114.

Laviosa, S., 2004. Corpus-based translation studies: Where does it come from? Where is it going? *Language Matters*, 35(1), pp. 6–27.

Laviosa-Braithwaite, S., 2005. Universals of translation. In M. Baker, ed., *Routledge Encyclopedia of Translation Studies*. London: Routledge Taylor & Francis Group, pp. 288–291.

LeBlanc, M., 2017. "I can't get no satisfaction!" Should we blame translation technologies or shifting business practices? In D. Kenny, ed., *Human Issues in Translation Technology*. Abingdon and New York: Routledge, pp. 45–62.

References 229

Lee, J. and Yeung, C., 2012. Extracting networks of people and places from literary texts. In R. Manurung and F. Bond, eds., *26th Pacific Asia Conference on Language, Information and Computation*. Indonesia: Faculty of Computer Science, Universitas Indonesia, pp. 209–218.Available at: https://aclanthology.coli.uni-saarland.de/volumes/proceedings-of-the-26th-pacific-asia-conference-on-language-information-and-computation

Leech, G., 2008. *Language in Literature: Style and Foregrounding*. Harlow: Pearson Longman.

Leech, G. and Short, M., 2007. *Style in Fiction,* 2nd ed., Harlow, England: Pearson Longman.

van Leeuwen, T., 2005. Typographic meaning. *Journal of Specialised Translation*, 4(2), pp. 137–143.

Levine, S., 2009. *The Subversive Scribe*. Champaign and London: Dalkey Archive Press.

Lewald, E., 1966. The 1965 Literary Scene in Argentina and Uruguay. *Books Abroad*, 40(2), pp. 145–148.

Lewis, B., 1982. Mario Benedetti and the Literature of Crisis. *Chasqui*, 11(2/3), pp. 3–13.

Lewis, P., 2004. The measure of translation effects. In L. Venuti, ed., *The Translation Studies Reader.* [ebook] London and New York: Routledge, pp. 264–283.

Lock, C., 2016. On roman letters and other stories: An essay in heterographics. *Journal of World Literature*, 1, pp. 158–172.

Lombardino, R., 2014. Why I use a CAT tool to translate books. *eWordNews*. Available at: http://ewordnews.com/literary-news/2014/4/11/why-i-use-a-cat-tool-to-translate-books?rq=swordfish

Maczewski, J.-M., 1996. Virginia Woolf's *The Waves* in French and German waters: A computer assisted study in literary translation. *Literary and Linguistic Computing*, 11(4), pp. 175–186.

Mahlberg, M., 2014. Corpus stylistics. In M. Burke, ed., *The Routledge Handbook of Stylistics*. London and New York: Routledge Taylor & Francis Group, pp. 378–392.

Malmkjaer, K., 2004. Translational stylistics: Dulcken's translations of Hans Christian Andersen. *Language and Literature*, 13(1), pp. 13–24. Available at: doi:10.1177/0963947004039484

Μανουσόπουλος, Ά., 2015. *Ο πόνος της επιστροφής*, Λάρισα. Available at: https://free-ebooks.gr/βιβλίο/3a4V/o-πόνος-της-επιστροφής

Marco, J., 2004. Translating style and styles of translating: Henry James and Edgar Allan Poe in Catalan. *Language and Literature*, 13(1), pp. 73–90. Available at: doi:10.1177/0963947004039488

Margolin, U., 2007. Character. In D. Herman, ed., *The Cambridge Companion to Narrative*. Cambridge: Cambridge University Press, pp. 66–79.

Martin, G., 1989. *Journeys Through the Labyrinth: Latin American Fiction in the Twentieth Century*. London: Verso.

Mathieu, C., 1983. *Los Cuentos de Mario Benedetti*. New York: Peter Lang.

Mattar, K., 2014. Orhan Pamuk and the limits of translation: Foreignizing *The Black Book* for world literature. *Translation and Literature*, 23(1), pp. 42–67. Available at: doi:10.3366/tal.2014.0135

230 References

May, R., 1994. *The Translator in the Text: On Reading Russian Literature in English*. Evanston: Northwestern University Press.

—— 1997. Sensible elocution: How translation works in & upon punctuation. *The Translator*, 3(1), pp. 1–20.

McCaw, J., 2013. A poetics sacralized: Luis de Góngora's *Soledades* as religious rhetoric in Luis de Tejeda's "Romance sobre su vida". *Hispanófila*, 167 (Enero 2013), pp. 3–22. Available at: https://muse.jhu.edu/article/508030/summary

McIntyre, D. and Walker, B., 2010. How can corpora be used to explore the language of poetry and drama? In A. O'Keeffe and M. McCarthy, eds., *The Routledge Handbook of Corpus Linguistics*. London and New York: Routledge, pp. 516–530.

McRae, E., 2010. *The Role of Translators' Prefaces to Contemporary Literary Translations into English*. M.A. University of Auckland. Available at: https://researchspace.auckland.ac.nz/bitstream/handle/2292/5972/whole.pdf;sequence=5

Meister, J-C., Petris, M., Gius, E., Jacke, J., Horstmann, J. and Bruck, C. 2018 (June 18). CATMA (Version v5.2). Zenodo. doi:10.5281/zenodo.1470119

Meylaerts, R., 2010. Multilingualism and translation. In Y. Gambier and L. van Doorslaer, eds., *Handbook of Translation Studies, Vol. 1*. Amsterdam and Philadelphia: John Benjamins, pp. 227–230.

Mitchell, D., 2015. Type-token models: A comparative study. *Journal of Quantitative Linguistics*, 22(1), pp. 1–21. Available at: doi:10.1080/09296174.2014.974456

Moorkens, J., Toral, A., Castilho, S. and Way, A., 2018. Perceptions of literary post-editing using statistical and neural machine translation. *Translation Spaces*, 7(2), pp. 240–262.

Morales, H., 2001. You Can't Say "Ain't" in Spanish--Or Can You? A conversation with Gregory Rabassa. *Hopscotch: A Cultural Review*, 2(4), pp. 116–127.

Moretti, F., 2011. Network theory, plot analysis. In F. Moretti, ed., *Distant Reading*. London and New York: Verso, pp. 211–240.

—— 2013a. *Distant Reading*. London and New York: Verso.

—— 2013b. *"Operationalizing": Or, the Function of Measurement in Modern Literary Theory*, Stanford Literary Lab Pamphlet 6.

Mosteller, F. and Wallace, D., 1964. *Inference and Disputed Authorship: The Federalist*. Reading, MA: Addison-Wesley.

Munday, J., 1997. *Systems in Translation: A Computer-Assisted Systemic Approach to the Analysis of the Translation of García Márquez*. PhD. University of Bradford.

—— 1998. Problems of applying thematic analysis to translation between Spanish and English. *Cadernos de Tradução*, 1(3), pp. 183–213. Available at: https://periodicos.ufsc.br/index.php/traducao/article/view/5387/4931

—— 2002. Systems in translation: A systemic model for descriptive translation studies. In T. Hermans, ed., *Crosscultural Transgressions: Research Models in Translation Studies II - Historical and Ideological Issues*. Manchester: St. Jerome, pp. 76–92.

—— 2007a. The relations of style and ideology in translaton: A case study of Harriet de Onís. In L. Pegenaute, J. DeCesaris, M. Tricás y E. Bernal, eds., *Actas del III Congreso Internacional de la Asociación Ibérica de Estudios de*

Traducción e Interpretación. La traducción del futuro: mediación lingüística y cultural en el siglo XXI. Barcelona: PPU, pp. 57–68.

—— 2007b. Translation and ideology. *The Translator*, 13(2), pp. 195–217.

—— 2008a. *Style and Ideology in Translation: Latin American Writing in English.* New York: Routledge.

—— 2008b. *Introducing Translation Studies*, 2nd ed., London and New York: Routledge.

—— 2011. Looming large: A cross-linguistic analysis of semantic prosodies in comparable reference corpora. In A. Kruger, K. Wallmach and J. Munday, eds., *Corpus-based Translation Studies: Research and Applications.* New York: Continuum, pp. 169–186.

Murray, T., 1995. *The Structure of English: Phonetics, Phonology, Morphology.* Boston: Allyn and Bacon.

Nan, C. and Cui, W., 2016. Overview of text visualization techniques. In *Introduction to Text Visualization,* Atlantis Briefs in Artificial Intelligence 1. Amsterdam: Atlantis Press, pp. 11–41. Available at: http://link.springer.com/10.2991/978-94-6239-186-4

Neto, P., 1962. The candombe, a dramatic dance from Afro-Uruguayan Folklore. *Ethnomusicology*, 6(3), pp. 164–174.

Newmark, P., 1983. Introductory survey. In C. Picken, ed., *The Translator's Handbook.* London: Aslib, pp. 1–17.

—— 1988. *A Textbook of Translation.* New York, London, Toronto, Sydney and Tokyo: Prentice Hall.

Nida, E., 2004. Principles of correspondence. In L. Venuti, ed., *The Translation Studies Reader.* [ebook] London and New York: Routledge, pp. 126–140.

Nord, C., trans. Nord, C. and Sparrow, P., 1991. *Text Analysis in Translation. Theory, Method, and Didactic Application of a Model for Translation-Oriented Text Analysis.* Amsterdam and Atlanta: Rodopi.

O'Bryen, R., 2011. McOndo, magical neoliberalism and Latin American identity. *Bulletin of Latin American Research*, 30(s1), pp. 158–174.

O'Halloran, K., 2012. Performance stylistics: Deleuze and Guattari, poetry, and (corpus) linguistics. *International Journal of English Studies*, 12(2), pp. 171–199.

O'Sullivan, C., 2013. Introduction: Multimodality as challenge and resource for translation. *The Journal of Specialised Translation*, 20, pp. 2–14.

O'Sullivan, E., 2003. Narratology meets translation studies, or, the voice of the translator in children's literature. *Meta: Journal des traducteurs*, 48(1–2), pp. 197–207. Available at: https://retro.erudit.org//revue/meta/2003/v48/n1-2/006967ar.html&gt

Olohan, M., 2001. *Spelling Out the Optionals in Translation: A Corpus Study.* UCREL Technical Paper No. 13. Lancaster: University of Lancaster.

—— 2011. Translators and translation technology: The dance of agency. *Translation Studies*, 4(3), pp. 342–357.

Pamuk, O., trans. Gün, G., 1994. *The Black Book.* New York: Farrar, Strauss & Giroux.

—— trans. Freely, M., 2006. *The Black Book.* New York: Vintage Books.

Paoletti, M., 1995. *El Aguafiestas: la Biografía de Mario Benedetti.* Madrid: Alfaguara.

Parkes, M., 1992. *Pause and Effect: An Introduction to the History of Punctuation in the West.* Aldershot and Burlington, VT: Ashgate.

232 References

Parks, T., 2014. *Translating Style: A Literary Approach to Translation - A Translation Approach to Literature*, 2nd ed., London and New York: Routledge.

Paz Soldán, E., 2018. *Desencuentros*. Madrid: Páginas de Espuma.

Pearson, L., 2003. *Usted*: a Re-examination of the Etymology of the Formal Spanish Word for "you". In *Linguistic Association of the South West Conference 2003*. Edinburg, USA.

Pekkanen, H., 2010. *The Duet of the Author and the Translator: Looking at Style through Shifts in Literary Translation*. Department of Modern Languages. PhD. University of Helsinki.

Pešková, A., 2013. Experimenting with Pro-drop in Spanish. *SKY Journal of Linguistics*, 26(2013), pp. 117–149. Available at: www.linguistics.fi/julkaisut/SKY2013/Peskova.pdf

Prince, G., 2014. Narratology and translation. *Language and Literature*, 23(1), pp. 23–31. Available at: doi:10.1177/0963947013510647

Prior, A., MacWhinney, B. and Kroll, J., 2007. Translation norms for English and Spanish: The role of lexical variables, word class, and L2 proficiency in negotiating translation ambiguity. *Behav Res Methods*, 39(4) pp. 1029–1038. Available at: www.ncbi.nlm.nih.gov/pmc/articles/PMC4109968/

Promis, J., 1966. "Mario Benedetti: Gracias por el Fuego." *Anales de la Universidad de Chile*, 139(julio-septiembre), pp. 252–257.

Pym, A., 1996. *On the Pragmatics of Translating Multilingual Texts*. Intercultural Studies Group. Tarragona: Universitat Rovira i Virgili. Available at: http://usuaris.tinet.cat/apym/on-line/translation/multilingual.pdf

—— 2011. What technology does to translating. *The International Journal for Translation and Interpreting*, 3(1), pp. 1–9.

—— 2012. *On Translator Ethics: Principles for Mediation between Cultures*. Amsterdam and Philadelphia: John Benjamins.

—— 2013. Translation skill-sets in a machine-translation age. *Meta: Translators' Journal*, 58, pp. 487–503. Available at: www.erudit.org/fr/revues/meta/2013-v58-n3-meta01406/1025047ar.pdf

Qun, L. and Xiaojun, Z., 2015. Machine translation: General. In S.-W. Chan, ed., *The Routledge Encyclopedia of Translation Technology*. London and New York: Routledge, pp. 105–119.

Rabassa, G., 1989. No two snowflakes are alike. In J. Biguenet and R. Schulte, eds., *The Craft of Translation*. Chicago, IL and London: University of Chicago, pp. 1–12.

—— 2005. *If This Be Treason: Translation and Its Dyscontents, a Memoir*. New York: New Directions.

Raffel, B., 1994. *The Art of Translating Prose*. Pennsylvania: Pennsylvania State University Press.

Rama, Á., 1966. *Cien años de raros*, Montevideo: Arca.

Riese, K., Bayer, M., Lauer, G. and Schacht, A., 2014. In the eye of the recipient: Pupillary responses to suspense in literary classics. *Scientific Study of Literature*, 4(2), pp. 211–232.

Rodríguez Monegal, E., 1965. *Literatura uruguaya del medio siglo*. Montevideo: Alfa.

Rommel, T., 2004. Literary studies. In S. Schreibman, R. Siemens and J. Unsworth, eds., *A Companion to Digital Humanities*. Malden, MA; Oxford; Carlton (Australia): Blackwell, pp. 88–96.

References 233

Rosa, A.A., 2015. Translating orality, recreating otherness. *Translation Studies*, 8(2), pp. 209–225.

Rosenwald, L., 2008. *Multilingual America: Language and the Making of American Literature*. Cambridge: Cambridge University Press.

Rothwell, A., 2009. Translating "Pure Nonsense": Walter Benjamin meets Systran on the dissecting table of Dada. *Romance Studies*, 27(4), pp. 259–272.

—— 2018. CAT tools and creativity: Retranslating Zola's La Joie de vivre. Oxford: Oxford University Press, pp. 1–7.

Ruffinelli, J., 1973. *Mario Benedetti: variaciones críticas*. Montevideo: Libros del Astillero.

—— trans. Smith, V., 1997. Mario Benedetti. In V. Smith, ed., *Encyclopedia of Latin American Literature*. London and New York: Routledge, pp. 209–213.

—— 2008. Conversación intemporal con el escritor "sin tiempo." In G. Dawes, ed., *Mario Benedetti, Autor Uruguayo Contemporáneo: estudios sobre su compromiso literario y político*. Lewiston, Queenston (Ca), Lampeter: Edwin Mellen Press, pp. 239–268.

Rybicki, J., 2013. Stylometric translator attribution: Do translators leave lexical traces? In T. Piotrowski and Ł. Grabowski, eds., *The Translator and the Computer*. Wrocław: The Philological School of Higher Education and C&M Localization Centre, pp. 193–204. Available at: www.wsf.edu.pl/upload_module/wysiwyg/Wydawnictwo WSF/The Translator and the Computer_Piotrowski_Grabowski.pdf

Rybicki, J. and Heydel, M., 2013. The stylistics and stylometry of collaborative translation: Woolf's Night and Day in Polish. *Literary and Linguistic Computing*, 28(4), pp. 708–717.

Saldanha, G., 2005. *Style of Translation: An Exploration of Stylistic Patterns in the Translations of Margaret Jull Costa and Peter Bush*. PhD. Dublin City University.

—— 2008. Explicitation revisited: Bringing the reader into the picture. *transkom*, 1(1), pp. 20–35. Available at: www.trans-kom.eu/bd01nr01/trans-kom_01_01_03_Saldanha_Explicitation.20080707.pdf

—— 2009. Principles of corpus linguistics and their application to translation studies research. *Tradumàtica*, 7, pp. 1–7. Available at: http://webs2002.uab.es/tradumatica/revista/num7/articles/01/central.htm

—— 2011a. Style of translation: The use of foreign words in translations by Margaret Jull Costa and Peter Bush. In A. Kruger, K. Wallmach and J. Munday, eds. *Corpus-based Translation Studies: Research and Applications*. New York: Continuum, pp. 237–258.

—— 2011b. Translator style: Methodological considerations. *The Translator*, 17(1), pp. 25–50.

—— 2011c. Emphatic italics in English translations: stylistic failure or motivated stylistic resources? *Meta: Translators' Journal*, 56(2), pp. 424–442. Available at: www.erudit.org/fr/revues/meta/2011-v56-n2-meta1821316/1006185ar.pdf

—— 2014. Style in, and of, translation. In S. Berman and C. Porter, eds., *A Companion to Translation Studies*. Chichester: John Wiley, pp. 95–106.

Saldanha, G., and O'Brien, S., 2013. *Research Methodologies in Translation Studies*. Manchester and Kinderhook, NY: St. Jerome.

234 *References*

Sanford, A. and Emmott, C., 2012. *Mind, Brain and Narrative.* Cambridge: Cambridge University Press.

Sari, D., 2016. Measuring quality of reading materials in English textbook: The use of lexical density method in assessing complexity of reading materials of Indonesia's curriculum -- 13 (K13) English textbook. *Journal of Applied Linguistics and Literature,* 2(2), pp. 30–39.

Schiaffino, R., 2016. CAT tools and translation style. *About Translation.* Available at: www.aboutranslation.com/2016/04/cat-tools-and-translation-style.html

Schiavi, G., 1996. There is always a teller in a tale. *Target,* 8(1), pp. 1–21.Schleiermacher, F., trans. Bernofsky, S., 2004. On the different methods of translating. In L. Venuti, ed., *The Translation Studies Reader.* [ebook] London and New York: Routledge, pp. 43–63.

Schneiderman, B., 1996. The eyes have it: A task by data type taxonomy for information visualizations. In *Proceedings of the IEEE Symposium on Visual Languages.* Boulder: IEEE, pp. 336–343.

Scott, C., 2010. Re-theorizing the literary in literary translation. In A. Fawcett, K. Guadarrama García and R. Hyde Parker, eds., *Translation: Theory and Practice in Dialogue.* London and New York: Continuum, pp. 109–127.

Screen, B., 2016. What does translation memory do to translation? The effect of translation memory output on specific aspects of the translation process. *Translation and Interpreting,* 8(1), pp. 1–18.

Shaw, D., 2008. Foreword. In G. Dawes, ed., *Mario Benedetti, Autor Uruguayo Contemporáneo: estudios sobre su compromiso literario y político.* Lewiston, Queenston (Ca), Lampeter: Edwin Mellen Press, pp. i–v.

Shen, D., 2005a. How stylisticians draw on narratology: Approaches, advantages and disadvantages. *Style,* 39(4), pp. 381–395.

———— 2005b. What narratology and stylistics can do for each other. In J. Phelan and P. Rabinowitz, eds., *A Companion to Narrative Theory.* Massachusetts, Victoria, London: Blackwell, pp. 136–149.

———— 2014. Stylistics and narratology. In M. Burke, ed., *The Routledge Handbook of Stylistics.* London and New York: Routledge Taylor & Francis Group, pp. 191–205.

Shen, G., 2010. Corpus-based approaches to translation studies. *Cross-Cultural Communication,* 6(4), pp. 181–187. Available at: www.cscanada.net/index.php/ccc/article/viewFile/j.ccc.1923670020100604.010/1017

Short, M., 1999. Graphological deviation, style variation and point of view in marabou stork nightmares by Irvine Welsh. *Journal of Literary Studies,* 15(3–4), pp. 305–323.

Simpson, P., 2004. *Stylistics: A Resource Book for Students.* London and New York: Routledge.

Šlancarová, D., 1999. On the use of italics in English and Czech. Brno Studies in English 25, Brno: University of Brno. Available at: www.phil.muni.cz/plonedata/wkaa/BSE/BSE_1999-25_Scan/BSE_25_05.pdf

Soubeyroux, J., 1985. Espacio y tiempo como base para una lectura sociocrítica de *Gracias por el fuego* de Mario Benedetti. *Anales de Literatura Española,* No. 4. Alicante: Universidad de Alicante, pp. 439–463. Available at: http://rua.ua.es/dspace/bitstream/10045/7566/1/ALE_04_19.pdf

—— 1986. Personnages, système normatif et idéologie dans *Gracias por el fuego* de Mario Benedetti. *Cahiers du monde hispanique et luso-brésilien*, 47(1), pp. 83–108. Available at: www.persee.fr/doc/carav_0008-0152_1986_num_47_1_2286

Sparavigna, A. and Marazzato, R., 2015. Analysis of a play by means of CHAPLIN, the characters and places interaction network software. *International Journal of Sciences*, 4(3), pp. 60–68. Available at: www.ijsciences.com/pub/pdf/V420150330.pdf

Sperber, D. and Wilson, D., 1995. *Relevance: Communication and Cognition*, 2nd ed., Oxford and Cambridge: Blackwell.

Spitaleri, M., 1972. *Gracias por el Fuego*: Estudio de dos variables temáticas. *Chasqui*, 2(1), pp. 31–44.

Stamatatos, E., 2009. A survey of modern authorship attribution methods. *Journal of the American Society for Information Science and Technology*, 60(3), pp. 538–556.

Stockwell, P., 2002. *Cognitive Poetics: An Introduction*. London: Routledge.

Stratton, F., 2004. "Hollow at the core": Deconstructing Yann Martel's *Life of Pi. SCLÉLC*, 29(2). Available at: https://journals.lib.unb.ca/index.php/scl/article/view/12746/13689

Stubbs, M., 2005. Conrad in the computer: Examples of quantitative stylistic methods. *Language and Literature*, 14(1), pp. 5–24.

Suchet, M., 2009. *Translating literary heterolingualism. Hijo de hombre's French variations*. Intercultural Studies Group. Tarragona: Universitat Rovira i Virgili. Available at: www.intercultural.urv.cat/media/upload/domain_317/arxius/TP2/suchet.pdf

Taylor-Batty, J., 2013. *Multilingualism in Modernist Fiction*. New York: Palgrave Macmillan.

Tenant, K. 1969. *Lady Weare and the Bodhisattva*. Bird, C. Victoria: Penguin.

Tognini Bonelli, E., 2010. Theoretical overview of the evolution of corpus linguistics. In A. O'Keeffe and M. McCarthy, eds., *The Routledge Handbook of Corpus Linguistics*. London and New York: Routledge, pp. 14–27.

Toral, A. and Way, A., 2015. Translating literary text between related languages using SMT. In *Proceedings of the Fourth Workshop on Computational Linguistics for Literature*, NAACL, Denver, Colorado, USA, pp. 123–132. Denver: Association for Computational Linguistics. Available at: www.aclweb.org/anthology/W15-0714

—— 2018. What level of quality can neural machine translation attain on literary text? In J. Moorkens, S. Castilho, F. Gaspari and S. Doherty, eds., *Translation Quality Assessment: From Principles to Practice*. Berlin, Heidelberg: Springer, pp. 1–26.

Toral, A., Wieling, M. and Way, A., 2018. Post-editing effort of a novel with statistical and neural machine translation. *Frontiers in Digital Humanities*, 5, pp. 1–11. Available at: http://journal.frontiersin.org/article/10.3389/fdigh.2018.00009/full

Toury, G., 2012. *Descriptive Translation Studies – and Beyond.*Amsterdam: John Benjamins.

Tsur, R., 2002. Aspects of cognitive poetics. In E. Semino and J. Culpeper, eds., *Cognitive Stylistics: Language and Cognition in Text Analysis*. Amsterdam and Philadelphia: John Benjamins, pp. 279–318.

References

Tymoczko, M., 2000. Translation and political engagement: Activism, social change and the role of translation in geopolitical shifts. *The Translator*, 6(1), pp. 23–47.

UK Translator Survey: Final Report, 2017. The European Commission Representation in the UK, the Chartered Institute of Linguists (CIOL) and the Institute of Translation and Interpreting (ITI).

Venuti, L. 2004. *The Translator's Invisibility: A History of Translation*. [ebook] London and New York: Routledge.

————— 2008. *The Translator's Invisibility: A History of Translation*, 2nd ed., Abingdon and New York: Routledge.

Vieira, L. and Alonso, E., 2018. *The Use of Machine Translation in Human Translation Workflows: Practices, Perceptions and Knowledge Exchange.* Bristol: University of Bristol and the Institute of Translation and Interpreting.

Wales, K., 2001. *A Dictionary of Stylistics*, 2nd ed., Harlow: Longman.

Winters, M., 2009. Modal particles explained: How modal particles creep into translations and reveal translators' styles. *Target*, 21(1), pp. 74–97.

Wright, C., 2007. *Translating the Exophonic Text. The German Prose Writings of Franco Biondi, Ermine Sergi Özdamar and Yoko Tawada*. PhD. University of East Anglia.

————— 2016. *Literary Translation*. London: Routledge.

Xanthos, A., Pante, I., Rochat, Y. and Grandjean, M., 2016. Visualising the dynamics of character networks. In *Digital Humanities 2016: Conference Abstracts*. Krakov: Jagiellonian University & Pedagogical University, Kraków, pp. 417–419. Available at: http://dh2016.adho.org/abstracts/407

Youdale, R., 2017. *Translating Literary Style: Close and Distant Reading in the Translation of* Gracias por el Fuego *by Mario Benedetti*. PhD. University of Bristol.

Zabalbeascoa, P., 2012. Translating heterolingual audiovisual humor: Beyond the blinkers of traditional thinking. In J. Muñoz-Basols, C. Fouto, L. González and T. Fisher, eds., *The Limits of Literary Translation: Expanding Frontiers in Iberian Languages*. Kassel: Edition Reichenberger, pp. 317–338.

Zanettin, F., 2002. Corpora in translation practice. In E. Yuste-Rodrigo, ed., *LREC Workshop No. 8: Language Resources in Translation Work*. Las Palmas de Gran Canaria: LREC, pp. 10–14.

Zunshine, L., 2011. Style brings in mental states. *Style*, 45(2), pp. 349–357.

Index

Note: **Bold** page numbers refer to major page reference and page numbers followed by "n" denote endnotes.

abusive fidelity 84, **90**
Aixelá, J. **99–100**, 106
Alonso, E. 14, 207; *see also* post-editing
Alvstad, C. 4, 42, 179
Amigas, Las 116; *see also* Fuentes, C.
Angels over Berlin 189
AntConc **32–4**, 51, 184
Arrebolarse 59, 202; *see also* rubify
ASLING 207
Association for Computational Linguistics in North America 207
authorship attribution: high-frequency function words 167; stylometry 3, 167, 183; translatorial presence in a text 207
auto-analysis of translator style 2, 25, 180, 188; Rybicki, J. 180; unconscious linguistic habits 189, 207; *see also* translator style
Automatic Language Processing Advisory Committee (ALPAC) 12

Baker, M. 4; corpora 16, 53; Descriptive Translation Studies (DTS) 16; pragmatics 114; punctuation 121, **144**; translator style **179**
Bassnett, S. 42, 126
Bell, A. 73, 75, 145
Benedetti, M.: as author 1, 9–10 (*see also* English Benedetti, creation of; Familia Iriarte; *Gracias por el Fuego*; *Tregua, La*); political views 49; use of commas 141–2; use of different languages 106–7; use of grammatical constructions 89, 127–8; use of y [and], 168–72, 201

Berman, A. 75, 80, 91, 110, 117, 135
Besacier, L. 17, 20
better informed translation and CDR **1–2**, 7, 40, 57, 72, 199
Biber, D. **25**, 26, 28
bilingual corpora *see* reference corpora
Blum-Kulka, S.: Descriptive Translation Studies (DTS) 16; explicitation 152, 184; length of translations 95
Boase-Beier, J.: style in translation 2, 3, 5; stylistic equivalence 82, 84; translation and narratology 42
Boom, Latin American: and Benedetti 10, 47; comparison of four novels with *Gracias por el Fuego* **126–7**, 142, 169
Burrows, J. 3, 201
Busa, R. 6
Bush, P. **82–3**, 103, 106

Campanella, H. 48, 79
Carter, R. 6
CATMA (Computer-aided Textual Markup and Analysis): functionalities **32–4**, 37, 51, 52, 98, 168; languages 31; lemma search 51; narratology and translation 42; sentence length 125, 157, 160 (*see also* sentence length); Word list and keyword-in-context (KWIC) **26–7**, 55, 160, 163
CAT tools 2, 19, 206, 221; definition and use of **13**; and literary translation 15–16, **17–18**; translator attitudes to 14–16, 199
CDR (close and distant reading) 1, **25**, 151–2

238 Index

Chesterman, A. 80, 85, 135
Cien Años de Soledad 126, 127, 142,
169; *see also* Márquez, G. G.; *One
Hundred Years of Solitude*
Ciudad y los Perros, La 126, 127,
169; *see also* Vargas Llosa, M.
close and distant reading *see* CDR
(close and distant reading)
close reading: definition 5 (*see also*
CDR (close and distant reading));
limitations 6–7, 59, **63**, 203–4;
partnership with distant reading 1,
7, 26, 40, 60, 94–5 (*see also* distant
reading); and visualisation 11, 34,
68–9
code-switching 109, 113–14
cognitive stylistics 43, 44, 187, 207
collocation 22, **26**, 30, 51, 33, 69
commas: auto-analysis of translator
style 179, 186–7, 189, 191, **194**;
Benedetti's use of **141–2**, 151;
French translation of *Gracias por el
Fuego* 146, 147
comparable corpora 32, 41
computational narratology 42; and
CDR 44; and Digital Humanities
40, 207
computer-aided literary analysis 1,
11, 206
computer-aided translation 1, 11, 40;
see also CAT tools
computer-assisted literary translation
(CALT) 199, 209
concordance: availability in software
programmes 26, 32, 190; definition
7; examples of use in translation 51,
52, 53, 57, 201; keyword-in-context
(KWIC) **26–7**
contrastive linguistics 23; French and
English 17; Spanish and English
132, 151, **160–2**, 172, 203
corpora *see* comparable corpora;
corpus; parallel corpora; reference
corpora
corpus: definition **16–17**, 25;
summary feature of software 33,
36, 41, **50–1**
corpus-based translation studies
(CTS): and CDR 207; development
16–17; translator style 8, 17, 24
Corpus del Español (CdE) *see*
reference corpora
corpus linguistics (CL): and CDR 11,
16, 17, 24; definition **25–6**; and

Descriptive Translation Studies
(DTS) 16; and the process of
literary translation 25–6, **31**, 203;
software **32–4**, 51, 59
corpus query language (CQL):
auto-analysis of translator style
190, **191**, 204; Four-stage model
of the CDR methodology 41;
grammatical analysis 127; lexical
density 195; proper noun extraction
61; sentence length 28
corpus stylistics: and corpus linguistics
(CL) **25**, 31; Digital Humanities 40,
44; *see also* stylistics
Cortázar, J. 10, 116, 126
culture-specific items (CSIs): Aixelá, J.
99–100; and CDR 98, 103; Davies,
E. 100–1; *falluto* 105, 106; *Rambla,
La* 88, 90, 104, 106; *sociedades de
padres demócratas* 106

dashes: auto-analysis of translator
style 179, 191; stylistic effect of
187, 189, **194**
Davies, E. **100**, 102, 103
Davies, M. 168
Dawydiak, E. 43, 87, 187
Descriptive Translation Studies
(DTS) 16
Desencuentros 189
Digital Humanities and the CDR
methodology 34, 37, **40**, 206
discourse analysis 57, **59–60**, 201
Discurso Vacío, El **182**, 183, 184,
185, 187, 219; *see also*
Levrero, M.
distant reading: auto-analysis of
translator style 177, 204; CDR **1**,
37, 40, 46, **54**, 205; contrast with
close reading **34**, 60, 72; Moretti, F.
1, 7, 61; text-visualisation 37
domestication 75, 76, **78**; *see also*
foreignisation
dynamic equivalence 74, 85; *see also*
equivalence of stylistic effect

Eagleton, T. 2, 98
Eco, U. 82, 109, 166
Edmundo (Budiño): CDR translation
of *el Viejo* 52, 58, 69–70, 155;
character 48, 50, 68, 81, **106**, 130;
conflict with Ramón 48, 52, 55,
68; discourse analysis **59–60**, 201;
network of relationships **63–8**;

Papá 133, 135–7; representation of Uruguayan elite 49; *usted* 117, 118, 119
effects on the reader 4, 5, 81, 82
Emerging Translators Network (ETN) 16
Emmott, C. 43, 86–7, 187
'English Benedetti', creation of 81, 84, **87–91**, 128, 131, 133
equivalence of stylistic effect 5, 42, 74, 80, **81–3**; as 'reverse engineering', 5; *see also* Nida, E.
Erupt 131, 162–6
Estallar, translation as erupt **162–6**
L'Étincelle 56, 57
explicitation 16, 101, 102, 103; translation universals 178, 180, 184; voluntary **161–2**, 203 (*see also* Frankenberg-Garcia, A.)

Familia Iriarte **91–3**, 94, **101–2**, 115, 116
Faulkner, W. 144, **147**
fingerprint 3, 179, 201
Fludernik, M. 41–2, 114
foreignisation 73, 75, 76, 77; and domestication 21, 72, 75, 78; Venuti, L. 74, **75–8**, 81
formal equivalence 74, **85**; *see also* equivalence of stylistic effect
four-stage model of the CDR methodology 11, 39, **41**, 50
Franco Arcia, U. 99, 109, 110
Frankenberg-Garcia, A. 31, 95, 152, 153
Frequency Dictionary of Spanish (FDS) *see* Reference corpora
Fuego **54–7**, 162–4, 202; *see also* *Gracias por el Fuego*
Fuentes, C. 116, 126
fully automated high-quality translation 12, 17

Gallego-Hernández, D. 28, 31
Genette, G. 80
Geng, Z. 39
Gracias por el Fuego: CDR standard analyses of **50–4** (*see also* auto-analysis of translator style); characterisation analysis 57, 61; comparison of ST and draft translation **152–3**; foreignising translation of 73, 74, **78–80**; French translation of 80, **90–1**, 145–6, 148,

149; interior monologue narrative format 10, 51, **122**, 124, 129, 131–2; long sentences 121, 123, **137–41**, **144–9**; most frequently used words 172; overall analysis 180–1; preservation in translation 151–2, 157, **159**, 183, 185, 197; short sentences 7, 59, 88, 96, **125–6**, **128–31**; use of italics 112; writing of **47**
Graham, B. 94, 95, 116
Greek 57, 179, **189–95**
Grossman, E. 7, 116
Gutt, E-A. 5, 84

Halliday, M. 123
Hamlet 61, 62
hapax legomena: definition **52**; measurement of lexical variety 53, 59, 152, 153, 183–5
Haywood, L. 73, 100, 115, 119, 133
Hermans, T. 4, 42, 75, 113, 179
Hervey, S. 73, 100, 115, 119, 132, 133
Higgins, I. 73, 100, 115, 119, 132, 133
high-frequency function words 3, 6, 152, 167, 177, **183**; *see also* authorship attribution
Holmes, D. 3, 166, 201
Hopscotch 47, 116; *see also* Cortázar, J.

International Association for Advancement in Language Technology *see* ASLING
Irizarry, E. 126, 140
Irvine, A. 17, 21

Jänicke, S. 34, 37
Jockers, M. 3, 201
Johnson, J. 69
Jones, R. 17, 21
Jull Costa, M. 103, 106

Keim, D. 37, 157
Kenny, A. 7, 8
Kenny, D. 14, 15, 209
Kerren, A. 37
key-word-in-context (KWIC) **26**, 27, 31, 32
keywords **26**, 52, 60
Klarer, M. 5
Kucher, K. 37

240 *Index*

language pairs and the CDR
methodology 31
Latin 106; Errare humanum est 107,
108; Mutus, Nomen, Dedit, Cocis
108–10
Laviosa, S. 16, 178, 184, 207
LeBlanc, M. 14
Leech, G. 2, 8, 9, 39, **46**, 86
lemma 33, 45n20, 51, 59, 163
Levine, S. J. 54, **92–3**, 102, 115, 133
Levrero, M. 182, 204
Lewis, P. **84**, 90
lexical density 53, 195
lexical diversity 53, 151, 153,
154, 203
lexical richness 41, **53**, 54, 152, 195
lexical variety 15, 51, 53, 153, 183;
see also type-token ratio (TTR)
LF Aligner 18, 30, 153–4, 190
limitations of the CDR methodology
8–9, 63, 195, **205–6**
literary translation: CAT tools **17–18**
(*see also* CAT tools); CDR and 6,
11, **25**, 28, 31, **41**; corpus linguistics
and 28, 30, **31–4** (*see also*
corpus linguistics (CL)); machine
translation and **19–23** (*see also*
machine translation (MT)); style
in **5**; technology and **1**, 11, 15–16,
199, 209
literary translators and the CDR
methodology 2; attitudes to
translation technology 1, 11, **15–16**,
18, 20, 21; auto-analysis of style
197–8 (*see also* auto-analysis of
translator style); stylistic analysis
25–31; training 31, **208–9**
LiteratureVis 157, 158

Mac Adam, A. 116
machine translation (MT): history
12–13; how it works **12**; impact
on translators **14–16**; literary
translation 19–23; post-editing
of 13, **19–21**, 23, 207; *see also*
post-editing
McRae, E. 80
Mahlberg, M. **5**, 7
Malmkjaer, K. 4, 17
Manousopoulos, A. 189
María dos Prazeres 116
Márquez, G. G. 10, 19, 47, 116,
126, 189

May, R.: punctuation **121–2**; sentence
translation 128, **135**, 140, **144–5**,
147; translator invisibility 73
memoQ 30
mirror-reflection translation 99, 110
monolingual corpora *see* reference
corpora
Montevideanos 74, 91, 102
Montevideo: Benedetti 50, **79**,
87, 93, 104, 107; Carnival 112,
129; Familia Iriarte 91, 101–2;
landmarks 80, 103; Rambla, la 88,
90, 104, 106
Morales, H.: translation of Familia
Iriarte **61–2**, 144, 206; translation
of *Tregua, La* 94–6
Moretti, F. **1**, 7, **61–2**, 206, 207
Mosteller, F. 3, 201
most-frequent-words analysis 180
Muerte de Artemio Cruz, La 126, 127,
142, 169; *see also* Fuentes, C.
Munday, J.: corpus linguistics 8, 167,
197; equivalence of effect 85–6;
translator presence in a text 75;
translator style 167

narratology: characterisation 57;
cognitive 43, 86, 207; stylistics
and **40**, 41, 42, 46; *see also*
computational narratology;
psycho-narratology
network visualisation **61–6**, 71n17
neural machine translation (NMT)
13, 19, 20, 21; *see also* machine
translation (MT)
Newmark, P. 80, 121
n-grams 32, 41, 50, **52**, 152, 200
Nida, E. 74, 85
Node 7, 26, 28
Nord, C. 43, 96
normalisation 79, 99, 117, 178, 180

Oelke, D. 37, 157, 158
Old Man, The *see Viejo, El*
Olohan, M. 14, 180
One Hundred Years of Solitude 47;
see also Márquez, G. G.

Paoletti, M. 48, 49, 50, 79, 81, 145
ParaConc 32–4
parallel corpora: compared with
dictionaries 29; MT systems 12,
19; search example 29, 156; use in

literary translation 29–30, 32, 41, 151, **153–5**, 190; *see also* reference corpora
paratext 80, 179
Parkes, M. 121
Parks, T. 4
part-of-speech (POS) tagging 28, 33, 41, 179, 190, **203–4**
Paz Soldán, E. 189, 192, 193, 194
PETRA-E Framework 209
philosophy of the CDR methodology **23–5**, 31
poetry 9, 23, 47, 72, 73, 75
post-editing 13, **19–21**, 23, 207
Prince, G. 42
pro-drop 153
psycho-narratology 44, 86
punctuation: functions of **121**, 140, 141, **144**; mirror-reflection 113; and translation 85, **121**, 123, 124, 128, 133; *see also* commas; dashes; Parkes, M.
Pym, A. 14, 15, 75, 77, 109, 208

Ramón (Budiño): CDR character analysis 57, 58; centrality in *Gracias por el Fuego* 48; character 48; conflict with Edmundo 47, **48**, 59; network of relationships 61, **63–70**; representation of Montevidean middle class 49, 56; *see also* Edmundo (Budiño)
Rayuela 115, 116, 126, 127, 142, 169; *see also* Hopscotch; Cortázar, J.
reader response 43, 86, 144
reference corpora 32, 178, 183, 201; bilingual corpora 29, 202; British English 2006 (BE06) 178; British National Corpus (BNC) 178; *Corpus del Español* (CdE) 29, **125**, 168, 169, 202; Frequency Dictionary of Spanish (FDS) 168, 169; monolingual corpora 29, 30, 32, 41, 202; TenTen Corpus Family 29, 202
repetition: detection by corpus linguistics 25, 41, 51, 151–2, **162–6**, 167; examples of 52, 56, 70, **83–4**, 88–9, 127–8; literary style and **24–5**, 88, 177
reverse engineering 5, 26
Rosa, A. A. 115, 117, 120
Rothwell, A. 17, **18**, **22**, 198, 209

Routledge Encyclopedia of Translation Technology 12
rubify 60, 202
Ruffinelli, J. 47, 49
Rybicki, J. 180, 207

Saldanha, G.: literary style **3**, 123, 180; translators as intercultural mediators 99, 101, 103; translator style **4**, **181**, 188; use of italics 111, 112, 197
Sanford, A. 43, 86–7, 187
Schiavi, G. 4, 75, 179
Schleiermacher, F. 75
Schwartz, L. 17, 20
Scott, C. 28, 121
segments: alignment **18**, 32, 41, 153–5; CAT tools 13, 16, 18; machine translation 12, 13, 19, 21
sentence length: average 33, 41, 46, 51, 59, **125–6**, 218; corpus query language (CQL) extraction 28; corpus summaries 33, 36, 41, **50–1**; in *Gracias por el Fuego* (*see Gracias por el Fuego*); registering as readers 6; visualisation 157–8
ShakerVis 37
Shen, D. 42, 207
Short, M. 2–3, **39–40**, 112
simplification: auto-analysis of translator style 180, 184, 187–8, **195**; translation universals 178, 180, 184
Simpson, P. 42
Sketch Engine: corpus creation 29, 30; corpus summary 50–1; list of functionalities **32–4**; multilingual use 31, 208; part-of-speech (POS) tagging 28, 33, 41, 179, 190, **203–4**; use in comparing ST and draft translation 152, 155, 203, 204; use in discourse analysis 58–9; word frequency views 35; Word Sketch 30, 202 (*see also* lemma); Reference corpora; N-grams; Parallel corpora; Part-of-speech
software for CDR **32–4**
Soga y cabrito 30–1, 202
Stamatatos, E. 3, 167, 183, 201
Stanford Literary Lab 61, 206; *see also* Moretti, F.

242 *Index*

statistical machine translation (SMT) 12, 19, 20, 21, 22; *see also* machine translation (MT)
strengths of the CDR methodology 7–8, **200–5**
students of translation 2, **208–9**
Style in Fiction 2, 39; *see also* Leech, G.; Short, M.
stylistics 2, 3, 5; cognitive 43, 44, 187, 207; computational **166**; empirical **86**; *see also* corpus stylistics; narratology
stylometry 3, **167**, 180, 183, 201, 207; *see also* high-frequency function words
subject-drop 160, 161; *see also* pro-drop

tagset 190
Text Visualization Browser 37, **38**
TextDNA 157
text-visualisation 11, 24, 31, **34–9**, 41, 199; *see also* Voyant Tools
theory: equivalence in translation 85; network **61–2**; and practice 2, 208; translation 5, 21, 72, 76
Thomas, D. 9
Tognini Bonelli, E. 26
Toral, A. 17, 19, 20, 23, 207
Toury, G. 16, 95, 117, 184, 207
Translational English Corpus 17
Translation Automation User Society (TAUS) 13, 44n6
Translation Memory eXchange (TMX) 18, 30, 155, 190, 203
translation memories 12, 14, 18
translation scholars and the CDR methodology 2, **206–8**
translator-as-reader 82, 122, 124, 144, 155
translator-as-writer 144
Translator's Invisibility, The 75–6, 78, 81; *see also* Venuti, L.
translator's preface **80–1**, 114, 179
translator style: auto-analysis of 25, 178, 183, **188**, 189, 191; research on 4, 17, **179–80**, 181
Tregua, La 74, 91, **93–5**, 115; *see also* Benedetti, M.
Tymoczko, M. 75, 76, 77

type-token ratio (TTR): definition **51**; examples of use 152, 183, 185, 203; limitations 53; *see also* lexical richness
typography 41, 106, **111–14**, 187

UK Translators Survey 2017, 14
unconscious linguistic habits 8, 189, 207
unconscious translation tendencies 178
unit of translation 151, 155
Uruguay: Benedetti 9, **47**, 49, 130; culture 103, 107, 110, 112, 204; dialect 105; politics 49, 56, 106
Usted: pragmatics 69, 98, **114**; translation of *Gracias por el Fuego* 99, **117–20**; translation of Latin American fiction **115–17**

Vargas Llosa, M. 126
Venuti, L. 74, 75–8, 81
Vieira, L. 14, 207; *see also* post-editing
Viejo, El 48, 49, 52, 63, 69–70, 155
visualisation: CDR and 11, 24, **34–9**, 147–8, 205; LiteratureVis 157, 158; network **61–6**, 71n17, 201; Sketch Engine 35, 127; Voyant Tools **36**, 51, 148–9; *see also* text-visualisation
Vizetelly, E. 18
Voyant Tools **32–4**, 35, **36**, 37, 50–1, 149

Wales, K. 3
Wallace, D. 3, 201
Way, A. 17, 18, 20, 23, 207, 209
Winters, M. 17, 180, 181, 184
Woolf, V. 144, 147
word cloud 41, 51
word list 26, 27, 32, 41, **51–2**, 59
Word Sketch 30, 33, 41, 202
WordSmith Tools 32, 34
Wright, C. 73, 74, 80

Youdale, R. 3, 10, 57, 206

Zanettin, F. 29, 31
Zola, É. 18, 198